SO LONG AS GAME
MAY BE FOUND
THEREON...

SO LONG AS GAME MAY BE FOUND THEREON...

—FORT BRIDGER TREATY, 1868—

Indian Treaty Hunting—from Fort Hall to Wyoming and Beyond

by

CLEVE DAVIS

Enrolled Shoshone-Bannock Tribal Member

Native Sciences Press

—2025—

Copyright © 2025 Cleve Davis

First edition

All rights reserved. No part of this book may be reproduced, stored in a retrieval system, or transmitted in any form or by any means—electronic, mechanical, photocopy, recording, or otherwise—without the prior written permission of the copyright holder, except for brief quotations in reviews, scholarly works, or articles.

ISBN: 979-8-9988178-0-9

Printed in the United States by:

Native Sciences Press
Fort Hall Indian Reservation

Artwork: Burdett Bird Osborne, Self-taught Bannock-Shoshone artist. *Huuzeevah Arts*, P.O. Box 110 Fort Hall, Idaho 83203.

Cover design and interior layout by Cleve Davis

This book is lovingly dedicated to my daughter, Isla Rain Davis. May you always understand your identity and roots.

TABLE OF CONTENTS

Acknowledgements iv
Author's Note on Terminology v
Preface vii
Chapter 1 - Where the Story Begins 1
Chapter 2 – What's in a Name 9
Chapter 3 - What Coyote Taught Us About Hunting 25
Chapter 4 – The Buffalo Nation 31
Chapter 5 - The Era of Suffering 47
Chapter 6 - The Jackson Hole Conspiracy................................... 85
Chapter 7 - In the Shadow of Race Horse 117
Chapter 8 – Species Conservation 133
Chapter 9 - Defining "Unoccupied"... 141
Chapter 10 - Make Said Reservations their Permanent Home .. 159
Chapter 11 - Concluding Remarks 177
The *Wihinakwate* Way.. 183
Appendix... 189
Glossary.. 193
Index... 198

Acknowledgements

My deepest gratitude goes to everyone who supported and inspired me along the way in writing this book. Special thanks to those who took the time to pass on knowledge and review drafts. To my relatives and friends—you know who you are. You've had my back when it counted, and I haven't forgotten that. Through good times and hard times, you shape who I am. I've learned a lot from you, and I carry those lessons and scars forward with pride.

Author's Note on Terminology

On the Use of the Word "Indian"

Throughout this book, I use the term Indian to refer to myself and others from my community. I do so intentionally and without hesitation. While some may prefer terms like Native American or Indigenous, I find those terms either too vague or culturally misplaced. The word Native can apply to anyone born in a particular place—including non-Indians born in America—while Indigenous is often used more broadly, even globally, to describe original peoples from regions outside North America. Neither term captures the legal, historical, and lived realities that define my experience.

Indian, on the other hand, is not only how I was raised to refer to myself and those around me on the Fort Hall Indian Reservation—it is the language used in federal law, in treaties, in the U.S. Constitution, and in landmark legal cases that define our rights, including the hunting rights discussed in this book. Most of the elders and reservation people I know use the word Indian without offense. For us, it carries weight, continuity, and legal recognition. It is the term used in our communities, in our ceremonies, and in our struggles.

So, if you're wondering why I don't use more politically correct alternatives—it's because Indian is who I am, how my people speak, and how our rights are written into the laws that continue to affect our lives. I use the word with pride, and with full awareness of its complex history.

On the Use of Bannock and Shoshone Language

The Bannock and Shoshone languages featured throughout this book are presented using two orthographies developed within the Fort Hall Indian Reservation. For assistance with pronunciation and understanding of these languages, please refer to the appendix titled "*Simplified Panakwate (Bannock) and Newe Daigwape (Shoshone) Pronunciation Guide and Orthography.*"

Additionally, to support readers unfamiliar with the Bannock and Shoshone terms used throughout the text, a *Glossary of Bannock and Shoshone Words* is provided at the end of the book. This glossary offers brief definitions and explanations to help readers better appreciate the cultural and linguistic richness embedded in the narrative.

Preface

Growing up on the Fort Hall Indian Reservation in southeastern Idaho, I've always known my Shoshone-Bannock heritage, with both parents enrolled in the Tribes. Yet it wasn't until I began to explore the history of my ancestors and the origins of my people that I truly grasped the depth of my identity. I grew up in a single-wide trailer and was raised mostly by my father, Joseph Davis Jr., who was a mechanic by trade. He played a significant role in my upbringing.

My father grew up poor, and he and his brothers often had to hunt to provide for the family. He still tells stories about those days—how there was plenty of game, unlike today. One of my favorite stories is about the time he and a friend brought home a deer on a single motorcycle, riding it from the Lincoln Creek district of the Reservation through a border town called Blackfoot, Idaho. That story always reminds me of the videos you see on social media of people in third-world countries, where three or four people are crammed onto a single motorcycle, making do with whatever they have.

My father was drafted into the Vietnam War before I was born, serving as a mobile artillery gunman in the Army. So, he is no stranger to weapons. Yet unlike many veterans today, he does not glorify his military service, often stating, "Those people never done nothing to me," expressing his belief that wars—whether in Vietnam or against the Indians—have always been driven by greed. My father is also an avid hunter, and some of my best memories are of salmon fishing, bobcat trapping, and hunting small and large game together. We continue to share these passions, although we no longer trap unless necessary. To this day, we spend time together reloading bullets, sighting in our guns, discussing strategies for hunting certain areas, and processing hides, furs, and meat side by side.

As for my mother, Marcia Racehorse-Robles, she was not consistently present in my life. She left my father, my brother, and me when we were young, resulting in only sporadic involvement during my childhood. Over time, however, she embraced Christianity, which brought a new stability to her life. Today, she is a talented seamstress, known for creating some of the finest cradleboards on the reservation.

When it comes to language, neither of my parents spoke our heritage languages, Shoshone or Bannock. On the other hand, my maternal grandmother, Caroline Teton-Racehorse, was fluent in both languages, and I was wise enough to spend time with her, picking up as much Bannock as I could during our time together. Her passing in 2022 marked the loss of one of the few remaining individuals in Fort Hall who could speak both languages fluently.

Hunting and fishing were more common activities on my father's side of the family, likely because there were more men involved. On my mother's side, however, I had only one uncle, and he struggled with alcoholism, which kept him from participating as much as my father and my other uncles. My grandmother Caroline, however, had a particular fondness for wild game, and she grew up in a time that was completely different from the one we know today. She would tell me childhood stories about being scared when a group of Bannock warriors came riding in, looking fierce and with their horses lathered in sweat. She also told me about her grandfather's people, who came from the Boise Valley and had to hide from the military. Their chief entrusted her grandfather with transporting all the people's money—likely gold and silver—to Fort Hall, but he lost it somewhere along the way.

Growing up in a family of modern reservation Indians, my sense of identity and heritage was often layered with questions and quiet wonder. However, two early spiritual experiences affirmed my connection to my Indian roots. One of these occurred when I was around eight years old. My brother, cousin, and I were playing a game called Killer, which is similar to hide-and-seek, amidst the sagebrush behind our house as dusk approached. As I hid with my dog Junior, a startling yet unexplainable phenomenon occurred: the sound of Indian drums enveloped my hiding spot under a canopy of sagebrush. My dog, sensing something unusual, laid down on the ground and whimpered. I remained perfectly still and scared. The drumbeats encircled us a few times before suddenly taking off in a different direction. Although nothing was visible to any of us, the drumming was unmistakably real. To this day, my brother, cousin, and I often reminisce about that mysterious and unexplainable evening.

The second spiritual incident occurred when I was about thirteen years old. I had a striking dream about participating in the *Daguwenede*, known as the "Standing Thirst Dance," or what the non-Indians refer to as the "Sundance." At the time, I had neither experienced the ceremony nor knew much about it. In Fort Hall, dreaming of the *Daguwenede* holds great spiritual significance. Shortly after, a dedicated dancer, who is now one of the leaders of the Buffalo Lodge Sundance in Fort Hall, came to talk to me about my dream and what it meant. He explained that it was an invitation for me to join the ceremony, a challenging ritual that involves several days of praying, fasting, and dancing under the scorching summer sun. He told me that participating at such a young age would be powerful.

In the Sundance, you learn the importance of water and food—and what it means to go without these necessities of life. Through sacrifice and purification, you become closer to *Damme Ape* or "Our Father" and the prayers are more powerful. The ceremony also imparts deeper lessons about the natural world, such as how the animals, like the buffalo, represent strength and perseverance, and how the eagle carries the prayers on its wings. But at that age, the thought of enduring such an intense spiritual experience was overwhelming, and I wasn't ready to take that step.

After completing high school, I struggled with alcoholism and heavy marijuana use, leading to legal issues and a mandatory rehabilitation program at the Four Directions Treatment Center in Fort Hall. There, my counselor, a fellow Shoshone-Bannock Tribal member and a recovering alcoholic himself, advised me to engage in our traditional practices for healing. Heeding his advice, I participated in my first Peyote meeting, sweat lodge ceremony, and later my first *Daguwenede* ceremony. Thus, I've consistently felt a spiritual presence in my life, offering guidance and protection throughout my journey. My experiences—and the lessons of the *Daguwenede*—stay with me to this day, reminding me of the strength that comes from sacrifice and suffering, as well as the deep connection between the Creator, the land, and our people.

Reconnecting with my Indian identity and hearing the Shoshone and Bannock languages used to conduct ceremonies stirred something deep within me. It also brought a sense of shame—I couldn't understand the prayers or the words. That feeling pushed me to begin learning these languages, a journey that quickly became a lifelong quest. Not long after I made the decision to learn these languages, I realized how inadequate the

English alphabet was for capturing the nuances and sounds of Shoshone and Bannock. As I delved deeper into my studies, I learned about the fragile state of the Bannock language—a language tied to my heritage.

Recognizing the limitations of using the English phonetic alphabet to document Numic languages, I pursued a master's degree in Anthropology, focusing on Bannock and Shoshone linguistics. As my understanding and experiences deepened, I began to see more clearly the profound and devastating impact of alcoholism, drug abuse, and unhealthy lifestyle choices on my friends, family, and community. These harsh realities reinforced what my counselor told me when I was 19—that one of the most effective ways to confront these challenges on the reservation is through the revitalization of our Indian languages and the active practice of our cultural traditions.

Every day, I begin with a prayer of gratitude and a glass of water—a simple ritual that reminds me of the blessings I've been given and the responsibilities I carry as an Indian man. Throughout the day, I prepare myself and my body the best way I can with the time I have to be able to protect and provide for my family amidst the challenges we face on the reservation. For me, this effort is not only about honoring the resilient legacy of my ancestors—who endured hardships I cannot begin to understand—but also about preparing for the new challenges I know lie ahead. Thus, I believe it is the fundamental responsibility of men to cultivate discipline, strength, and competence—to provide for their families and protect the vulnerable, to develop the capacity to defend their people, to endure the demands of hard physical labor, and to confront life's inevitable challenges with courage. Only by mastering these burdens can men create order out of chaos and secure a future where their families and communities can thrive. I hope to instill these values in my own family, ensuring that they not only recognize the potential difficulties ahead but also develop the discipline and mindset needed to face life's challenges with resilience and a smile—just as our ancestors had.

Yet today, our communities face a crisis. While some men are capable of fighting, many are misguided—fighting for the wrong reasons, under the wrong flag, or worse, becoming burdens to their own families and communities. In too many cases, women have had to step up and fill the void left by the absence of real men. Too many remain "man-boys," trapped in the bodies of grown men but lacking the heart and discipline that true manhood requires. This void is not just a personal failing. It's a threat to the survival of our families, culture, and identity.

And this is where hunting comes in…

Hunting, in our traditional culture, was never merely about securing meat. It was about safeguarding the family during travels, preserving food through expert processing, caring for animals like horses and dogs, crafting tools, and accumulating wealth through the acquisition of resources. It involved devising strategies for defense, maintaining community order, and fostering individual and collective self-reliance through discipline. Hunting was not a "sport" but a sacred responsibility that demanded expertise, precision, teamwork, and unwavering commitment to the well-being of the community.

Our leaders understood this deeply, which is why they fought to enshrine hunting as a fundamental right in the Fort Bridger Treaty of 1868—an acknowledgment of its central place in our identity and cultural legacy. This book delves into these tribal hunting traditions, narratives, and histories, shedding light on what it truly means to be an Indian hunter-warrior—a role defined by resilience, discipline, and the ability to persist through impossible adversity.

But treaty rights alone are not enough to preserve this sacred tradition. While federal Indian law has affirmed our off-reservation hunting rights as a Tribal right, the responsibility to uphold and honor this right rests with each individual Indian hunter. It is not merely a legal privilege—it is a sacred obligation. To truly honor the spirit of the Treaty, we must actively exercise this right and ensure that our hunts reflect the discipline, respect, and reverence that our ancestors demonstrated.

As Indian men, we must reclaim our role as providers, protectors, and leaders. By doing so, we not only safeguard our families and communities but also preserve the values and traditions that define us. Through the hunt, we reaffirm our connection to the land, to our ancestors, and to the Creator—fulfilling a promise that was made long before we were born.

Chapter 1 - Where the Story Begins

This story begins on the move—traveling, hunting, fishing—following the seasons my people have for generations. That's where I'll begin this journey. I think often about my younger years joining my father on trips to central Idaho to fish for salmon or hunting big game with my uncles on and off the reservation. Back then, some of our fellow Tribal fishermen would share stories about how the cowboys from the East Fork of the Salmon River fired shots at them while they attempted to access the river. In the early 1980s, as a youngster, I remember we were careful to avoid run-ins with both the Idaho Fish and Game and Tribal game wardens. We kept quiet about the quantity of fish we caught and made efforts to conceal our haul. Our distrust of the white game wardens was evident, while with the Tribal game wardens, we were aware that they kept track of fish counts. If our catch was tallied, it meant fewer fish available for our fellow tribal members, so we did not want to spoil opportunities for others hunting fish.

But it wasn't always about avoiding trouble. I remember the times when I witnessed vast schools of salmon, some as large as sharks. I also recall spearfishing what we called "dog salmon" in the Yankee Fork. Additionally, I remember the first time I witnessed a steelhead being speared. It happened while hiking with my uncle Mike Davis above the rattlesnake-infested Herd Creek, a tributary of the East Fork of the Salmon. From the cliffs overlooking the creek, we spotted the fish in its narrow waters. My uncle quickly fashioned a spear pole from a small crooked aspen tree he found nearby. With stealth, he crept up to the stream, hiding behind willows until he was close enough. In a flash, he struck the steelhead with the spear pole and pulled an unbelievably large and thrashing fish out of the water. To me, it seemed to be twice as large as when it was swimming. To subdue the fish, my uncle quickly stabbed it in the head with a knife. Witnessing such a large fish in such a small stream was amazing, and I can still feel the excitement of the moment in my heart to this very day.

You might be wondering, why am I telling stories about fishing in a book about hunting? Well, it is because, according to our Indian language and culture, the actions of fishing, gathering, and hunting are considered one and the same. In essence, whether you're fishing, hunting, or gathering, these activities all fall within the broader category of "hunting."

Traveling to hunt has probably always been exciting and had its risks, but it was a lot more dangerous in the past than it is today. Nevertheless, there are still inherent risks in the present day. In May of 2023, I attended a Tribal fisherman's meeting in Fort Hall and a Shoshone-Bannock woman recounted an unsettling encounter from the previous season, where a white man told her that "he should just kill her" for no other reason than she was an Indian. Another man in the same meeting shared he had a confrontation with a group of armed Nez Perce fishermen who apparently bullied him out of his fishing spot. The history of disputes and conflicts involving the Nez Perce dates back to ancient times and, regrettably, these tensions continue in the present. The friction between our Tribes in this day and age has become an unfortunate tradition.

I also remember a time when I shot a nice bighorn sheep in central Idaho and when I reported my kill to the Tribal wildlife biologist, he said, "Where did you poach this one?" Even though my hunt was legitimate under treaty hunting rights and I had the necessary tribal tag, I couldn't help but chuckle. When I killed it, I anticipated confrontations. I quickly gutted the animal, navigated it down a cliff, across the Salmon River, and threw the very heavy animal into my truck all by myself within 45 minutes. I had heard stories of tribal hunters facing scrutiny from spectators, some of which even reached the media. I didn't want to become the subject of an article from Custer County, Idaho - a county predominantly inhabited by extremely conservative white residents - that would likely present a skewed perspective on the legitimacy of Indian hunting rights.

These days, I find myself concerned with the well-being of my wife and youngest daughter, who often accompany me on outdoor adventures. The crisis of American Indian women disappearing or being murdered has recently entered the public consciousness, despite being a pervasive issue among American Indians for generations. The abduction of Indian children throughout history is also a serious concern that tends to be neglected, as does the deaths of American Indian men. While I acknowledge the tragic reality that Indian women are subject to violence at the hands of Indian men, I also believe that many these crimes are perpetrated by non-Indian individuals, exploiting the insufficient and overwhelmed justice system present in Indian Country. Sometimes I wonder: could the descendants of the miners and cowboys who tormented my ancestors be the ones perpetuating these crimes, or is it just the evil of men in general? Perhaps the latter.

Identifying those who still harbor such deep-rooted animosity against Indians is not easy these days. Yet, it's worth noting that many people in the Western United States (U.S.) are armed, be it openly or concealed. While it is true that many present-day challenges facing Indians can be attributed to historical trauma, I argue that a significant part of our ongoing struggle stems from enduring historical hate. Although this narrative delves into the off-reservation Indian hunting and fishing rights from a historical and contemporary standpoint, I ask the reader to question how race, language, or prejudices may have factored into the events that have shaped history.

You might be wondering why I am writing about Indian hunting rights. The answer lies in a personal bond that runs deeper than academic interest. I am a direct descendant of *Pohave* (1863–1926), also known as John Race Horse Sr., and through him, I inherit not only a connection to these treaty rights but a responsibility to understand and defend them. *Pohave* played a pivotal role in the inaugural off-reservation treaty rights test-case for the Bannock Tribe. The case was ultimately decided by the U.S. Supreme Court, which concluded that the hunting rights accorded to the Bannock Tribe under the Fort Bridger Treaty of 1868 were not sustained following Wyoming's attainment of statehood in 1890. The case is now known as Ward v. Race Horse[1].

For over a hundred years, the repercussions of the Ward v. Race Horse case have deeply affected the Shoshone-Bannock, Eastern Shoshone, and Crow Tribe. The case is particularly unsettling because it stemmed from a calculated conspiracy involving hunting guides and Wyoming state and federal officials, all concerted in their efforts to undermine the Tribes' off-reservation hunting rights. This specific collusion, steeped in the prevailing prejudices of the late 19th century, not only incited violent incidents that tragically led to the deaths of a Bannock elder and an infant, but it also set a federal Indian law precedent that touched other federally recognized tribes. While the more recent Minnesota v. Mille Lacs Band of Chippewa Indians[2], and Herrera v. Wyoming[3] decisions overturned aspects of the Race Horse verdict, the struggle persists, as the State of Wyoming remains reluctant in providing the necessary redress. Compounding the injustice, those responsible for the initial violence were never held accountable, leaving the wrongful deaths of the Bannock people an open wound.

---

[1] *Ward v. Race Horse*, 163 U.S. 504 (1896)
[2] *Minnesota v. Mille Lacs Band of Chippewa Indians*, 526 U.S. 172 (1999)
[3] *Herrera v. Wyoming*, 587 U.S.__(2019)

This book examines the enduring hunting traditions and cultural heritage of the Shoshone-Bannock Tribes, particularly those from Fort Hall, Idaho, who trace their roots within the territories of Wyoming as recognized by the 1868 Fort Bridger Treaty. It explores the intricate history and the cultural significance of hunting for these tribes, shedding light on a conspiracy leading to the landmark Race Horse decision and subsequent hunting right court cases and history. The Race Horse case set a harmful precedent and influenced future legal interpretations and policies across Indian Country, playing a pivotal role in shaping federal Indian hunting laws. Therefore, the scope of this book extends beyond Wyoming, providing a comprehensive overview of the intricate legal framework that governs hunting and, to a certain degree, fishing rights of Indians across the U.S. This approach situates the discussion of federal Indian hunting rights within the broader context of the American West, emphasizing that the denial of these treaty-protected rights is foremost a violation of tribal sovereignty and federal law, while also intersecting with issues of environmental justice.

Today, *Pohave* rests in the Sand Hill cemetery located on the Fort Hall Indian Reservation. The name *Pohave* can be interpreted as "One Who Has Power" or "One Who Possesses Power." In my lineage, he is my *kusi-tzo* or "gray grandfather," a Bannock term that translates to "great-great-grandfather" in English. As stories from my family have been passed down to me, I've learned he was born in what is now known as Montana[4], probably to a family and band of buffalo hunters. John Race Horse Sr. is my mother's, Marcia Claudia Racehorse-Robles' (1955-present) great-grandfather. She is the child of Cleveland Brooks Racehorse (1920-1971) and Caroline Teton-Racehorse (1929-2022). Cleveland was born to Nelson Racehorse (1905-1938) and Maude Pocatello-Racehorse (1897-1963), with Nelson being the son of John Race Horse Sr. (1860-1906) and *Hahveedziah* (1878-1924), whose name translates as the "Laying Girl."

Today, what was once the "Race Horse" surname has evolved to a single word: "Racehorse." I once sought the origins of this name from a now deceased Tribal elder and relative, Lonnie Racehorse. He shared that the name was derived from our ancestor's ability to steal horses and evade or outrun enemy

---

[4] Velda Racehorse, personal communication, August 2021.

pursuers while riding horseback. To this day, our family legacy lives on as family members partake in horse racing events, including the Indian Relay racing and the Bannock Warrior Challenge, an event in which I have proudly competed.

Exploring my family heritage and being an avid hunter myself, I became intrigued by the story of John Race Horse Sr. When I embarked on exploring this tale, I hadn't anticipated its profound connection to events like the Bear River Massacre and the pivotal Treaty-making period. This journey also afforded me the opportunity to delve into the life and times of another forebear, Chief Pocatello, who is my *gaihitsi* or "great-great-great grandfather" in Shoshone. It's rather amusing, however, that in Shoshone, the term *gaihitsi* translates to "no longer related". On my paternal lineage, Chief Eagle Eye also stands out as another ancestor, notably, perhaps one of the last *Dukudeka* chiefs to exist outside reservations within the lower 48 states. Chief Eagle Eye's granddaughter, Josephine Thorpe was my paternal great-grandmother or *tso'o*, in Shoshone. Josephine and her family were the final group of Indian people in Idaho to surrender their autonomy to colonial powers and transition to life on a reservation[5]. Notwithstanding the tribulations faced by my predecessors, I hold immense pride in their defiance against colonization and their indelible mark on the rich history of the American West.

It's important to recognize that much of the historical record about my ancestors has been shaped through the lens of non-Indian writers—accounts that, while sometimes valuable, often lack the cultural grounding and lived understanding found in Tribal oral traditions. I always wanted to research the information myself and combine what has been passed on to me through the oral traditions to come up with my own interpretation. As time passed, I observed the devastating loss of knowledge with Tribal elders walking on and now I know how fast a life can be lived. Family have, over time, entrusted me with documents and prior research accomplished by relatives before their demise, with an expectation that I might further the cause. As I get older, I also feel an urgency to chronicle what I have

---

[5] Jon P. Dayley, "An Ethno-Historical Shoshone Narrative PIE NIMMIN NAAKKANNA 'HOW WE LIVED LONG AGO'," *Idaho Archaeologist* (1986): 3.

learned on my journey to leave for my children and do my part to ensure this legacy persists for future generations. Consequently, "*So Long As Game May Be Found Thereon...*" embodies my humble attempt at this end. I ardently hope this inspires fellow Indians to write their distinct narratives, as they are worth telling.

Chapter 1 – Bibliography

Dayley, Jon P. "An Ethno-Historical Shoshone Narrative: PIE NIMMIN NAAKKANNA 'How We Lived Long Ago'." Idaho Archaeologist (1986): 3.

Herrera v. Wyoming, 587 U.S.__(2019).

Minnesota v. Mille Lacs Band of Chippewa Indians, 526 U.S. 172 (1999).

Ward v. Race Horse, 163 U.S. 504 (1896).

Chapter 2 – What's in a Name

The Shoshone Indians have long been skilled hunters, with their traditional hunting territories once stretching deep into the northern plains of what are now Montana and southern Alberta, Canada. Prior to the exposure of smallpox and before the acquisition of the gun, the imposing stature of the Shoshone was recognized in David Thompson's accounts of the war between the "Peeagans" and the "Snake Indians" around the year 1730.[1] Additionally, in 1742, the de la Verendrye brothers chronicled the presence of the powerful "Gens du Serpent" - French for "People of the Serpent" - who were involved in conflicts with the Blackfeet and other northern Great Plains tribes.[2] The term "Gens du Serpent" or "Snakes" stems from the unique hand sign used by the Shoshone to describe themselves in Plains Indian Sign Language. The hand sign involved a forward motion with a side-to-side wave, similar to or perhaps a mimic of a snake's movement.

The heart of the conflict lay across the plains stretching from Canada's Bow River to the Missouri River in the U.S., lands rich in resources and vital to the hunting traditions of the Kootenai, Salish, and Snake Indians.[3] The Shoshone were the first mounted buffalo hunters of the Northern Plains, and initially, horses gave the Shoshone a distinct tactical advantage.[4] However, the dynamics shifted when the Blackfeet, who had traders among them, acquired firearms, which quickly altered the power balance.[5] This shift in technological armament allowed the Blackfeet to push the Shoshone and possibly their ally the Bannock southward, gradually seizing control of the plains. Compounded by the devastation of the smallpox epidemic in 1781, the retreat of the Shoshone was accelerated. By the winter of 1787–1788, as observed by Thompson, these once-contested

---

[1] David Thompson, *Narrative of His Explorations in Western America, 1784-1812,* ed. J. B. Tyrrell (Toronto: The Champlain Society, 1916), 328.
[2] Robert F. Murphy and Yolanda Murphy, "Shoshone-Bannock Subsistence and Society," *Anthropological Records* 16, no. 7 (Berkeley and Los Angeles: University of California Press, 1960), 294-295.
[3] Thompson, *Narrative of His Explorations in Western America,* 325.
[4] Murphy and Murphy, "Shoshone-Bannock Subsistence and Society," 294.
[5] Ibid., 294.

plains had become the established hunting grounds of the Blackfeet.[6]

David Thompson, a significant British fur agent, surveyor, and cartographer for Western Canada and the U.S. recorded one of the earliest accounts of the Snake name origin. He relayed a story from the 1730s, told by a Piegan elder of the Blackfeet Tribe, confirming the association of this hand sign with the term "snake" for these Indian people. The Piegan elder described the Shoshone with a certain skepticism to say the least, stating,

> "no one believes what they say, and [they] are very treacherous; everyone one says they are rightly named Snake People, for their tongue is forked like that of a Rattle Snake, from which they have their name"[7]...

and further elaborated, "the Snake Indians, that race of liars, whose tongues are like rattle snakes, have already made war on us"[8].

The Skeen Pah and the Tribes of Celilo Falls, who are likely the ancestors to the people who now comprise the Nez Perce Tribe, Confederated Tribes of Warm Springs, Yakama Nation, or Umatilla Tribes, apparently referred to the Bannocks as *Wahkpuch Pel*, meaning the "Rattlesnake People".[9] This name was attributed to their vigilant and formidable nature. As described, the Bannocks were "[L]ike a rattler, the Bannock was always watching for somebody he could strike," and it was widely acknowledged that "[e]verything knew and feared the fierce Bannock, or river warrior". The description highlights the respect and caution the Bannock Indian warrior commanded among their enemies. However, the perspective that the sign literally represented a snake, was contrasted with yet another viewpoint from a Nez Perce named War Singer, who offered a different explanation regarding the origin of the name "Snake".

---

[6] David, Thompson, *Travels in Western North America*, 1784-1812, reprint ed., Victor G. Hopwood, ed. (Toronto: Macmillian of Canada, 1971), 191.
[7] Thompson, *Narrative of His Explorations in Western America*, 338.
[8] Ibid., 340.
[9] L. V. McWhorter, *Hear Me, My Chiefs! Nez Perce Legend & History* (Caldwell, Idaho: Caxton Press, 2001), 10.

These tribes [Shoshones, Bannocks, Lemhis, Utes, Comanches, and some Paiutes], all of the same people, termed themselves as belonging to the River of Many Curves. When they showed this name in sign language to the whites, the sinuous arm and hand movement was mistaken for a crawling snake, hence the name was fastened on both Indians and their River.[10]

Besides the snake reference, two other possible meanings have been proposed. Some believe the sign was a gesture to mimic salmon and indicated they were the "people who live where the salmon spawn"[11] or the "Salmon People".[12] Others maintain that the sinuous motion of the hand indicated that they were the "grass-weaver people".[13] Nonetheless, the Snake River has been named in honor of my people, a river system that flows through much of our homelands. I have inquired amongst my friends and family here in Fort Hall on the interpretation of the meaning without any confirmation either way. It should also be noted that very few tribal members today use or know Indian Plains Sign Language and it, like the Shoshone and Bannock languages is in danger of extinction.

Even the etymology of the word "Shoshone" is somewhat murky and open to debate. The term may very well be an Anglicized adaptation of the word *sosoni*, whose origins are also not definitively known. One possibility is that *sosoni* originates from the Shoshone word *sonigahni*, meaning "grass lodge," or it might come from *sonipe*, the Shoshone term for grass. Consequently, I believe there isn't a definitive or accurate pronunciation of the English word "Shoshone." Some people stress the high front [i] vowel phoneme at the end of the term, like the pronunciation in "heed," while others omit the vowel entirely. It is quite common for tribal members today to pronounce "Shoshone" in the term 'Shoshone-Bannock Tribes' without the final vowel feature. In contrast, the origin of the term "Bannock" is relatively

---

[10] Ibid., 10.
[11] Lalia Boone. *Idaho Place Names A Geographic Dictionary* (Moscow: The University of Idaho Press, 1988), 349.
[12] Brigham D. Madsen. *The Bannock of Idaho* (Moscow: University of Idaho Press, 1996), 19.
[13] Aubrey L. Haines, *The Yellowstone Story Volume 1* (Yellowstone National Park: Yellowstone Library and Museum Association in cooperation with Colorado Associated University Press, 1977), 22.

clearer, being a corrupt English version of *Panakwate*, the name the Bannock people use for themselves. *Panakwate* can be translated as "from the water" and it is possibly a reference to a geographical origin[14] or that they originally came from the direction of the ocean or other large water body.

Despite the Shoshone-Bannock Tribes establishing a Language and Culture Preservation Department and the introduction of the Chief Tahgee Elementary Academy Shoshone language immersion school for K–7th grade, the everyday use of the Shoshone language in Fort Hall remains infrequent and has a diminishing domain of use. Regarding the Bannock language, there is a small cohort of committed students, me included, who are actively immersed in its study. However, there are only a handful of elders who learned Bannock as their first language. Unfortunately, the Shoshone-Bannock High School, funded by the Bureau of Indian Education, does not currently offer instruction in either Bannock or Shoshone languages. Apparently, the school has encountered challenges in hiring and retaining qualified language instructors for these languages. We can only hope that the investments made by the Shoshone-Bannock Tribes and the dedication of the students, along with potential technological aids, will be adequate to uphold the language within the community for future generations.

In the Shoshone language, the term *Newe* translates to "the People," and is probably a better term to broadly describe our larger community. The Bannock people also refer to themselves using this designation, although in some Bannock dialects, the word *Neme* is used instead. *Newe* and its allophone *Neme* can also mean "a person speaking our native tongue".[15] From here on when the term *Newe* is used, it implies the Shoshone and Bannock, especially those Indians from Fort Hall. For many years, most European-Americans who encountered the *Newe* did not realize they were in fact two separate peoples who spoke related but mutually unintelligible languages. The confusion of the outsiders could have also been attributed to similarities between the Tribes and their close relations, as they often lived together in peace, traded, intermarried, and collaborated in subsistence and

---

[14] Sven Liljeblad, *Indian Peoples in Idaho* (Pocatello: Idaho State College, 1957), 88.
[15] Ibid., 23.

ceremony. Compounding the confusion among the non-Natives was the *Newe*'s tendency to switch their identity group names. Moreover, it is important to acknowledge that, even today, distinction remains between some Shoshone and Bannock people within the Fort Hall community, despite mixed heritage among many of us. This confusion is also compounded when you consider the fact that the name Shoshone-Bannock Tribes implies two separate and distinct tribes but is legally acknowledged as a single federally recognized tribe among 574 other federally recognized Indian tribes in the U.S.[16]

Historically, the *Newe* have a rich tradition of naming distinct *Newe* groups based on sustenance activities, geographical regions, or some other ethnographic criterion.[17] Thus, *Newe* group names for themselves can vary from foods to wealth. For example, the Shoshone and Bannock people of the Tetons and Jackson Hole area were dubbed *Badeheyadeka*. In this name, *baa-* signifies "water", *deheya* stands for deer, and *deka* means "eater". Thus, *Badeheyadeka* can be translated as "Water Deer Eaters" or "Elk Eaters" and the name also signifies that many elk live in that region. The horse-owning groups that pursued buffalo into the Northern Plains were labeled *Gutsundeka* or "Buffalo Eaters". This title also pertained to the *Newe* living on the Lemhi and upper Snake River. However, the same inhabitants of the Lemhi River region could also be recognized as the *Agaideka* or the "Salmon Eaters". In the mountainous regions of western Idaho and into eastern Oregon, where many deer once existed, lived the *Deheyadekane'e,* the "Deer Eater People".

The nomenclature extended beyond specific animals, as some *Newe* groups were named after the animal parts they consumed or the condition of the meat. The Wind River Shoshone, for instance, were known as *Gogohi'* due to their preference for eating or making use of the "guts" or "intestines" of buffalo, highlighting the importance of the buffalo stomach. Regions rich

---

[16] Indian Entities Recognized by and Eligible To Receive Services From the United States Bureau of Indian Affairs," Federal Register 87, no. FR 4636 (January 28, 2022): 4636-4641, Department of the Interior, Bureau of Indian Affairs, updated from the notice published on January 29, 2021 (86 FR 7554) and corrections on April 9, 2021 (86 FR 18552), Document Number 2022-01789.

[17] Liljeblad, *Indian Peoples in Idaho*, 54-56.

in rabbits bore the name *Ga'mmudeka'* or the "Rabbit Eaters". Additionally, the *Newe* residing near the Boise River and the lava fields of southcentral Idaho, where rock chucks, also called the yellow-bellied marmot, live in abundance, were named *Yahandeka* or the "Rock Chuck Eaters". Later and during colonization and conflict with European Americans, these same people became known as *Dedebiwa'ne'e*, or in Bannock *Tedebiwa'a* both of which translate to the "Poor People".

Delving further into the *Newe* naming convention, as it relates to plants, the tribes labeled those who consumed edible seeds like wild wheatgrass as *Hekandeka,* the "Wheat Grass Seed Eaters" and later after native bunchgrass communities were decimated by the livestock of emigrants, *Hukandeka* or the "Dust Eaters". The *Newe* whose wintering ground was near present day Fort Hall, Idaho, could also be called *Bohogoi* or the "Sagebrush Butte People". *Bohogoi* is also the Shoshone place name for a landmark called Ferry Butte, which literally translates as "Sagebrush Butte". The Indians who went south to collect pine nuts from the single-leaf pinyon pine near the City of Rocks and northern Nevada were called the *Debadeka* or the "Pine Nut Eaters". However, this name could also be applied to the *Newe* who used seeds from the limber pine tree, which has a greater range in their territory. The mixed bands of Shoshone and Bannock who lived along the Weiser and Payette Rivers in southwestern Idaho were known as *Sewoki'i* or *Sehewoki'i*, which can literally be translated as "Willows Standing in a Row". They could also be called the *Seheewooki'nee'* or the "Willows Standing in a Row People". The *Pihaguyudeka'*, known as the "Sweet Root Eaters", lived along the Portneuf River, near its headwaters. The Bannock original name for this river is *Pihaguye Nahukwa*, or the "Sweet Root River." They also frequented the area of *Paaguchuha*, which translates to "Warm Water" and is now known as Lava Hot Springs. An alternative way to say Lava Hot Springs is *Paaguchuhaade.* Some Indians from Fort Hall also simply refer to Lava Hot Springs as *Boha Baa*, which can be translated as "Power Water", which is a fitting name if you ever had the experience of soaking your sore muscles or bones in the pools.

As mentioned earlier, *Newe* groups could also be named after fish. For example, the Snake River, specifically below the Shoshone Falls, was renowned for massive salmon, leading to the people of that region being dubbed *Bia'agaideka'* or the "Big

Salmon Eaters". Interestingly, any group of people could earn different identity names contingent on their seasonal activities and to this day, *Newe* individuals and families continue to identify as belonging to one or more group names of their forebears. Another name that was ascribed to the Boise Valley Indians, especially during the massive salmon migrations that once came into the basin, was the *Soho'agaideka* or "Cottonwood Salmon Eaters". This was because, prior to European arrival, the area was lush with woodlands of willow and cottonwood, a verdancy nurtured by major rivers like the Snake, Boise, Payette, and Weiser. Moreover, the *Newe* groups that lived by or often visited the Bear River, and the Big and Little Lost Rivers were termed *Baingwideka*, known as the "Fish Eaters". This rich tapestry of nomenclature not only identifies but also connects the *Newe* people to their homelands and activities.

As for what is now Wyoming, certain Shoshone groups from the Yellowstone region were known as *Duuwihi*, or the "Black Knife" Shoshone. This designation was influenced by the dark color of the obsidian they utilized to craft their *wihi*, meaning "knife". In contrast, Western Shoshone communities from northeastern Nevada were often termed *Dosawihi*, known as the "White Knife" Shoshone. As iron knives became prevalent among the *Newe*, the term *wihi* expanded its meaning to also denote "iron." Consequently, some *Newe* groups were named after abundant geological resources or tool materials specific to certain regions of their homelands.

A more general term for the people of Yellowstone, or other mountainous areas for that matter, was the *Dukudeka* or *Doyanee*[18]. The *Dukudeka'* are the only Indians known to have held year-round residence in what is now known as Yellowstone National Park.[19] LaSalle Pocatello, a respected elder of the Shoshone-Bannock Tribes, described their homelands as:

> Tukudeka'a Around ... Fork of the Salmon River. Around Mt. Borah. Back of the Sawtooth mountains. Up in the high country. When they got down in the valley, they were the

---

[18]David Dominick, "The Sheepeaters," in *Annals of Wyoming*, vol. 36, No. 2, ed. Lola M. Homsher and Katherine Halverson (Wyoming State Archives and Historical Department, 1964), 136.
[19] Haines, *The Yellowstone Story Volume One*, 22 and 29.

same as agaide'ka'a or the Boise Indians Sewoki'i. The Sewoki'i went as far as Warm Springs[20]

In the Shoshone and Bannock languages, *Duku* or *Tuku* means "meat", because this particular group of Indians consumed a lot of bighorn sheep, which they also called "meat", their name translates as "Meat Eaters". In Western academic literature they are colloquially known as the "Sheep Eaters", or the "Bighorn Sheep Eaters", as domestic sheep are alien species to North America.

Various sources have mistakenly referred to the *Dukudeka* as "Tukuarika"[21] or perhaps these authors used the "r" to describe the "d" phoneme, as there is no r's in the Shoshone or Bannock languages. Additionally, the terms Bannock or Bannack are corrupt versions of *Panakwate*, which is the authentic name for my people. In my family, there's a running joke about the term Bannack, where we humorously emphasize the 'nack' part of the word, which always brings laughter to everyone. I cannot explain why it is funny to us, I guess it is just an Indian thing, kind of like Baby Yoda being a papoose. This humorous emphasis on 'nack' typically occurs during our journeys in southern Montana, where that state preferred the term 'Bannack' over 'Bannock'. This region of Montana is dotted with various place names, such as the notable gold mining ghost town of Bannack, as opposed to the alternative, yet also corrupted version, Bannock, commonly used in southern Idaho. Anyway, I digress. Let's return to the story of the *Dukudeka*.

The *Dukudeka*, who also included the *Seheewooki'nee'*, were among some of the last American Indian groups in the lower 48 states to be forcibly relocated to reservations. The exact timing and circumstances surrounding the relocation and removal of the Wyoming *Dukudeka* is not known, but the second Superintendent of Yellowstone National Park, Philetus W. Norris, wrote in his 1881 Annual Report,[22]

---

[20] Sven Liljeblad, interview with La Salle Pocatello, 1966, in "Field Notebook #3," Sven Liljeblad Papers, box 86, folder 14, page 6.
[21] Steward, *Basin-Plateau Aboriginal Sociopolitical Groups*, 186.
[22] Joel C. Janetski, *Indians in Yellowstone National Park* (Salt Lake City: The University of Utah Press, 2002), 65.

> To prevent these forays [referencing travel into the Park], in council at their agency on Ross Fork of Snake River, in Idaho, and in Ruby Valley, Montana, in early 1880, I obtained a solemn pledge from them to not thereafter go east of Henry's Lake, in Montana, or north of Hart Lake in Wyoming, to which . . . they faithfully adhered.

Although Norris made efforts to prevent this, both the Shoshone and Bannock travelled into the region throughout the 1880s and Park Superintendents expressed frustrations about Shoshone and Bannock sightings near the Park, where they camped and hunted. In some correspondence from May 23, 1888, the Park Superintendent noted:

> ... That a considerable number of Indians from your agency have been hunting near the Park during the past summer is a well established fact. The presence of these Indians in close proximity to the Park is a serious annoyance to those charged with its protection as a constant watch as supervision is necessary to prevent them from getting into the park, the boundaries of which are unmarked. The Park is visited by many people from the East who are unaccustomed to seeing Indians and the mere rumor of the presence of Indians in the Park is sufficient to cause much excitement and anxiety amount the tourist visitors.

Despite the *Dukudeka* being the sole inhabitants of the Yellowstone Plateau, their land rights were never acknowledged by the U.S. government. This oversight reflects a broader pattern of disregard for Indian land claims. Numerous families from the Fort Hall Reservation know their ancestral roots intertwine with the Yellowstone area, with tribal elders affirming that the *Dukudeka* comprised both Shoshone and Bannock. Additionally, descendants of the *Dukudeka* from Yellowstone have also made their home on the Wind River Reservation[23] and the Shoshone of Wind River have their own names and histories for Western Wyoming.

The Yellowstone Plateau, known for its harsh and challenging environment, was the home of the Yellowstone family of the Shoshone-Bannock Tribes. According to the oral history passed down by Martha Yellowstone Seaman, born in Yellowstone,

---

[23] Liljeblad, *Indian Peoples in Idaho*, 94.

this family depended on the park's geysers for warmth during harsh winters[24]. The Bannock say, *"Newe o Patotonoi Wakwamikwai manipenni yakwi. Oteu iwau tekkapema pemma nana'atakussu tekkapekayu,"* which translates as "We Indians used to live in Yellowstone, largely due to its abundance of food resources."

In historic times, the evolution of identity names went beyond representation of primary subsistence activity or geographic location. The names began to symbolize social standing. In the Shoshone language, some *Newe* from the Fort Hall region were referred to as *Wihinai*. In Bannock, they're called *Wihinakwate*. Both terms can be translated as "on the knife side", "from iron", or "on the iron side", which was ascribed to them as a sort of acknowledgment of technological superiority to other Shoshone and Northern Paiute groups[25]. Therefore, it is probably safe to say that this group of Shoshone and Bannock Indians were among the first to begin trade with Europeans. The *Gutsundeka* or "Buffalo Eater" people were also equated with affluence and high social status because they were a group of people recognized as being owners and masters of the horse and often earned war honors on hunting excursions or raids— frequently near or within enemy territory. Collectively, the *Newe* community from Fort Hall has ancestral ties to over 30 unique groups, each distinguished by their own names, territories, mobility and sustenance patterns, and cultural practices. A compilation of some Shoshone and Bannock linguistic names representing different groups scattered across modern-day regions of Idaho, Montana, Wyoming, Utah, and Nevada is provided in Figure 1.

The map in Figure 1 reveals the historical expanse of the *Newe* across Idaho, Montana, Wyoming, Utah, and Nevada, emphasizing the rich cultural heritage and the varying identities shaped by their environment and lifestyle. It also shows the challenge of preserving these traditional identities within the context of modern legal and territorial boundaries, particularly in areas like Yellowstone and Grand Teton National Parks where traditional Indian uses conflict with conservation policies.

---

[24] Lori Ann Edmo, "Yellowstone Family Wintered Near Geysers," *Sho-Ban News Festival Edition*, August 8, 2022, 38.
[25] Sven Liljeblad, *The Idaho Indians in Transition, 1805-1960* (Pocatello: Idaho State University Museum, 1972), 13.

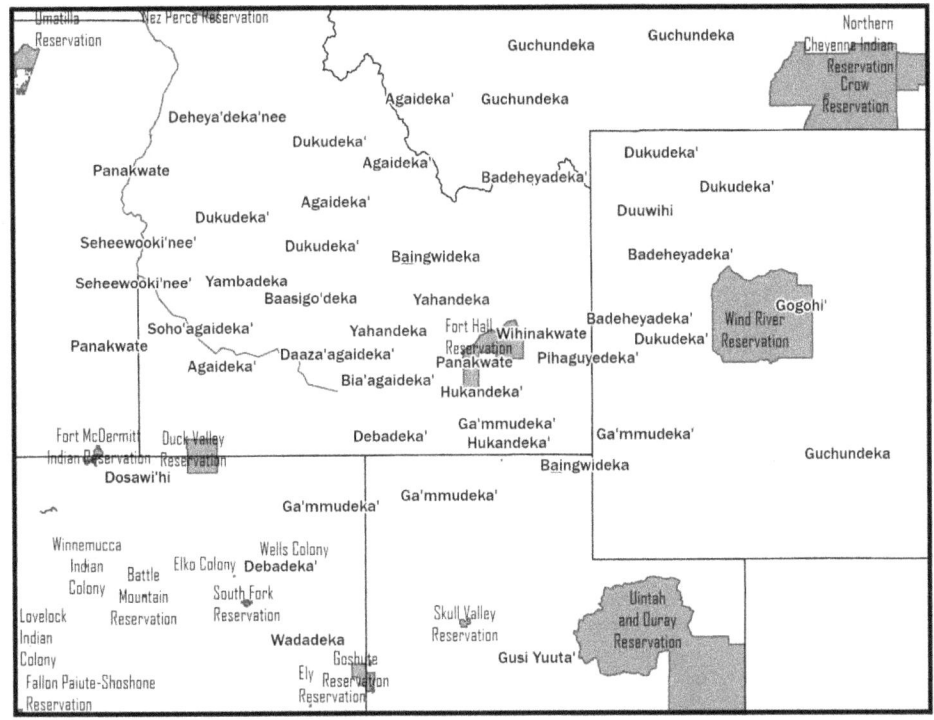

Figure 1. This map illustrates the diverse names and locations of some Shoshone and Bannock groups, as denoted in their respective languages, juxtaposed within present-day political boundaries.

It is crucial to understand that these group names were not rigid labels for distinct bands. Instead, they were adaptive classifications rooted in seasonal and regional resources. Unlike the English expressions "to live" and "to travel", the Shoshone used words that merged the two into one. For example, the nouns *nemi* and *yemega* in the Shoshone language are the singular and plural forms of a word that describes "travel, wander, roam, and live".[26] In other words, where a Shoshone person lived and where they moved were one and the same in their native tongue, and not limited to a single location but a multitude of places where they secured their subsistence. For example, the Bannock term *tebiwa* can mean "Indian land" or "one's own country" and when Chief Taghee (*Taggi*) signed the 1868 Fort Bridger Treaty, a Bannock Indian's native land was "anywhere he could find something to

---

[26] Beverly Crum and Jon Dayley, *Shoshoni Texts Occasional Papers and Monographs in Cultural Anthropology and Linguistics* (Boise: Boise State University, 1997), 285.

eat...and could safely pitch his tipi".[27] As the *Newe* subsistence rested heavily upon a wide variety of foods and materials, their hunting, fishing, and gathering activities required the group to be highly mobile. They would move place to place, disband and regroup, ever moving with the seasons as the natural bounty increased and waned. Thus, it is not surprising that the Bannock and Shoshone were perceived as athletic,[28] a trait likely nurtured by their nomadic and highly active lifestyle, rich in the diet of lean meats and diverse plant-based foods and cold clean river water.

The social structure of the Bannock and Shoshone tribes was notably dynamic, with members frequently forming various loosely connected groups. It was not uncommon for families to move and align with different groups as situations and alliances changed. As a case in point, those identified as Shoshone often joined Bannock bands, leading to intermarriages and the creation of mixed communities. Even with linguistic disparities between the two tribes, communication wasn't a significant issue; many among them were trilingual if one considers the inclusion of the Plains Indian Sign Language. Some could have also spoken the language of neighboring tribes, such as the Nez Perce, Crow, and others.

Language is a powerful carrier of identity and historical memory. While Shoshone and Bannock share many cultural and linguistic features, particularly in how they describe social groups—they are not mutually intelligible. Both, however, descend from a common proto-language[29] and belong to the Numic branch of the Uto-Aztecan Language Family, alongside Northern Paiute. This ancient language family is one of the oldest and most geographically widespread in the Western Hemisphere, stretching from central Mexico's Aztecoidan languages to the Great Basin and northward into present-day Idaho, Wyoming, and—historically—even Montana. Today, Bannock is spoken primarily on the Fort Hall Reservation in Idaho, where it is considered critically endangered, with only a handful of fluent speakers remaining. Shoshone, while also endangered, continues to be

---

[27] Liljeblad, *Indian Peoples in Idaho*, 51-52.
[28] Brigham D. Madsen, *The Bannock of Idaho* (Moscow: University of Idaho Press, 1996), 19.
[29] Cleve Davis, "*A Comparative and Historical Linguistic Analysis of the Bannock Dialect of the Northern Paiute Language*" (master's thesis, Idaho State University, 2010), 40.

spoken more widely—across the Fort Hall and Wind River Reservations, as well as among small communities in Nevada, Utah, and even parts of eastern California. Historically, both languages once covered a much broader landscape across the Intermountain West, long before the confinement of Tribal peoples to reservation boundaries.

Although Shoshone and Bannock have branched from a singular ancestral tongue, their mutual intelligibility is only about 65%, similar to the relationship between English and German.[30] Yet despite these linguistic divergences, both languages continue to serve as powerful vessels of cultural memory and identity, maintaining the deep bond between the *Newe* and the natural world that sustained them.

The names our ancestors gave to their bands were more than labels—they were reflections of the land itself. Band names often marked the natural plant and animal communities where life was most abundant, signaling the regions where water, roots, game, and fish could be found. In this way, language preserved the map of our survival across the landscape. However, with colonization, many of these names changed. Groups once known for the resources they gathered became known instead as the "Poor People" or the "Dust Eaters"—a stark testament to the loss and depletion of traditional food sources, and the forced exile to marginal lands where settlers would not contest their presence. When I reflect on the realities of reservation life today, I often wonder: what names would our Shoshone and Bannock ancestors give us now? What words would they choose to describe the way we live today?

The original homelands of the Fort Hall Shoshone and Bannock once stretched across vast, living territories—spanning from the high deserts of eastern Oregon to the headwaters of the Salmon, Snake, Missouri, Humboldt, Yellowstone, and Colorado Rivers.[31] In their quest for sustenance, these people collectively

---

[30] Davis, "A Comparative and Historical Linguistic Analysis," 40.
[31] Catherine S. Fowler and Sven Liljeblad, "Northern Paiute," in *Handbook of North American Indians*, vol. 11, *Great Basin*, ed. Warren L. D'Azevedo, gen. ed. William C. Sturtevant (Washington, DC: Smithsonian Institution, 1986), 435.; Steward, *Basin-Plateau Aboriginal Sociopolitical Groups*, Territorial Map; Liljeblad, *Indian Peoples in Idaho*, 63; Omer C.

embraced a vast notion of territory,[32] not measured in fences or deeded plots. They followed the migrations of animals and fish, the cycles of the seasons, and the leadership of those who could skillfully navigate the dangers posed by other Tribal nations. These lands are more than mere geographic areas; they are integral to our identity and survival as Shoshone and Bannock peoples. Today, these rivers and deserts remain a part of who we are, even if the reservation boundaries tell a different story. The land continues to speak our history, and through it, so do we.

Considering the unjust appropriation of our lands through treaties and other means, and the rigid territorial boundaries depicted in academic research, it has become increasingly vital to assert and reaffirm our enduring relationship with western Wyoming and other regions from which we originate. It's crucial to acknowledge that the traditional territorial perspectives of the Bannock and Shoshone starkly contrast with Western concepts of land ownership. The fluidity highlights the complexity in defining our original homelands and the origins of our people. It's a process steeped in nuance and one that should be left to us, the Indians, to articulate and define.

Although many of us now make our home on the Fort Hall Indian Reservation, we know we come from our larger original territories. Our historical names for ourselves draw from the very heart of nature and the landscapes that nurtured us and shaped our language and culture. Such names encapsulate our profound bond with the environment and our place within it.

Chapter 2 - Bibliography

Boone, Lalia. Idaho Place Names: A Geographic Dictionary. Moscow: University of Idaho Press, 1988.

Stewart, "The Question of Bannock Territory," in *Languages and Cultures of Western North America*, Essays in Honor of Sven S. Liljeblad, ed. Earl H. Swanson, Jr. (Pocatello: Idaho State University Press, 1970), 214, 219; Peter Nabokov and Lawrence Loendorf, "Visitors on the West: Bannock and Nez Perce," in *American Indians and Yellowstone National Park* (National Park Service: Yellowstone National Park, Wyoming, 2002), 170, 176; John C. Ewers, *Indian Life on the Upper Missouri* (Norman: University of Oklahoma Press, 1988), 16; Dominick, "The Sheepeaters," 131; Janetski, *Indians in Yellowstone*, 65.
[32] Ibid., 52.

Crum, Beverly, and Jon Dayley. Shoshoni Texts: Occasional Papers and Monographs in Cultural Anthropology and Linguistics. Boise: Boise State University, 1997.

Davis, Cleve. "A Comparative and Historical Linguistic Analysis of the Bannock Dialect of the Northern Paiute Language." Master's thesis, Idaho State University, 2010.

Dominick, David. "The Sheepeaters." In Annals of Wyoming, vol. 36, no. 2, edited by Lola M. Homsher and Katherine Halverson, 131–136. Wyoming State Archives and Historical Department, 1964.

Edmo, Lori Ann. "Yellowstone Family Wintered Near Geysers." Sho-Ban News Festival Edition, August 8, 2022.

Ewers, John C. Indian Life on the Upper Missouri. Norman: University of Oklahoma Press, 1988.

Fowler, Catherine S., and Sven Liljeblad. "Northern Paiute." In Handbook of North American Indians, vol. 11, Great Basin, edited by Warren L. D'Azevedo, general editor William C. Sturtevant, 435. Washington, DC: Smithsonian Institution, 1986.

Haines, Aubrey L. The Yellowstone Story, vol. 1. Yellowstone National Park: Yellowstone Library and Museum Association in cooperation with Colorado Associated University Press, 1977.

Janetski, Joel C. Indians in Yellowstone National Park. Salt Lake City: University of Utah Press, 2002.

Liljeblad, Sven. Indian Peoples in Idaho. Pocatello: Idaho State College, 1957.

Liljeblad, Sven. The Idaho Indians in Transition, 1805–1960. Pocatello: Idaho State University Museum, 1972.

Liljeblad, Sven. Interview with La Salle Pocatello, 1966. In "Field Notebook #3," Sven Liljeblad Papers, box 86, folder 14, page 6.

Madsen, Brigham D. The Bannock of Idaho. Moscow: University of Idaho Press, 1996.

McWhorter, L. V. Hear Me, My Chiefs! Nez Perce Legend & History. Caldwell, Idaho: Caxton Press, 2001.

Murphy, Robert F., and Yolanda Murphy. "Shoshone-Bannock Subsistence and Society." Anthropological Records 16, no. 7. Berkeley and Los Angeles: University of California Press, 1960.

Nabokov, Peter, and Lawrence Loendorf. "Visitors on the West: Bannock and Nez Perce." In American Indians and Yellowstone National Park, 170, 176. National Park Service: Yellowstone National Park, Wyoming, 2002.

Steward, Julian H. Basin-Plateau Aboriginal Sociopolitical Groups. Washington, DC: U.S. Government Printing Office, 1938.

Stewart, Omer C. "The Question of Bannock Territory." In Languages and Cultures of Western North America: Essays in Honor of Sven S. Liljeblad, edited by Earl H. Swanson, Jr., 214, 219. Pocatello: Idaho State University Press, 1970.

Thompson, David. Narrative of His Explorations in Western America, 1784–1812, edited by J. B. Tyrrell. Toronto: The Champlain Society, 1916.

Thompson, David. Travels in Western North America, 1784–1812, edited by Victor G. Hopwood. Reprint edition. Toronto: Macmillan of Canada, 1971.

U.S. Department of the Interior, Bureau of Indian Affairs. "Indian Entities Recognized by and Eligible To Receive Services From the United States Bureau of Indian Affairs." Federal Register 87, no. FR 4636 (January 28, 2022): 4636–4641.

Chapter 3 - What Coyote Taught Us About Hunting

When I was a boy, my father made me give away the first deer I killed. I didn't understand it then. I wanted to keep that animal. I felt that I had earned it. But he made me give it away. That one act taught me more about generosity and responsibility than any lesson in school ever could. For the *Newe* people, hunting was never just about getting meat. It was about survival, hard work, and providing for those who could not provide for themselves. And for thousands of years, those lessons were passed down not through books, but through stories—oral traditions carried by elders and shaped by the rhythms of the seasons. One of our stories is about *Izahpe'a*, or Coyote, and how he changed the way our people hunt. The story goes something like this.

A very long time ago the birds and animals were the people and they all spoke the same language and understood each other. The people lived together in a lush meadow below a mountain. The leaders of the animal people were the *Isha,* the Wolf, and his little brother the *Izahpe'a*, the Coyote. Near their village, there was a long tunnel running beneath the mountain, leading to its other side. When the people got hungry, they could go through this mountain to get their food on the other side. There was a little gate on the tunnel that everyone was required to close when traveling to and from the place where they gathered their food. *Isha* and *Izahpe'a*, leaders of the people, instructed everyone to close the gate when they went out to hunt and upon returning. This measure was taken to prevent the animals from escaping.

In the area where they got their food, the food animals and cranes were unafraid of the people. The people could pass through the tunnel, select the crane or animal they wanted, walk up to it, and kill it. It was a very easy life. It was easy hunting because the cranes and animals did not fear the people. The people always did like they were told by *Isha* and *Izahpe'a*. Their leaders had warned that if the gate remained open, the animals would escape and become scared of humans, making the hunt difficult. This is the way it was a very long time ago and it was not like it is today.

One day, *Isha* and *Izahpe'a* made a plan to go hunt on the other side of the mountain together. They always hunted together, but when it came time to go hunt, *Izahpe'a* said, "I am going to hunt by myself." *Isha* did not want to argue, so he said, "Little brother, remember to close the gate so the food animals won't get out." *Izahpe'a* heard him but thought to himself, "I don't like it when someone tells me what to do." *Izahpe'a* didn't like to listen to his elder brother or anyone for that matter. He didn't believe what anyone else said either. *Izahpe'a* always did as he pleased.

When *Izahpe'a* went into the tunnel to hunt, he shut the gate behind him. After he got through the tunnel, he climbed up a hill to see all the animals below. There he sat and gazed at all the animals—the cranes, elk, buffalo, and deer. He thought to himself, "there is a lot of good food here!" As *Izahpe'a* sat and watched the animals, they looked back at him with blank stares on their faces. A big river flowed around the animals, keeping them in place. As *Izahpe'a* sat there watching them, he thought to himself, "I do not think it is fair that the people should kill all these tame animals." Then he said, out loud, "There is no honor in killing these animals. They don't move fast and they have nowhere to run and hide." As *Izahpe'a* continued to watch, he then made a decision and said,

> It's not fair for the people to come here and kill these animals when they are like this. I will open the gate and leave it open so all these animals can run out and be free. When they escape, they will be afraid of people. For here on out the people will have to earn their food through skill and sweat.

So, *Izahpe'a* opened the gate, and all the animals escaped. Once they reached the other side of the mountain, they became afraid of people and quickly scattered into the forests and were scared of the people.

Since that day, People cannot get near these animals—the elk, deer, and other game—because of what *Izahpe'a* did long ago. That is how *Izahpe'a* wronged his people by letting the animals out. After *Izahpe'a* did that, whenever his people needed food, they had to work for it. The people were not happy with what *Izahpe'a* had done and sometimes they went hungry and some even died, but *Izahpe'a* felt satisfied with his decision. *Izahpe'a* thought it was good that when you wanted something, you had to work for it. Ever since then, when the People wanted meat, they had to earn it. And when they finally got it, they appreciated it more because they had earned it. This also made them take better care of the meat, and they devised ways to preserve it for hard times. *Izahpe'a* did these things a long time ago and things have been different ever since.

There are many versions of this story, each meant to entertain but also to teach—especially to children. It reminds us that hard work is part of hunting, and that's just the way it is. It teaches respect for elders, like Wolf, who warned Coyote to close the gate. And most of all, it shows that when something is earned through effort, it's valued and not wasted. In other words, by letting the animals go free, *Izahpe'a* didn't just change the hunt—he made us value what we earn through hard work.

Many people outside our culture laugh at these old stories, calling them myths or children's tales. But those stories carry deep truth. You've probably seen what happens when someone gets something they didn't earn. A child gets a new toy, plays with it once, and leaves it in the dirt. Adults do the same—whether it's money, food, or opportunity. If you don't sweat for it, you won't take care of it.

Today, we have long-range rifles, UTVs, drones, critter cams, scents, decoys, digital maps, and many other devices to make the hunt easier. Some hunters kill out of habit, pride, or worse for trophies—not out of need. It makes me wonder if a kill still holds meaning when the hunt requires so little effort.

At Fort Hall, we have a tradition: when a boy kills his first animal—whether it's a deer, elk, or anything else—he gives the whole thing away to someone in need. And that gift should be clean, well-cared for, and in good condition—not half-spoiled or neglected. Better yet, it should already be cut up and packaged! Now that is a good gift. That's how we begin to teach what hunting really means. It's not about showing off or chasing the biggest rack. It's about feeding people when they need it most. And let's be honest—these days, many of us have more than enough to eat. Take only what is needed.

I still remember my first deer. It was a doe, and I didn't want to give it up. But my dad made me. And I've never forgotten how that felt. That lesson stuck with me. These stories and traditions didn't just entertain, they shaped us. They taught discipline, respect, and generosity without ever needing a raised hand. In fact, they were a preferred method of discipline over physical punishment[1].

In our traditional culture, ideas like "regulations" or "conservation measures" didn't exist—because we did not need them. Waste, disrespect, and overharvesting weren't issues that had to be controlled by law. They were prevented through teachings. In Shoshone, we call that *Deniwape*. In Bannock, it's *Tenichui*. These words go far beyond instruction—they carry spiritual weight. And in Bannock, *Tenichui* can also serve as a warning: if you don't follow the teachings, there will be consequences.

Our people understood the purpose of conservation long before the word existed. We harvested only what we needed, we used everything we took, and we honored the animal or plant that gave its life. That wasn't law—it was tradition. It was survival.

Boys were taught by their fathers, uncles, and grandfathers. Girls were guided by their mothers, aunts, and grandmothers. Everyone had a role. And those roles carried weight in the hunting or food gathering process. You didn't become a man just because you got older—you became a man because you took responsibility for your people, showed courage, and had the discipline and know-how to provide food. One elder, Andrew Johnson (*Tuwahbahba*), put it this way:

> Our people learned from generation to generation, beginning at conception, the ways that teach you life's lessons. A mother must change her lifestyle through her love and compassion to accommodate the needs of the child. Every emotion, thought, and food that is ingested while pregnant is experienced by the child. Once the child is old enough, they will learn through trial and error, good mentors will teach them the ways of nature... After you understand who you are and how to discipline yourself, you become your best friend or your worst enemy. You must always balance yourself with everything in the universe. There are teachings and ceremonies that make this possible. Listen to traditions and following prayer ways will help you keep your positive mind. Your mind will lead you

---

[1] Laine Thom, *Becoming Brave* (San Francisco: Chronicle Books, 1992), 21.

down that path of goodness. We are all together in this life and we can help each other through our prayers and encouragement.[2]

In the old days, being a man meant something. You were expected to hunt, fight, and protect your people. And you didn't always make it home. That is why our ancestors built responsibility into the language. In Shoshone, a child didn't just call one man "*appe*" (father)—he used that word for his father's brothers, too. If a man died, his brothers stepped in to raise the children. That was their duty. It was the same for women. A wife called her husband's brothers *guhaape'e*—also meaning husband. If her husband died, one of his brothers took responsibility for her and the children. This wasn't about control. It was about survival. No child was left behind. No woman was left alone.

Sometimes, this way of life meant a man could have more than one wife—not because of lust, greed, or some selfish desire for dominance, as many outsiders have assumed. That's how the Western world often sees it: through a lens shaped by their own culture, religion, and moral superiority. Outsiders call this polygamy, like it was some perverse system. But that's not what it was—not for our people. It was a duty. When men died in battle or while hunting dangerous animals, there were widows and children left behind. Someone had to step in, provide for them, and protect them. A man didn't take on another wife to serve himself—he did it to serve his community. To hold a broken family together. To keep the people strong. It wasn't something to mock. It was something to respect. It was a beautiful thing.

Even now, those old expectations haven't gone away entirely—at least based on my observations here in Fort Hall. If you want respect as a man, especially as a *Newe* man, you have to earn it. And very few even try. It's certainly not earned by being angry, bitter, self-pitying, violent, lazy, or strung out on alcohol and drugs—dragging others down and becoming a burden to your own family. A respectable man is dangerous—but he controls it. He's disciplined, steady, and willing to suffer. He trains his mind and body for hardship because he knows life will test him. He speaks the truth, which is part of *Deniwape*, even when it costs

---

[2] LaNada War Jack, *Native Resistance* (Brookfield, MO: The Donning Company Publishers, 2019), 30.

him. He doesn't chase recognition. He doesn't complain. He takes responsibility—for his family, his work, and his future. He protects the people he loves. He brings order, not chaos. His wife and kids sleep better because they know he's there. He doesn't just carry the weight—he carries it with purpose. He builds. He provides. He leads.

That's real strength. That's the hunter-warrior standard. And it still matters. Now more than ever.

Chapter 3 - Bibliography

Thom, Laine. Becoming Brave. San Francisco: Chronicle Books, 1992.

War Jack, LaNada. Native Resistance. Brookfield, MO: The Donning Company Publishers, 2019.

Chapter 4 – The Buffalo Nation

While the North American bison, also known as buffalo, holds a prominent place in our cultural heritage and lifestyle, it is crucial to recognize that our dependency extended beyond this one species. The diverse ecosystems of Wyoming's high mountain parks offered a rich tapestry of wildlife, such as elk, bighorn sheep, moose, and deer, as well as a multitude of smaller game species. The importance of these animals went beyond mere subsistence, and many played a role in our stories and legends. Additionally, the region's aquatic systems — its lakes and streams — were vibrant habitats for various fish species, contributing significantly to food reliability. Fertile lands and unique soils nurtured a wide range of plant life that provided berries, roots, and other edible vegetables. These plants met essential dietary and medicinal needs, supporting the health and well-being of our people. For thousands of years the abundance of natural food sources in Wyoming's mountains, plains, lakes, and streams played a critical role in sustaining our people, highlighting the rich natural bounty that the region historically provided.

At one time the buffalo roamed widely throughout the homelands of the Fort Hall Shoshone and Bannock. In fact, before European contact, some estimates suggest that the Buffalo Nation could have numbered as many as 60 million[1] and historical records indicate its habitat spanned most of the North America continent.[2] It is thought that the *Newe* acquired the horse sometime in the late 1600s or early 1700s, and that they obtained the horse from their Comanche[3] relatives or perhaps the Utes,[4] who in turn acquired it from the Spanish who were colonizing in the southwest. While certain parts of Wyoming's terrain are unsuitable for horseback travel, much of the terrain is navigable on horseback. In fact, crossing mountain passes in the Tetons and

---

[1] Philip W. Hedrick, "Conservation Genetics and North American Bison (Bison bison)," *Journal of Heredity* (2009): 411.
[2] R. List, G. Ceballos, Curtin C., G. Gogan PJP, J. Pacheco, and J. Turetts, "Historical Distribution and Challenges to Bison Recovery in the Northern Chihuahuan Desert," *Conservation Biology* (2007): 1487-1494.
[3] Sven Liljeblad, *The Idaho Indians in Transition, 1805-1960* (Pocatello: Idaho State University Museum, 1972), 9.
[4] Steward, *Basin-Plateau Aboriginal Sociopolitical Groups* (Salt Lake City: The University of Utah Press, 1938), 201.

Yellowstone, even at altitudes exceeding 10,000 feet, was often preferred to the more circuitous and lower elevation trails where ambushes could be more easily laid.

Although the origin of the horse with the Shoshone and Bannock is not definitively known, there is an oral tradition of the "Little Bu'ngu (Horse)".[5] The story goes that the *Newe* once used two pack animals during hunting season, one would eat anything from spoiled soup to meat bones. This animal was the *sadee'* or what we now call the "dog". The other four-legged animal would eat grass and weeds, and it was called the *bu'ngu*, the "horse". The story goes that one-day, Little *Bu'ngu* told the people that he had to go away but said he would return someday and would be bigger. After Little *Bu'ngu* left and many winters following, there were two hunters out on the prairie, and they came across a very strange animal. They tried to get close, but it ran away. When they got to camp and told what they saw no one knew what the animal was. So, they traveled to another village to ask them if they knew what it was. At that village an old man spoke up and said,

> "Maybe it is the Little One that came back. When I was a little boy they told stories about the bu'ngu, and said that someday he would return". The old man than asked how big was the animal and did it have four legs? The hunter replied, "[i]t is big like an paa'teheya (elk), or dupatehe'ya (moose), and it has four legs".[6]

This is not the only story about the horse among the *Newe*. I have also heard another oral history of how the horse came among the Shoshone to the north. The story goes something like this, once, two brothers had a yearning to explore the land to the south. They ventured far into the south, encountering various tribes along the way. In these lands, both brothers took wives from the other tribes and lived among the other tribes for a long time. It was here that the brothers first came across the horse, which they acquired and mastered. As time passed, one brother wanted to return home. The other, however, had grown fond of his new life in the south and chose to stay behind. The brother that returned home to his relatives introduced the horse to his people.

---

[5] Donna E. Houtz McArthur, *When the Smoke Goes Straight Up* (Pocatello: Gateway Printers, 2012), 104-105
[6] Ibid., 105-106.

Although it is pure speculation on my part, I wonder if the story of Little *Bu'ngu* and the Two Brothers are related. Perhaps the two brothers are the same two hunters who encountered the horse on the prairie. I also wonder if the brother who stayed in the south started the Comanche Nation? Nonetheless, the modern horse transformed our culture. With the enhanced mobility and carrying capacity that horses provided, the *Newe* became more adept in hunting, facilitating an increase in the accumulation of food, hides, and other valuable commodities. Consequently, this had a major impact upon their diet, economic structures, social interactions, and contributed to changes in language and culture. Furthermore, the possession of horses and the subsequent buffalo hunting activities in the Plains engendered distinct cultural nuances between the *Newe* to the east and *Newe* who resided in Nevada and southeastern Oregon.

Before the transformation occurred, some scholars speculated that the migration of the Shoshonean speaking people to the Great Plains started somewhere in the Great Basin or Southwest[7]. At one time, the Shoshonean frontier had extended north to the Saskatchewan plains of Canada,[8] and southwards, with the Comanche raiding into Mexico.[9] To the east, by the mid-seventeenth century, the Shoshone had expanded their domain as far as the Black Hills and had contact with the Kiowa and other eastern tribes.[10] Mounted bands of Shoshone and Bannock retained all their traditional food-gathering skills, and their vast knowledge of plants subsidized the reliance upon animal life. *Newe* equestrian groups had their own distinct style to differentiate themselves from other Plains Indians, but they also lived in skin teepees like many other tribes of the Great Plains. Skin containers took the place of basketry, the former being better suited for travel by horse. Groups began to unite to travel in large numbers as a defense tactic against enemies. In times of defense, they organized under the most distinguished and wisest of the warriors, called *nabidenge dai'gwahni,* who were chosen for their abilities to lead in battle and in matters of defense. In *Newe*

---

[7] Pekka Hämäläinen, *The Comanche Empire* (New Haven: Yale University Press, 2008), 350-351.
[8] Brigham D. Madsen, *The Lemhi: Sacajawea's People* (Caldwell, Idaho: Caxton Press, 2000), 23.
[9] Hämäläinen, *The Comanche Empire*, 350-351.
[10] Ibid., 21-22.

society, a person's reputation was everything. It wasn't just what people said about you—it was what earned you respect and gave you influence. Your name carried weight because of how you lived and the words that came out of your mouth.

As a living testament to the lesson of Coyote—that what we earn through hard work must be respected and never wasted—I want to share a glimpse into how the *Newe* used the animals they killed. Among the most important of these was the buffalo. It wasn't just meat—it was shelter, tools, clothing, and ceremony. Our people found a purpose for nearly every part of it, not only out of survival, but out of appreciation and gratitude. What follows is more than a list—it's a reflection of how far our ancestors would go to make the most of a kill. And after showing how central this animal was to our way of life, I'll speak to its tragic loss—the role colonization played in its destruction, and what that loss meant for the *Newe* and other Tribal Nations.

As outsiders arrived, linguistic shifts reflected the changing times. Originally, the Bannock referred to buffalo as *kuchu*. However, with the introduction of cattle, this term evolved to *Newekuchu*, translating to "Indian cattle." Presently, *guchu* is utilized to denote cattle. Additionally, Bannock have incorporated the Shoshone word *bozheena* for buffalo, adapting it to their own variation, "*pozena*." Over time, the *Newe* developed a rich history of interaction with large animals, particularly the buffalo and horse. Every part of the buffalo was utilized with great ingenuity, often serving multiple purposes. For example, the buffalo's brain could be consumed as a food source, or it could also be used in the hide tanning process. The hide could be fashioned into a myriad of items, including robes, lodges, sacks, rafts, saddles, whips, quivers, knife-scabbards, parfleche, and the travois cradle. Moreover, the thicker portions of buffalo hides could serve as moccasin soles or war shields.

Buffalo rawhide was also used in crafting baby cradles, with the fur facing inward for warmth during winter, and these cradles were commonly carried on the mothers' backs. Other innovative uses included turning the tail into a quirt (whip) and creating cordage and lariats from the buffalo's shaggy forehead and mane. The bones were also versatile, serving as materials for arrowheads or tools for straightening arrow shafts. The horns, referred to as *aa*, being transformed into items such as powder horns, weapons, cups, spoons, and they also played roles in various healing rituals.

When on the move or settling in for the winter, both Bannock and Shoshone tribes erected tepees. The central role of the buffalo in their lifestyle becomes evident when noting that constructing a modest-sized tepee required stitching together between seven to eight treated buffalo hides, and a more expansive teepee demanded up to 20 hides.[11] Structurally, tepees featured a cone shape, had an internal fire at the center, and included an opening at the peak for smoke ventilation. The design allowed the structure to be stable, even when the wind blew hard as it often does in the Northern Plains. The door typically faced east to greet the rising sun and to shield the entrance from prevailing winds. Hides were smoked to make them more resistant to the elements and helped in preservation. Some Shoshone and Bannock men would paint symbols or exploits on their teepees above the doorway.

The act of painting exploits on tepees above the doorway served multiple purposes. Firstly, it was a way of recording history and significant events, much like a visual journal. This was especially significant in cultures where oral traditions were dominant. These paintings could represent a power or protection symbol given to the painter through dream or vision quest. The paintings communicated personal identity, power, accomplishments, and/or experiences. Each design was unique to the individual or family and often contained symbolic meanings known to the tribe.

Even hooves had diverse applications. They could be melted down in stone pots to produce adhesive substances. Hooves could also be hung in juniper trees which could serve as a survival food source, if needed. The buffalo's sinew, termed *Newe da'mmu*, was utilized for crafting slender cords, bow strings, and for reinforcing bows. The rumen could be adapted into a sack, which, apart from storage, doubled as cooking pouches. The small intestine, once cleaned and reversed, was used as a casing for various meat fillings and seasonings, subsequently roasted over an open flame. Bones became the basis for a wide range of tools and weaponry.

---

[11] Brigham D. Madsen, *The Bannock of Idaho* (Moscow: University of Idaho Press, 1996), 27.

Culinary delights included the buffalo's tongue and bone marrow, which were esteemed as delicacies. Teeth could even be crafted into decorative necklaces and were also incorporated into medicine rattles. Overall, the buffalo provided a comprehensive dietary range, from meat, hide scrapings, internal organs to blood, and these were not only consumed but also held significance in various healing ceremonies. During journeys across the plains, where traditional wood fuel was scarce, dried buffalo dung, colloquially known as "buffalo chips," became an invaluable fuel source. Symbolically, the buffalo was perceived as a formidable and most powerful creature of the animal world. Its mounted head, showcased during the *Daguwenede* ceremony, epitomized attributes like strength.

Historically, large herds of buffalo were present near Fort Hall in 1834 and prehistorically buffalo could be found as far west as Nevada.[12] However, by 1832, these herds had already disappeared from northern Utah, and by approximately 1840, they were no longer found in Idaho[13]. After the buffalo became extinct in Nevada, Idaho, and Utah, the Shoshone and Bannock began pursuing the ever-dwindling populations into what is now Montana and Wyoming via the Great Bannock Trail (Figure 2). Prior to decimation of buffalo populations these animals were hunted year-round throughout the *Newe* homeland. However, with dwindling buffalo populations, *Newe* buffalo hunting seasons were reduced to the spring or autumn, when conditions allowed.[14] Due to early snowfalls in Yellowstone obstructing routes from Idaho, the tribes would typically winter in Montana and Wyoming. The goal of each hunt was to amass enough meat and materials to last until the subsequent hunting season.

---

[12] Steward, *Basin-Plateau Aboriginal Sociopolitical Groups*, 200.
[13] Ibid, 200.
[14] Liljeblad, *Indian Peoples in Idaho* (Pocatello: Idaho State College, 1957), 64-65.

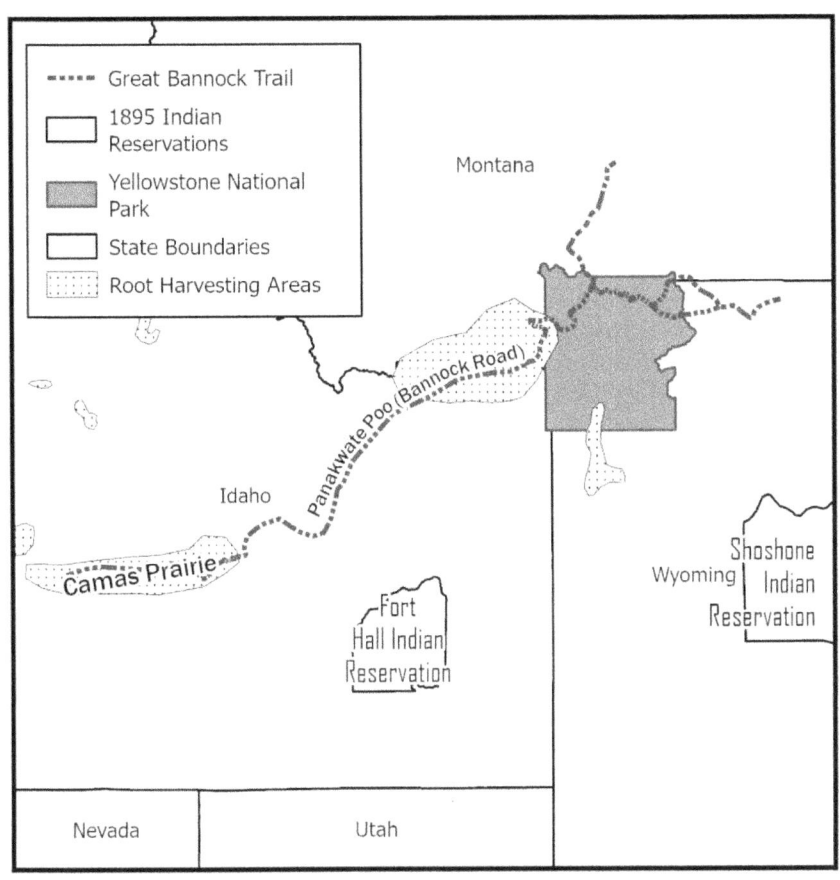

Figure 2. This map illustrates the primary travel routes used by the Bannock and Shoshone people as they followed the dwindling buffalo herds into Montana and Wyoming. As the animals were pushed farther north and east, the last wild herds found refuge in what is now Yellowstone National Park. The Great Bannock Trail—stretching from Idaho's Camas Prairie through key mountain passes and valleys—was essential to the tribes' survival and way of life until the 1880s.

Mounted bands of Shoshone and Bannock could travel into eastern Montana to an area known in Shoshone as *Gutsunambihi* or "the buffalo heart." This name originated from a heart-shaped rock situated approximately forty miles northwest of the present-day location of Billings[15]. Between approximately 1868 and 1878, the Fort Hall Indian community maintained their yearly journey for sustenance, traversing from Idaho through Wyoming into Montana via the Great Bannock Trail. Although, during these years the Shoshone and Bannock of Fort Hall were to remain on the newly established Fort Hall Reservation, the rations provided

---

[15] Ibid, 64.

by the U.S. government were often insufficient, compelling the Indian agent at Fort Hall to permit the Indians to depart, as they faced the threat of starvation. Traveling off the reservation to hunt was a treaty right, the Eastern Shoshone and Bannock expressly retained in the 1868 Fort Bridger Treaty, 15 Stat., 673, where it reads:

> The Indians herein named agree, when the agency house and other buildings shall be constructed on their reservations named, they will make said reservations their permanent home, and they will make no permanent settlement elsewhere; but they shall have the right to hunt on the unoccupied lands of the United States so long as game may be found thereon, and so long as peace subsists among the whites and Indians on the borders of the hunting districts.

The buffalo hunting pattern persisted until the 1880s.

While there are certain variations in the trajectory of the Great Bannock Trail, a significant stretch started from the Camas Prairie in Idaho and traversed what is now the northwest boundary of the Idaho National Laboratory. It proceeded to cross Targhee Pass and traverse the Madison River, subsequently ascending the Gallatin Mountains before descending into the Gardner River valley. Following this, the route encompassed Snow Pass toward Mammoth Hotsprings, continuing its path along Lava Creek and through the meadows of Blacktail Deer Creek. The Yellowstone River was crossed near Tower Falls at a site named Bannock Ford[16]. The trail proceeded through the Lamar Valley, surmounting the Absaroka Range, and descending into the Clarks Fork Valley. From this strategic position, the *Newe* could access buffalo herds either along the Yellowstone River or within the confines of the Wyoming Basin. It is here where the Shoshone and Bannock of Fort Hall also likely met up with their Eastern Shoshone allies before traveling onto the plains. Portions of the trail are still used today by tribal members on our annual buffalo hunts in the Gardner Valley of Montana.

---

[16] Aubrey L. Haines, *The Yellowstone Story Volume 1* (Yellowstone National Park: Yellowstone Library and Museum Association in cooperation with Colorado Associated University Press, 1977), 27.

Historically, the buffalo roamed across the vast territories of the Shoshone and Bannock, inhabiting regions from the Arctic Circle to northern Mexico and covering almost the entire breadth of the continent[17]. However, the Buffalo Nation, as I call it, underwent a holocaust parallel to the devastating impact experienced by American Indians following the arrival of Europeans. But the Buffalo Nation's Holocaust was more extreme and possibly as many as 60 million were wiped out as result of European emigrant spread. In the mid-west and eastern front of the Rocky Mountains, the greatest loss of the iconic American bison occurred from 1871-1883, especially in the Great Plains and along the eastern frontiers of the Rocky Mountains[18]. The primary culprits behind this drastic reduction were commercial hunters, whose ruthless pursuits mirrored the ferocity of Indian scalp bounty hunters. The buffalo hunters were enticed by the potential profits from selling buffalo hides in both eastern and international markets, as well as to the railroad companies. These hunters, equipped with advanced long-range rifles, such as the Sharps .50 caliber rifle, slaughtered vast herds of bison. A buffalo hunter named George Reighard described his hunt with Sharps rifles[19].

> In 1872 I organized my own outfit and went south from Fort Dodge to shoot buffaloes for their hides. I furnished the team and wagon and did the killing. [My partners] furnished the supplies and the skinning, stretching and cooking. They got half the hides...I had two big .50 Sharps rifles...
>
> Usually, I went to the top of some rise to spy out the herd, [then I'd] sneak up to within good ranges. Between 200 and 350 yards was all right...I carried a gun rest made from a tree crotch...

---

[17] Rurik List, Gerardo Ceballos, Charles Curtin, Peter J. P. Gogan, Jesús Pacheco, and Joe Truett, "Historic Distribution and Challenges to Bison Recovery in the Northern Chihuahuan Desert," *Conservation Biology* (2007), 1487.
[18] John Hanner, "Government Response to the Buffalo Hide Trade, 1871-1883," *Journal of Law and Economics* (1981), 239.
[19] Wayne van Zwoll, "Going the Distance with the Sharps Rifle," *Gun Digest*, November 10, 2014, https://gundigest.com/more/classic-guns/going-the-distance-with-the-sharps-rifle, quoting George Reighard in the Kansas City Star, 1930.

The time I made my biggest kill I lay on a slight ridge behind a tuft of weeds 100 yards from a bunch of 1,000 buffaloes... After I had killed about 25 my gun barrel became hot and began to expand. A bullet from an overheated gun does not go straight, it wobbles, so I put that gun aside and took the other. By the time that became hot the other had cooled, but then the powder smoke in front of me was so thick I could not see through it; there was not a breath of wind to carry it away, and I had to crawl backward, dragging my two guns, and work around to another position on the ridge, from which I killed 54 more. In 1½ hours I had fired 91 shots, as a count of the empty shells showed afterwards, and had killed 79 buffaloes, and we figured that they all lay within an area of about 2 acres of ground. My right hand and arm were so sore from working the gun that I was not sorry to see the remaining buffaloes start off on a brisk run ... .

Following the pursuits of buffalo hunters, with some notable names like William F. "Buffalo Bill" Cody, Frank Mayer, Billy Dixon, "Prairie Dog" Dave Morrow, and Tom Nixon, vast quantities of buffalo were killed. Primarily focusing on the valuable hides and tongues, these hunters led to the wasteful discarding of millions of pounds of meat. Their actions significantly contributed to the near-extinction of the American bison, an event that resulted in profound ecological and cultural impacts. This not only affected the Shoshone and Bannock but also numerous other American Indian tribes who relied on the bison for their survival.

Railroad companies of the transcontinental railroad further facilitated the onslaught. Not only did the rail line make hunting more accessible to emigrants, hunting from the train turned into a spectacle. Railroad companies were known to organize shooting sprees or hunting excursions where passengers could shoot buffalo directly from their carriages. The railroads were also utilized by the commercial buffalo hunters to transport the hides to eastern markets. For the Shoshone-Bannock of Fort Hall, the last hunts of free roaming buffalo ended in the 1880s.

At this time, Montana stockmen, a potent political force, took offense at the off-reservation hunting rights of the Indians under various Treaties. They concluded that the most expedient approach to displacing the Indians would involve eradicating the buffalo herds[20]. By the 1880s, a consortium of stockmen, backed by the U.S. military and commercial hunters, nearly eradicated the buffalo population, driving them to the brink of extinction. The combined efforts of the frontier army, professional hunters, and so-called sportsmen decimated the buffalo. With no herds left to follow, off-reservation hunting rights were being stripped of meaning—pushing Tribes into dependency and deeper confinement on reservations[21]. This was a calculated move by the U.S. government and one of the most devastating steps taken to break the Indians' independence and force them into dependence. They were now corralled into poverty, and had no choice but to rely on the very system that sought to erase them.

Fortunately, the buffalo was saved from extinction in the late 1800s by five private herds established by ranchers and by a sixth herd at the New York Zoological Park. These herds were established with less than 100 wild-caught founders[22]. A small remnant wild population also survived in what is now Yellowstone National Park (NP). This population declined to an official estimate of 23 animals in 1902[23]. In other words, nearly all the present-day plains bison in the United States are descended from a founder population of 100 or less, and probably an effective founder number substantially less than 100, because of the small sizes of the herds in the initial generations[24].

The period of buffalo hunting represents a somber part of American history, a brutal consequence of westward expansion, where so-called "progress" came at the cost of an entire way of life and the near destruction of a sacred animal. Today, the once expansive Buffalo Nation is now largely limited to the confines of Yellowstone National Park, and if the buffalo attempt to migrate out of the Park they are killed through state and Indian treaty harvests. Although several federally recognized Tribes, including

---

[20] Liljeblad, *Indian Peoples in Idaho*, 69
[21] David D. Smits, "The Frontier Army and the Destruction of the Buffalo: 1865-1883," *The Western Historical Quarterly* 25, no. 3 (Autumn 1994): 312-338, http://www.jstor.org/stable/971110.
[22] Philip W. Hedrick, "Conservation Genetics and North American Bison (Bison bison)," *Journal of Heredity* 100, no. 4 (2009): 411, doi:10.1093/jhered/esp024.
[23] Margaret M. Meagher, *The Bison of Yellowstone National Park* (Washington DC: National Park Service, 1973), 17.
[24] Hedrick, "Conservation Genetics and North American Bison," 411.

the Shoshone-Bannock Tribes participate in these hunts, the primary purpose of the harvest is to prevent the free roam of buffalo outside of Yellowstone National and Grand Teton National Parks.

Brucellosis in wildlife, especially in bison and elk populations, poses health risks to both animals and humans. Brucellosis, a contagious disease caused by the *Brucella* bacterium, is notable in various species, with *B. abortus* causing bovine brucellosis, *B. melitensis* affecting sheep and goats, and *B. suis* impacting swine[25]. While cattle are the primary hosts of *B. abortus* in North America, the bacterium also persists in wildlife, especially bison[26] and elk, with artificial winter feeding contributing to its maintenance in elk populations[27]. Brucellosis in humans is a noteworthy zoonotic disease, where prevention relies heavily on controlling or eradicating the disease in animal populations[28], along with adopting hygienic measures and proper cooking practices. This disease manifests in humans with symptoms such as recurrent fevers, night sweats, joint and back pain, flu-like symptoms, and arthritis. Additionally, both in animals and humans, brucellosis has the potential to remain in the body for extended durations[29]. In bison, brucellosis can cause reproductive issues and increased transmission risk during calving or abortion[30]. The disease's transmission among animals primarily occurs through direct contact with infectious fluids[31].

---

[25] J. Godfroid, "Brucellosis in Wildlife," *Revue scientifique et technique de l'Office international des Epizooties* 21 (2002): 277.

[26] Jack C. Rhyan, Keith Aune, Thomas Roffe, Darla Ewalt, Steve Hennager, Tom Gidlewski, Steve Olsen, and Ryan Clarke, "Pathogenesis and Epidemiology of Brucellosis in Yellowstone Bison: Serologic and Culture Results from Adult Females and Their Progeny," *Journal of Wildlife Diseases* 45, no. 3 (2009): 729.

[27] Jack C. Rhyan, Pauline Nol, Christine Quance, Arnold Gertonson, John Belfrage, Lauren Harris, Kelly Straka, and Suelee Robbe-Austerman, "Transmission of Brucellosis from Elk to Cattle and Bison, Greater Yellowstone Area, USA, 2002–2012," *Emerging Infectious Diseases* 19, no. 12 (December 2013): 1992.

[28] M. J. Corbel, "Brucellosis: An Overview," *Emerging Infectious Diseases* 3, no. 2 (April–June 1997): 214.

[29] Rhyan et al., "Transmission of Brucellosis from Elk to Cattle and Bison," 1992

[30] Ibid., 1993.

[31] Ibid., 1993.

Due to its agricultural implications, brucellosis is a 'reportable disease' in countries like the U.S. and Canada, where control and eradication programs are implemented[32]. Despite these efforts, the complete eradication of brucellosis in wild populations remains a daunting challenge, and the complex dynamics of disease transmission among wildlife, livestock, and humans make it difficult to determine the direct impact of the disease on each group. Nonetheless, the existing buffalo management practices implemented in the Greater Yellowstone Area are highly controversial and have led to debate between wildlife advocates, ranchers, tribes, and state agencies.

In 2008, I had the profound opportunity to join a buffalo hunt at the National Elk Wildlife Refuge, nestled near the breathtaking landscapes of Jackson Hole, Wyoming. This unique experience was part of a joint effort between the State of Wyoming and the National Elk Refuge to manage the burgeoning buffalo population, which had grown excessively due to the absence of natural predators and restricted hunting. The burgeoning populations were impacting the local ecology, overgrazing, and stripping woody vegetation along the streams. In response, the U.S. Fish and Wildlife Service, the federal agency that oversees the management of the refuge, sanctioned controlled hunts of various species including elk, bison, pronghorn, and white-tailed deer to help regulate the numbers. Similar wildlife management practices are also implemented within the confines of Grand Teton National Park. A significant breakthrough came when Claudio Broncho and Chad Colter, both members of the Shoshone-Bannock Tribes and serving as the Tribes Fish and Wildlife Policy Representative and Fish & Wildlife Director respectively, successfully negotiated with the U.S. Fish and Wildlife Service permission to harvest five buffalos. To many of us, who would never buy a tag from the state of Wyoming, it was the first time we were allowed to hunt legally within Wyoming.

---

[32] United States Department of Agriculture (USDA), *Bovine Brucellosis Eradication: Uniform Methods and Rules, Effective October 1, 2003*, APHIS 91-45-013 (Washington, DC: USDA, 2003), 121 pp.; Government of Canada (GOC), *Health of Animals Regulations (C.R.C., c. 296)*, Department of Justice (Ottawa, ON, 2009), accessed October 31, 2009, http://www.canlii.org/en/ca/laws/regu/crc-c-296/latest/crc-c-296.html.

However, the Wyoming Game and Fish Department made it clear to us that this was not a "Treaty hunt." On the day of the hunt and as dawn approached, Claudio, a respected elder and veteran, offered a prayer in the Shoshone language and outlined the distribution and handling of the meat. He instructed that all the meat was to be returned to our Tribe, while we were permitted to keep the guts, bones, and hides. To assist in the task of transporting the large, heavy animals, my uncle, Leo Teton, brought horses. Due to the Racehorse family's historical ties to Treaty hunting rights in Wyoming, highlighted in the Ward v. Race Horse case, my uncle, Sherwin Racehorse, was chosen to initiate the hunt as one of the primary hunters. The other hunters selected were either elders or veterans, all respected within the Tribe. The rest of us helped with the dragging and gutting of the buffalo.

We were only allowed to take five buffaloes. However, my uncle Sherwin exceeded our limit, which initially caused a bit of commotion but eventually resolved itself. I couldn't help but laugh, thinking back on our discussions about treaty hunting rights in Wyoming. Sherwin, known in Fort Hall as a true Bannock for his defiant spirit, once told me about his plan to call the Wyoming Game and Fish Department, boldly declaring his intention to hunt an elk right in front of them. I cautioned him against such a confrontational approach, stressing that if he were to hunt, it should be for the right reasons - for food, in line with our traditions and needs. While many of our hunters were equipped with high-caliber rifles, it often took more than one bullet to bring down the buffalo. The most effective shot was found to be just behind the ear, which proved to be the most reliable method for a swift conclusion.

Before we started gutting, I approached a wildlife biologist from the Wyoming Game and Fish Department to inquire whether we should use rubber gloves as a precaution against brucellosis transmission. His response, delivered in a whisper and accompanied by an odd look, was to not worry about it and that gloves weren't necessary. I found this advice peculiar, especially considering that one of the reasons for thinning the buffalo herd was to curb the spread of brucellosis, which was believed to be prevalent in these animals. After several strenuous hours and an incident where a horse injured its leg pulling the heavy animals, we finally managed to load all the buffalo. I think we ended up killing 8 total. Amidst the effort, we joked around with Sherwin, and I accused him of "flock shooting" the buffalo. Although I cannot recall his exact words in response, he suggested that they ought to permit us to hunt more than just five buffalo. Claudio was upset with Sherwin for exceeding the quota, since he was the one who had to deal with the white guys. I'm not sure what he said, but we were able to keep our animals.

This hunt held deep significance for me, not just as a participant but also symbolically, as it was the first time we were legally allowed to hunt in Wyoming again. Though it was not classified as a treaty hunt, it represented a chance to hunt on our own terms, and there was a profound sense of unity in traveling as a tribe to our original homelands. It's worth mentioning that while standard hunting permits are accessible to us like they are to anyone else, to my knowledge, no tribal member has ever purchased a hunting tag from the State of Wyoming. Thus, this was the first opportunity in over a century for us to hunt in Wyoming according to our own terms and traditions. To me, hunting in Wyoming should be conducted under the rights reserved by the Fort Bridger Treaty. The historical and ongoing conflicts around independent Indian hunting, along with the longstanding grievances of my Tribe and the Racehorse family against the state of Wyoming, are topics I plan to delve into more deeply in the next chapter.

Chapter 4 – Bibliography

Corbel, M. J. "Brucellosis: An Overview." Emerging Infectious Diseases 3, no. 2 (April–June 1997): 213–221.

Godfroid, J. "Brucellosis in Wildlife." Revue scientifique et technique de l'Office international des Epizooties 21 (2002): 277–286.

Haines, Aubrey L. The Yellowstone Story. Volume 1. Yellowstone National Park: Yellowstone Library and Museum Association in cooperation with Colorado Associated University Press, 1977.

Hämäläinen, Pekka. The Comanche Empire. New Haven: Yale University Press, 2008.

Hanner, John. "Government Response to the Buffalo Hide Trade, 1871–1883." Journal of Law and Economics (1981): 239–252.

Hedrick, Philip W. "Conservation Genetics and North American Bison (Bison bison)." Journal of Heredity 100, no. 4 (2009): 411–420. https://doi.org/10.1093/jhered/esp024.

Liljeblad, Sven. The Idaho Indians in Transition, 1805–1960. Pocatello: Idaho State University Museum, 1972.

———. Indian Peoples in Idaho. Pocatello: Idaho State College, 1957.

List, Rurik, Gerardo Ceballos, Charles Curtin, Peter J. P. Gogan, Jesús Pacheco, and Joe Truett. "Historic Distribution and Challenges to Bison Recovery in the Northern Chihuahuan Desert." Conservation Biology 21, no. 6 (2007): 1487–1494.

Madsen, Brigham D. The Bannock of Idaho. Moscow: University of Idaho Press, 1996.

———. The Lemhi: Sacajawea's People. Caldwell, ID: Caxton Press, 2000.

McArthur, Donna E. Houtz. When the Smoke Goes Straight Up. Pocatello: Gateway Printers, 2012.

Meagher, Margaret M. The Bison of Yellowstone National Park. Washington, DC: National Park Service, 1973.

Rhyan, Jack C., Keith Aune, Thomas Roffe, Darla Ewalt, Steve Hennager, Tom Gidlewski, Steve Olsen, and Ryan Clarke. "Pathogenesis and Epidemiology of Brucellosis in Yellowstone Bison: Serologic and Culture Results from Adult Females and Their Progeny." Journal of Wildlife Diseases 45, no. 3 (2009): 729–739.

Rhyan, Jack C., Pauline Nol, Christine Quance, Arnold Gertonson, John Belfrage, Lauren Harris, Kelly Straka, and Suelee Robbe-Austerman. "Transmission of Brucellosis from Elk to Cattle and Bison, Greater Yellowstone Area, USA, 2002–2012." Emerging Infectious Diseases 19, no. 12 (December 2013): 1992–1995.

Smits, David D. "The Frontier Army and the Destruction of the Buffalo: 1865–1883." The Western Historical Quarterly 25, no. 3 (Autumn 1994): 312–338. http://www.jstor.org/stable/971110.

Steward, Julian H. Basin-Plateau Aboriginal Sociopolitical Groups. Salt Lake City: University of Utah Press, 1938.

United States Department of Agriculture (USDA). Bovine Brucellosis Eradication: Uniform Methods and Rules, Effective October 1, 2003. APHIS 91-45-013. Washington, DC: USDA, 2003.

van Zwoll, Wayne. "Going the Distance with the Sharps Rifle." Gun Digest, November 10, 2014. https://gundigest.com/more/classic-guns/going-the-distance-with-the-sharps-rifle.

Government of Canada (GOC). Health of Animals Regulations (C.R.C., c. 296). Department of Justice. Ottawa, ON, 2009. Accessed October 31, 2009. http://www.canlii.org/en/ca/laws/regu/crc-c-296/latest/crc-c-296.html.

Chapter 5 - The Era of Suffering

In 1803, the U.S. acquired approximately 828,000 square miles west of the Mississippi River basin, from the Emperor of France Napoleon Bonaparte for about five cents per acre[1]. To put the size of this land acquisition into perspective, the purchase was approximately 44.5 million acres larger than the country of Mexico. This transaction, which became known as the Louisiana Purchase, effectively doubled the size of the U.S., and significantly bolstered its global stature[2]. However, the land involved in this purchase was already governed and home to numerous Indian tribes, and neither France nor the U.S. fully grasped the true extent of this territory. Thus, France sold lands to the U.S. which it had no real authority or ownership over. Although the purchase was initially met with some skepticism, the land acquisition from France is now recognized as a pivotal moment in U.S. history[3]. The purchase not only legitimized but also amplified support for an already planned expedition being pulled together by President Thomas Jefferson. The purchase gave the U.S. exclusive right to deal with Indian tribes through treaties or conquest, sidelining other colonial powers.

The expedition of the Louisiana country that President Jefferson was planning materialized two years later and is now known as the Corps of Discovery. It was led by none other than Captains Meriwether Lewis and William Clark. For the *Newe*, members of the Corps of Discovery became the first contact with *Daibo'o* or whites. The word *Daibo'o* literally means "the man who writes things down" in Shoshone. The first encounter of the Corps of Discovery with a group of Lemhi Shoshone occurred in what is now southwestern Montana near where Clark Canyon Reservoir[4] has been established. Their primary village was located on the banks of the Lemhi River, a river the Shoshone knew as *Agaibaa*

---

[1] Britannica, The Editors of Encyclopedia. "Louisiana Purchase." Encyclopedia Britannica. Last modified December 26, 2023. https://www.britannica.com/event/Louisiana-Purchase.
[2] Stephen E. Ambrose, *Undaunted Courage* (New York: Simon & Schuster Paperbacks, 1996). 101.
[3] Ibid., 101-102.
[4] Gary E. Moulton, ed. *The Definitive Journals of Lewis & Clark: Through the Rockies to the Cascades* (Lincoln: University of Nebraska Press, 1988), 68.

or the "Salmon Water". During this historic meeting, Lewis presented Ca-me-ah-wait, the Shoshone leader, with an American flag. The name Ca-me-ah-wait was likely the Shoshone word *Gai Miawaite*, which means "no walk" and probably an indication that he rode horse everywhere. Lewis described the U.S. flag to Ca-me-ah-wait as "an emblem of peace among whitemen and now that it had been received by him it was to be respected as the bond of union between us"[5].

Although it is unknown how Ca-me-ah-wait may have perceived the gift, it is now hard to not think of how the American flag represented the coming conquests and colonization despite Lewis' words of peace. In fact, European settler-colonists had already been involved in several significant conflicts with American Indian Tribes, including the Pequot War, King Philips War and Tuscarora War and it is likely Lewis did know what would ultimately come to the Lemhi Shoshone and other Indians for that matter. Later the U.S.'s approach of systematic removal and legal discrimination against American Indian Nations and individuals would serve as a case study for Nazi Germany's Third Reich in its efforts to translate racist ideologies into enforceable laws[6]. Today, like Christopher Columbus, Lewis's actions can be viewed in light of a legacy of Western or Euro-American exploratory expeditions, where initial moments of contact and exchange often preceded deeper and more troubling chapters of history.

The Corps of Discovery looked at the Shoshone mostly as a means to an end. They required horses, packing services, food, and a guide to get through the mountainous terrain of central Idaho. The Shoshone who Lewis first encountered were recently attacked by the *Baki'ehe* or the "Raw Hide People", who are now known as the Blackfeet. Despite losing a great part of their horse herd and all their lodges, except the one they erected to accommodate Lewis[7], they accommodated the Corp of Discovery with berry cakes, root foods, antelope meat, salmon, and horses.

---

[5] Moulton, *The Definitive Journals of Lewis & Clark: Through the Rockies to the Cascades*, 79-80.
[6] Miller, Robert J. 2020. "Nazi Germany's Race Laws, The United States, And American Indians." St. John's Law Review 94: 751.
[7] Moulton, *The Definitive Journals of Lewis & Clark: Through the Rockies to the Cascades*, 83.

Both Lewis and Clark noted in the journals on several occasions that although the Shoshone were in a destitute state, they shared what little they had with great joy[8], which still speaks to our *Newe* culture of humor today.

On August 17, 1805, Lewis, through interpreters Labuish, Charbono, and Sah-cah-gar-weah, communicated to the Shoshone people the expedition's intent to travel through their territory. He expressed "good wishes" and the "care of our government," highlighting their dependence on the government for essential merchandise and conveying the government's strength and amicable attitude towards them[9]. Lewis mentioned their quest to find a more direct western route to the ocean, which would facilitate easier trade with the Shoshone. He explained that no trade could commence until their return journey and exaggerated the benefits the Shoshone would receive for providing aid. What Lewis really wanted was acquisition of Shoshone horses and services. The diplomatic Chief Ca-me-ah-wait expressed gratitude for Lewis's words of friendship and a willingness to help. However, he lamented the delay in receiving firearms but accepted that his people could continue to live as before until the promised firearms were delivered[10]. Nonetheless, the Shoshone were able to obtain some firearms. Out of desperation, Captain Clark traded his "Pistol 100 Balls Powder & a Knife" and a musket for horses[11]. These were the only firearms obtained by the Shoshone. Ca-me-ah-wait desired to obtain guns was for two purposes, first they greatly help while hunting buffalo and secondly for defense against enemies already equipped with such weapons[12]. Ca-me-ah-wait told Lewis,

> "we could then live in the country of buffaloe and eat as our enimies do and not be compelled to hide ourselves in these mountains and live on roots and berries as the bear do. We do not fear our enemies [sic] when placed on an equal footing with them"[13].

---

[8] Ibid., 119, 139
[9] Ibid., 111.
[10] Ibid., 111.
[11] Ibid., 178.
[12] Ibid., 91
[13] Ibid., 91.

Now knowing the tumultuous history between the U.S. and my people to this very day, it is humorous to me that although the Shoshone Indians were initially awestruck with the Corp of Discovery and traded horses for trivial items, perhaps they leveraged the situation to their advantage. For the Corps acquired a total of 29 horses from the Shoshone and Clark made some remarks on the quality of the horses they received.

> they were nearly all Sore Backs and Several pore, & young Those horses are indifferent, maney Sore backs and others not accustomed to pack, and as we Cannot put large loads on them are compelled to purchase as maney as we Can to take our Small proportion of Baggage of the Parties.[14]

Lewis, as a representative of the U.S., assured Ca-me-ah-wait and his people of future trade and support in return for their help. However, these commitments were never realized, reflecting a historical pattern of unfulfilled promises by European explorers and their successors. This trend of broken promises, including those explicitly stated in treaties, persists today. For instance, Ca-me-ah-wait's anticipation of receiving firearms remains unmet, symbolizing the ongoing wait for promises to be honored. The Shoshone and Bannock tribes from the Lemhi and Salmon River regions were once provided the Lemhi Reserve[15], an area spanning approximately 100 square miles in their home territory. However, following the land cession in 1889 this land was also confiscated and open for settlement, resulting in the forced relocation of the descendants who helped Lewis and Clark to the Fort Hall Reservation[16].

In his records, Lewis also observed that the Shoshone, a tribe previously unacquainted with white men, had already been afflicted with European diseases like gonorrhea and smallpox[17]. These illnesses passed from human to human through their interactions with other tribes who had prior contact with European immigrants. Lacking effective treatments for these diseases, the Shoshone and Bannock usually died after contraction, highlighting the dire consequences of European

---

[14] Ibid., 178.
[15] Executive Order, February 12, 1875, 1 Kappler 839.
[16] 25 Stat. 687, February 23, 1889, 1 Kappler 314.
[17] Moulton, *The Definitive Journals of Lewis & Clark: Through the Rockies to the Cascades*, 122.

contact on Indian populations[18]. It is unknown to what extent the Corp of Discovery may have introduced venereal, or other, diseases to the Shoshone during their extended stay, but nearly every man in the Corps of Discovery suffered from at least syphilis[19].

The story of first contact with the Bannock began in the early 1790s when successful trading ventures of the English Captain James Cook, inspired New England merchants to establish trade with Northwest Indian Tribes for sea otter furs to sell in China[20]. Captain Robert Gray, an American sea captain, followed Cook's lucrative trade route. He commanded a ship named the Columbia and in 1792 discovered the mouth of a large river in the Pacific Northwest. Recognizing the importance of his discovery, he named this river the "Columbia" after his ship and laid claim to the entire region drained by the river and its tributaries for the U.S.[21] The discovery was crucial in establishing the foundation for the U.S.' claim to the vast region west of the Rocky Mountains, known as Oregon Country. This claim was later bolstered by the Louisiana Purchase in 1803 which demonstrated the nation's intent to expand westward and set the stage for further territorial claims into the Oregon Country. However, like the Louisiana Purchase, the Columbia River Basin was unexplored by Euro-Americans and home to numerous Indian tribes, including the Bannock. The actions of explorers like Gray, coupled with political acquisitions like the Louisiana Purchase, set the stage for the U.S.'s continued territorial expansion into *Newe* territory.

While the initial interactions between the Shoshone and the Corps of Discovery were friendly and cooperative, the Bannock's first documented contacts with Euro-Americans were marked by conflict. The first recorded encounter between the Bannock and Europeans occurred in 1814 in what is now western Idaho[22]. This incident occurred roughly a year after John Reed and his Astorian group established Fort Boise along the Snake River. In a violent

---

[18] Ibid., 122.
[19] Ambrose, *Undaunted Courage,* 196-197.
[20] Floyd R. Barber and Dan W. Martin, *Idaho in the Pacific Northwest* (Caldwell, Idaho: The Caxton Printers, Ltd., 1956), 2.
[21] Ibid., 2-3.
[22] Darcy Williamson, *River Tales of Idaho* (Caldwell, Idaho: The Caxton Printers, Ltd.), 26.

clash, nine members of Reed's party were killed by a group referred to as the "Ban-at-tees"[23]. The term "Ban-at-tees" is obviously the Shoshone term *Bannaite*, which is used by the Shoshone to describe the Bannock Indian. Later in 1819, Donald McKenzie established the Northwest Fur Company post near the site of Reed's post, and the Bannock attacked again[24]. Among neighboring tribes and later the whites, the Bannock were renowned for their fierce and warlike nature. Despite their smaller numbers, Bannock men would frequently attain the status of war chief, leading not only their own people but also the Shoshone into battle.

Up until the 1840s, explorers and fur trappers represented the main Euro-American contacts for the *Newe*. Interactions with the outsiders had profound impacts on the Indians, introducing them to diseases, alcohol, and the trade items which had significant impacts, negative and positive. The contact led the tribes to adapt to the cultures and habits of the white men, creating a dependency on them for essential trade items like guns and iron tools. The *Newe*, and other tribes, were active participants in the Rocky Mountain rendezvous, first established in 1825 at Green River, Wyoming[25]. These rendezvous were gatherings where Indians could trade their furs, hides, and other Indian curios with the outsiders. However, by the 1840s, the region had been largely trapped out. Lockstep with the decline in the fur trade, Euro-American emigrants began to traverse through *Newe* territory marking a significant change in the nature of interactions with outsiders.

The *Newe's* lifestyle was inherently nomadic, adapting to the changing seasons, which led to their seasonal campsites being temporarily abandoned until the appropriate time of year. However, early settlers, either unaware or indifferent to the *Newe's* way of life, rapidly took over their favorite hunting spots and camping sites. They established permanent settlements, particularly targeting the most fertile and hospitable areas that were traditionally used by the *Newe* for thousands of years. The

---

[23] Brigham D. Madsen, *The Bannock of Idaho* (Moscow: University of Idaho Press, 1996), 43 and 48.
[24] Ibid., 44.
[25] Brigham D. Madsen, *The Northern Shoshoni* (Caldwell, Idaho: Caxton Press, 2007), 27.

colonists were highly destructive to the soil and quickly overhunted the game, such as bighorn sheep, and destroyed native plant communities with livestock and introduced invasive species, as well as impairing water quality.

Combined setter-colonist actions led to widespread famine and suffering for the *Newe*, some of whom began to raid, while others begged along the immigrant trails[26]. This behavior at times elicited impulsive, fearful reactions from the colonists who would indiscriminately shoot any Indian person they encountered[27]. The introduction of alcohol by Europeans, an unfamiliar chemical substance to Indian communities, did not help matters and brought long-term harmful effects upon all Indian communities in the U.S.[28]. Some colonists even went as far as engaging very evil acts, like purposely poisoning dead livestock carcasses with strychnine, as a type of booby trap to kill the starving Indians who would consume the meat and die[29].

It is no surprise that the Indians considered the occupation of their lands as trespass. As a result, the *Newe* began to demand payment and if payment was not met, they took what they believed to be owed. On the other hand, the actions of the Indians led the settler-colonists to believe that the Indians were stealing from them! Conversely, such measures were misconstrued by settlers-colonists as theft. Looking back, it becomes evident that the true act of taking without permission was overwhelming on the part of the settlers. Especially when you consider that the settlers squatted on the most beautiful and choice lands that had be used by the Indians for millennia, they also cut the timber and wiped out the game, especially bighorn sheep. Nonetheless, the taking of property as payment for trespass caused the Mormons and other colonists to demand that the U.S. government punish the Indians. In 1863, an Annual Report of the Commissioner of Indian Affairs said:

> The scarcity of game in these Territories, and the occupation of the most fertile portions thereof by our

---

[26] Brigham D. Madsen, *The Shoshoni Frontier and the Bear River Massacre* (Salt Lake City, UT: University of Utah Press, 1985), 25-39.
[27] Madsen, *The Shoshoni Frontier and the Bear River Massacre*, 47.
[28] Lamarine, Roland J. "Alcohol Abuse Among Native Americans." *Journal of Community Health* 13, no. 3 (1988): 143.
[29] Madsen, *The Shoshoni Frontier and the Bear River Massacre*, 47.

settlements, have reduced these Indians to a state of extreme destitution, and for several years past they have been almost literally compelled to resort to plunder in order to obtain the necessaries of life. It is not to be expected that a wild and warlike people will tamely submit to the occupation of their country by another race, and to starvation as a consequence thereof.[30]

It is also important to note that the swift colonization of the *Newe* territories by settler-colonists was undertaken without legal authorization, even according to U.S. norms. At this time, no formal treaties had been ratified to legitimize such occupation. Tension between the two races manifested itself in various forms and conflicts occurred increasingly along the immigrant trails. However, a lot of the raiding that occurred was also done by Euro-American bandits dressed as Indians[31]. Although Colonel Albert Sidney Johnston was one the first U.S. military commanders dispatched to the area, his primary purpose was to keep an eye on the Mormons[32]. However, it was not until Colonel Patrick Edward Connor and his California Volunteers were dispatched to Utah territory that real trouble began for the *Newe*[33]. Connor and the California Volunteers' aim was to subdue and displace the *Newe* by using unlimited warfare tactics to achieve these objectives.

Major Edward McGarry, who was under Connor's command, was particularly brutal and ruthless. He and his troops carried out many executions and indiscriminate killings of Indians, which incited retaliation by the Indians against the whites[34]. The retaliation and increased frequency of conflicts ultimately led to the Bear River Massacre, where on January 29, 1863, not long after the Shoshone held their annual Warm Dance, Connor and his troops indiscriminately massacred Shoshone men, women, elders, children, and infants near the Idaho-Utah border. Although relatively unknown, this event is one of the largest, if not the largest, single massacres in U.S. history. Darren Parry, who was the Chairman of the Northwestern Band of the Shoshone Nation, wrote in his book.

---

[30] Madsen, *The Northern Shoshoni*, 38.
[31] Madsen, *The Shoshoni Frontier and the Bear River Massacre*, 99-100.
[32] Ibid., 77.
[33] Ibid., 157-200.
[34] Madsen, *The Shoshoni Frontier and the Bear River Massacre*, 168-169.

Connor and his men slaughtered what has been estimated to be more than 400 Shoshone men, women, and children, the largest massacre of Native Americans in the West, much larger than the horrors of Sand Creek, Wounded Knee, or Washita.[35]

For the Indians the carnage lasted all day. After the initial attack soldiers walked among the fallen and killed the wounded with axes, including babies still clutching to their dead mothers. Wounded Indian women were raped, some while in the agony of their death[36]. Chief Bear Hunter was captured and tortured to death, but as a warrior he did not utter a word[37]. This angered the soldiers and one put his bayonet into a fire until it was glowing red and ran it through the chief's ears. Bear Hunter left a wife and child behind. The Indians fought mostly by hand. After the massacre it was now apparent to the *Newe* that the whites intended to take everything, including their lives. From then on, the Indians could only hope to survive. A quote from Mae Timbimboo Parry's "Massacre at Boa Ogoi",

> The morning after the massacre, the few Indians that remained looked at their destroyed village in horror and disbelief. They now saw things they had not noticed the night before. The ground was covered in various colors, red from blood, black from the fires of their teepees and food, and brown from the many seeds and nuts which had been scattered. There were also blue and purple areas made up of their dried berries. They noticed pieces of the teepee poles which the soldiers had burned to keep themselves warm.[38]

Mae Perry's description of the aftermath is called "scorched-earth" military tactics. The scorched-earth tactic aims to destroy anything that might be useful to the enemy. It has since been banned under the 1977 Geneva Conventions. Although Connor was promoted for the massacre, today it would be recognized as a crime against humanity and a form of ethnic cleansing. Shamefully, the U.S. government originally touted this the "Battle

---

[35] Darren Parry, *The Bear River Massacre: A Shoshone History* (Salt Lake City, Utah: By Common Consent Press, 2019), 37.
[36] Madsen, *The Shoshoni Frontier and the Bear River Massacre*, 191.
[37] Ibid., 234.
[38] Ibid., 237.

of Bear River", but today it is known more aptly as the Bear River Massacre. The Bear River Massacre marked the beginning of the U.S. campaign of systematic and forced removal of the *Newe* from their homelands.

However, despite its scale, the Bear River Massacre has not received as much attention as other historical events. Perhaps this is due to factors such as its occurrence during the Civil War, publicity tactics and fake news of the time that labelled it as a mere battle, less national scandal and governmental scrutiny, and its location in a then-remote area. Additionally, the narrative of the massacre has been overshadowed by other incidents that sparked greater public outcry and subsequent investigation, like the Sand Creek Massacre. Efforts to raise awareness about this tragic event have increased in recent years, yet it remains lesser-known in the broader context of American history.

The tragic events of the Bear River Massacre catalyzed the commencement of the treaty-negotiation period for the *Newe*. Washakee, alternatively spelled as Washakie, the Chief of the Eastern Band of Shoshone, became the inaugural signatory of such a treaty, signed on July 2, 1863, at Fort Bridger. Renowned for his benevolence and amiability towards the white settlers[39], Washakee procured $10,000 as compensation for the decimation of game. It also affirmed the U.S.' right to maintain and establish travel routes, military posts, and settlements within Shoshone territories without impediments. This also included the continuation of telegraph and overland stage lines, and the construction of a railway from the plains to the Pacific.

Following the Bear River Massacre, Connor and his troops persistently pursued my great-great-great-grandfather, Tonaioza who became known as Chief Pocatello, regarded as the most formidable figure within the Shoshone Nation[40]. Peace only became a possibility when James Duane Doty, alongside the now promoted Brigadier-General Connor, conveyed to the Indians that halting their attacks would lead to them receiving the same gifts

---

[39] The Editors of Encyclopedia Britannica, "Washakie," *Encyclopedia Britannica*, February 16, 2023, https://www.britannica.com/biography/Washakie. Accessed December 24, 2023.

[40] Brigham D. Madsen, *Chief Pocatello The "White Plume"* (Salt Lake City: University of Utah Press, 1985), 68.

as those given to Washakie's Shoshone. This assurance led Pocatello and his subchiefs to seek reconciliation, culminating in the signing of the 1863 Treaty of Box Elder. Indeed, Pocatello and his people were the very targets Connor sought to destroy during the Bear River Massacre. Being one the Shoshone Nations most capable *Nabidenge dai'gwahni* "war chiefs", Pocatello had the foresight to vacate Bear River a day before the attack[41].

Although promises were made to provide the same gifts Washakie received, Doty and the now Brigadier-General Connor, representing white negotiators, exhibited less generosity towards Pocatello in their dealings. Under Article 3 of the treaty, a mere $5,000 was allocated in "provisions and goods" for the entirety of the Tribe. Furthermore, an acknowledgment detailed a payment of $2,000 to the Northwestern Bands in an attempt to alleviate their dire circumstances, given their described state of "utter destitution" following the war. Echoing this sentiment, a note from Mormon Bishop Nichols shortly before the treaty mentioned the particularly challenging situation of Pocatello's family[42]. Across their expansive homelands, the Fort Hall *Newe* entered into eight treaties with the U.S. government. Of these, only four received ratifications. While Pocatello eventually settled on the Fort Hall Reservation, home to many of his descendants who are now part of the Shoshone-Bannock Tribes, the Northwestern Band of the Shoshone Nation leveraged the Treaty of Box Elder as a foundational document in their journey to achieve federal recognition, which was officially granted in 1987[43].

The final ratified treaty involving the Eastern Shoshone and Bannock was formalized on July 3, 1868, at Fort Bridger. Article IV of the 1868 Fort Bridger Treaty stipulates:

> "The Indians herein named agree, when the agency house and other buildings shall be constructed on their reservations named, they will make said reservations their permanent home, and they will make no permanent settlement elsewhere; but they shall have the right to hunt on the unoccupied lands of the United States so long as game may be found thereon, and so long as peace subsists

---

[41] Madsen, *The Bannock of Idaho,* 137.
[42] Ibid., 57-58.
[43] Northwestern Band of Shoshone Nation, "History," accessed February 13, 2024, https://www.nwbshoshone.com/history/.

among the whites and Indians on the borders of the hunting districts."[44]

In the treaty negotiations between the U.S. and Indian leaders, Article IV emerges as a pivotal clause. Though J. Van Allen Carter acted as the official interpreter during these dialogues, the precise words articulated by the Indian leaders and the translations relayed to them remain unknown. Nevertheless, records of the discussions have been preserved through the documentation of C.C. Augur, the Brevet Major General of the U.S. Army Commissions. During these sessions, General Augur informed the Shoshone and Bannock leaders of the growing white population within their territories and anticipated further influx. Consequently, the government expressed its intent to procure tribal lands, relocating the Indian populations to a designated reservation. Augur conveyed the President's wish by saying, "Upon this reservation he [President] wishes you to go with all your people as soon as possible, and to make it your permanent home, but with permission to hunt wherever you can find game"[45]. Augur also wrote that the head Shoshone Chief Washakie said as a response,

> "I want for my home the valley of Wind river and lands on its tributaries as far east as the Popo-agie, and want the privilege of going over the mountains to hunt where I please"[46].

The Bannock Chief Taggie said,

> "As far away as Virginia City our tribe has roamed. But I want the Porte-neuf country and Kamas plains. . . we are friends with the Shoshones and like to hunt with them, but we want a home for ourselves"[47].

It's worth highlighting that the language in Article IV of the Fort Bridger Treaty of 1868 is identical to that found in the earlier 1868 Treaty of Fort Laramie with the Crow. This similarity's significance will become evident in subsequent chapters.

---

[44] "Treaty with the Eastern Band Shoshoni and Bannock," July 3, 1868, 15 Stat. 673.
[45] Augur, C. C. Transcript of Fort Bridger Treaty Negotiations, October 4, 1868. Reproduced at the National Archives, p. 260.
[46] Ibid., 265.
[47] Ibid., 266.

Additionally, a crucial element of the Fort Bridger Treaty of 1868 was Article 1, often referred to as the "Bad Men" clause.

> "Article 1. From this day forward peace between the parties to this treaty shall forever continue. The Government of the United States desires peace, and its honor is hereby pledged to keep it. The Indians desire peace, and they hereby pledge their honor to maintain it.
>
> If bad men among whites, or among other people subject to the authority of the United States, shall commit any wrongs upon the person or property of the Indians, the United States will, upon proof made to the agent and forwarded to the Commissioner of Indian Affairs, at Washington City, proceed at once to cause the offender to be arrested and punished according to the laws of the United States, and also re-imburse the injured person for the loss sustained..."[48]

The purpose of the "Bad Men" clause was to guarantee justice in cases where individuals under U.S. jurisdiction committed wrongs against Indians. This process begins with the presentation of evidence to the designated Indian Agent, currently known as the Bureau of Indian Affairs (BIA) Superintendent. The matter is then escalated to the higher authority, previously the Commissioner of Indian Affairs, but now termed the Assistant Secretary for Indian Affairs, who oversees the BIA. Once informed, the U.S. government is obligated to swiftly carry out legal actions to apprehend and appropriately punish the offender under federal law. Furthermore, the U.S. is required to compensate the Indian party for any losses sustained.

Though the 1863 Treaty of Box Elder and the 1868 Treaty of Fort Bridger initially brokered peace between Indians and whites, this peace was short-lived. Just a decade after signing the Fort Bridger Treaty, the Bannock tribe went to war against the U.S. The reasons for this conflict were manifold, with one significant factor being the unfulfilled promise concerning the Camas Prairie, which was to be reserved for the Bannock as stipulated in the Fort Bridger Treaty. Article II of this Treaty intended to secure one large reservation for the Bannock in their

---

[48] "Treaty with the Eastern Band Shoshoni and Bannock," July 3, 1868, 15 Stat. 673.

original homelands. Chief Taggie, spelled *Taggi* in the Bannock alphabet, identified the importance of the Camas Prairie not once, but twice during the treaty negotiations[49]. In one instance, Chief Taggie delineated their territories, leading Augur to note, the first time was when Chief Taggie described their territories, where Augur wrote, "The Bannacks in terms more general even, all the country about Soda Spring, the Porteneuf river and the big Kamas prairie to the north west of it"[50].

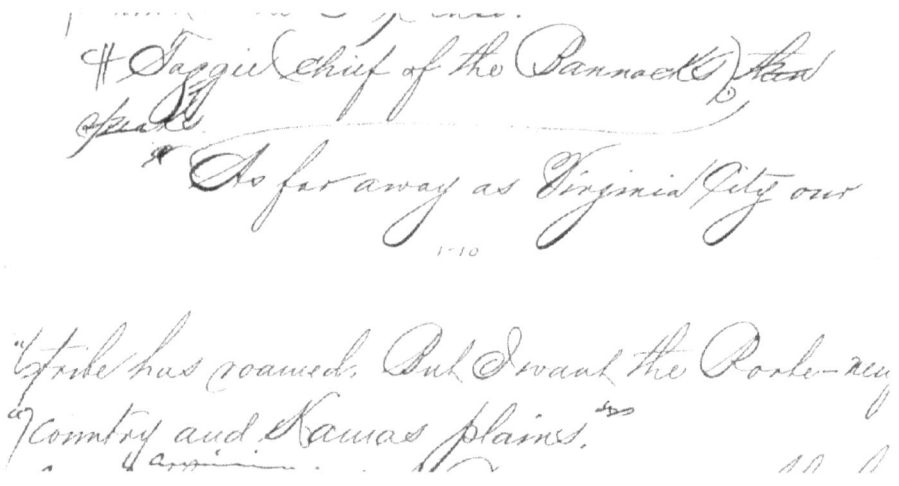

Figure 3. Brevet Major General United States Commissioners C.C. Augur handwritten transcript identifying Chief Taggie's desire to reserve the Portneuf Country and "Kamas Plains". The actual writing reads, "Taggie (Chief of the Bannacks) 'As far away as Virginia City our tribe has roamed. But I want the Porte-neuf Kountry and Kamas plains'." Augur tended to use "k" instead of "c" in his spellings.

The second occasion Taggie mentioned the area was when specifying his preferred location for the reservation. Despite the U.S. Commissioners of the Fort Bridger Treaty being fully aware of this detail, as recorded in the negotiation transcripts, a significant error occurred in the final Treaty document: the Camas Prairie was mistakenly referred to as the "Kansas Prairie". This oversight persisted into the text that was ultimately used in the Treaty and ratified by the Senate.

> ARTICLE 2. It is agreed that whenever the Bannacks desire a reservation to be set apart for their use, or whenever the

---

[49] Augur, *Fort Bridger Treaty Negotiations*, 3, 11.
[50] Ibid, 10-11.

President of the United States shall deem it advisable for them to be put upon a reservation, he shall cause a suitable one to be selected for them in their present country, which shall embrace reasonable portions of the "Port neuf" and "Kansas Prairie" countries, and that, when this reservation is declared, the United States will secure to the Bannacks the same rights and privileges therein, and make the same and like expenditures therein for their benefit, except the agency-house and residence of the agent, in proportion to their numbers, as herein provided for the Shoshonee reservation...."[51]

However, the U.S. never fulfilled the treaty's implied promise of establishing a reservation that encompassed both the Portneuf and the so-called "Kansas Prairie" (Camas Prairie) regions. Instead, it designated only a portion of the Portneuf Valley for the creation of the Fort Hall Reservation. This decision was particularly calculated, as Fort Hall had already been established in an 1867 Executive Order—one year prior to the signing of the 1868 Fort Bridger Treaty—originally intended for the Boise and Bruneau bands[52]. Through the Fort Bridger treaty and the Executive Order establishing the Fort Hall Reserve, the Bannock, including those under the leadership of Taggee, were subsequently assigned to this existing reservation. In effect, the federal government consolidated multiple bands—both Shoshone and Bannock—onto a single small reservation, despite the treaty's language suggesting a very large reservation within their traditional homelands. The promise of land encompassing both the Portneuf and Camas Prairie was never realized. Instead, experienced treaty negotiators, adept in legal interpretation and the abrogation of treaty obligations, strategically guided the Bannock toward accepting Fort Hall as their designated reservation, thereby streamlining federal responsibilities while failing to deliver the broader territorial assurances originally outlined.

Despite the U.S. government's legal maneuvers, the Indians understood and recognized the Camas Prairie/Plains as their

---

[51] "Treaty with the Eastern Band Shoshoni and Bannock," July 3, 1868, 15 Stat. 673
[52] Executive Order, "Fort Hall and Coeur d'Alene Reservations," June 14, 1867.

designated reservation lands. However, after the Fort Bridger Treaty was signed, white settlers consistently pushed their cattle, horses, and hogs to graze and uproot the camas bulbs on the Camas Prairie. The violation of the Indians' rights was clearly articulated in a letter by Idaho Governor Brayman, which shed light on the persistent difficulties the Bannocks encountered in claiming their rightful access to these lands.

> It seems to be understood that Kansas Prairie is a misprint – there being no prairie of that name west of the mountains, and that "Camas Prairie" is meant. The Indians understand it thus and without exception or doubt insist that the Big Camas Prairie is theirs by that treaty.
>
> In proof of the sincerity of this belief, it is true that they have each year, during the season for digging camas roots and hunting, resorted in great numbers to and occupied this tract of country. The camas root is to them the equivalent of our potato, and it grows spontaneously in vast quantities on these grounds. I have been visited by a great number of Indians who uniformly claim "Camas Prairie" as their garden. They declare their right by this treaty, whether the word should be "Kansas" or "Camas." These Indians did, evidently, in making the treaty of 1868, and do now in their verbal way, confirm by their "unbroken practice," understand "Camas Prairie" to be rightfully theirs.[53]

In Brayman's letter to General O. O. Howard, who commanded the Department of the Columbia, he emphasized that the climate and soil conditions of the Fort Hall Reservation were less conducive for cultivating vegetables compared to the Camas Prairie. He pointed out the significance of the camas plant for the tribes, noting that its bulbs, which could be preserved throughout the seasons, were a crucial food source. Without access to the Camas Prairie, Brayman noted, the tribes would face considerable hardship. He elaborated on these points saying,

> our advancing population have for years invited increasing encroachments upon this prairie. Herders crowd upon it with thousands of cattle, destroying the product, and bands

---

[53] "Annual Report of the Secretary of War, 1878, Vol. 1, pt. 2," *U.S. Congressional Serial Set* (1878): 151.

of "hogs" that dig up the roots, destroying not only the growing crops but the seed of the future.[54]

Every year, the whites ran more and more hogs and cattle on the Prairie and the Indians were beginning to lose patience and the situation was edging towards conflict. Brayman urged for a definitive resolution from the President and Congress, requesting a clear declaration of whether the area would officially be part of the reservation or not. Regrettably, to the Bannock tribe this provision of the Treaty was never fulfilled by the U.S.

Like the buffalo, the camas plant of southcentral Idaho was a vital staple for the Indians and provided a food source to supplement the meager rations now being provided to the Indians at Fort Hall. From 1869 to 1877 the Fort Hall Indian Agents consistently struggled to secure adequate food and clothing from the government to support all the reservation's population.[55] Apparently, there often wasn't enough game left on or near the reservation to sustain people through the winter months—likely the result of overhunting at a time when no game laws existed, and Idaho had not yet become a state. Among the two tribes, the Shoshone were generally more passive and tended to remain on the reservation, relying more heavily on federal rations, while the Bannock, especially in times of hardship, were more likely to venture out in search of buffalo. In some instances, Shoshone hunters only left the reservation at the urging of the Indian agent, who understood that available supplies would not meet the tribes' needs. On April 20, 1876, Agent W.H. Danilson reported the complete depletion of food rations and documented the desperation faced by the people under his charge.

> The rations of more than a thousand Indians were thus cut off, and they were thrown upon their own resources for a living. This, too, in a season of the year when the mountains and foothills were covered with snow, and in a country where, under the most favorable circumstances, game is hard to obtain. Large numbers came to the office

---

[54] Ibid., 151.
[55] Madsen, *The Bannock of Idaho*, 174.

begging most piteously for food, stating that their children were crying for bread, which I well knew was the truth.[56]

The chronic food shortages on the Fort Hall Reservation were primarily a result of congressional budget cuts, reflecting the low priority given to providing adequate rations for the large Indian population there at the time. These ongoing scarcities frustrated the Bannock, and each spring, as supplies invariably dwindled, most of the Bannock population would relocate to the Camas Prairie, where they could rely on their traditional food sources.[57]

Chief Taggie, distinguished for his outstanding leadership through the 1860s and who was principally involved with the negotiation of two treaties with the U.S. government,tragically met his end in a battle during a buffalo hunting expedition in Montana, near the Crow Reservation, in the winter of 1870-1871[58]. His demise marked the close of a significant chapter for the Bannocks, with leadership passing to Pat Tyhee and then to Buffalo Horn (Figure 4). Buffalo Horn is probably best known for being the War Chief during the Bannock War of 1878.

---

[56] W. H. Danilson, "Report of Agents in Idaho, Fort Hall Indian Agency," in *Annual Report of the Commissioner of Indian Affairs to the Secretary of the Interior for the Year 1876* (Washington: Government Printing Office, 1876), 43.
[57] Ibid., 88.
[58] Madsen, *The Bannock of Idaho*, 176.

Figure 4. Chief Buffalo Horn, former leader U.S. Indian Scout and War Chief of the Bannocks during the Bannock War of 1878.

However, he was also a former U.S. military scout who was known for his bravery. He had previously served as a leader of Indian scouts under various army commanders. His notable feats include volunteering in 1876 to carry a dispatch through Sioux enemy territory from the Powder River to General Nelson A. Miles on the Yellowstone River, a dangerous mission he undertook alongside a Crow scout, Leforge, and "Buffalo Bill" Cody[59]. This successful delivery highlighted his courage and resourcefulness.

---

[59] Thomas H. Leforge, *Memoirs of a White Crow Indian*, vol. 584 (Lincoln: University of Nebraska Press, 1974), 262.

Cody, inspired by his adventures, later established "Buffalo Bill's Wild West," a circus-like show that enjoyed widespread popularity in the U.S. and Europe for three decades. Buffalo Horn also distinguished himself in skirmishes against the Northern Cheyenne in the same year, further cementing his legacy as a formidable leader and warrior[60].

Buffalo Horn's leadership inspired his scouts to persevere through extreme difficulties. One notable instance of his leadership occurred while pursuing the Nez Perce in 1877. General O. O. Howard documented Buffalo Horn's ability to rally his Bannock scouts during a challenging moment. After a grueling ride of over 200 miles from Boise to meet up with Howard, amidst a treacherous rainstorm, Buffalo Horn galvanized all but three of his men to continue down a perilous path. Howard's account highlights Buffalo Horn's exceptional motivational skills and his unwavering determination to lead his people through adversity. Howard wrote,

> we had, this day, our first trouble with the Bannock scouts. They had come from Boise; were tired, and did not mean to go any further. Buffalo Horn, a young Indian, very handsomely decked off with skins and plumage, fortunately, for this time, took the side of their white chief, Robbins, and induced all but three to keep on with us for the present[61].

The complex character of Buffalo Horn is vividly showcased through his dealings with General Howard concerning the Nez Perce Indians. During a pursuit near Henry's Fork of Idaho, Buffalo Horn and his Bannock scouts, along with the U.S. military, paused for a night. Here, Buffalo Horn sought permission from General Howard to perform a war dance, which was granted. However, tensions arose post-midnight when Buffalo Horn, accompanied by a mixed-heritage Bannock named Raine, approached Howard with a grave request—to execute three Nez Perce Indians whom they accused of treachery. These Nez Perce were aligned with Howard, assisting in herding stock. Despite Raine's allegations, Howard denied their request, leading to significant discontent from Buffalo Horn.

---

[60] Ibid., 273-275.
[61] O. O. Howard, *Nez Perce Joseph* (Boston, 1881), 175.

> He [Buffalo Horn] was very angry in consequence, and never quite forgave me for this refusal. The third Indian may have been guilty. He, at any rate, so much feared these suspicious and exacting Bannocks, that he escaped into the forest that night, and went back to Kamiah.[62]

Buffalo Horn's actions reflect a man committed to his integrity and Indian cultural ways, embodying a rigid sense of justice shaped by the severe conditions of war and survival. His determined, albeit controversial, stance on the perceived Nez Perce traitors exemplifies a sense of duty and his willingness to take extreme actions in times of war. However, Buffalo Horn was killed not long after the war broke out when he led the charge against a volunteer force of 26 men from Silver City near South Mountain[63]. The volunteers had Paiute scouts accompanying them and a scout named Piute Joe claimed the credit for killing the war chief. He stated,

> I saw that I could not get away when they [Bannock] were all mustered on me, so I jumped off my horse and placed my horse between me and them, and laid my gun over the saddle, and fired at Buffalo Horn as he came galloping up, ahead of his men. He fell from his horse, so his men turned and fled when they saw their chief fall to the ground, and I jumped on my horse again and came to Silver City as fast as I could.[64]

The U.S. military and militias have a long history of utilizing Indian scouts to achieve their military agendas against other Indian tribes, and Buffalo Horn himself exemplified this very fact. This practice became particularly notable during the westward expansion of the U.S. in the 19th century where American Indian scouts were valued for their unparalleled knowledge of the land, including terrain, trails, water sources, and seasonal variations. Their tracking skills and ability to move stealthily in the wilderness provided a strategic advantage to U.S. forces navigating unfamiliar or hostile environments. Scouts also often served as interpreters and mediators between U.S. forces and Indian tribes. Their linguistic skills and understanding of

---

[62] Ibid., 233.
[63] Sarah Winnemucca Hopkins, *Life among the Piutes: Their Wrongs and Claims* (New York: G.P. Putnam's Sons, 1883), 148.
[64] Ibid., 148-149.

cultural nuances were crucial in negotiations, gathering intelligence, and preventing misunderstandings during military campaigns.

The U.S. military's recruitment of Indigenous people to achieve broader U.S. objectives continues to this very day in places like the Middle East and elsewhere. By enlisting members of certain tribes as scouts in campaigns against rival tribes, the U.S. government easily exploited existing rivalries and tensions, weakening Indian resistance to westward expansion and consolidation of U.S. territories. Indian scouts were often promised rewards for their service, including pay, food, and clothing. However, once these scouts were utilized to their end they were usually discarded and subjected to the same hardships as the Indians they helped subdue. Some famous units of Indian scouts were the Apache Scouts, used by the U.S. Army during the Apache Wars in the late 19th century[65]. The scouts were instrumental in tracking down Apache leaders such as Geronimo. Similarly, Crow and Shoshone scouts played a crucial role in the campaign against the Sioux and Northern Cheyenne during the Great Sioux War of 1876-77[66]. The Umatilla were in turn used against the Bannock[67] and Shoshone in both the Bannock War and the so called 1879 Sheepeater War in central Idaho[68]. Indeed, following the end of the Bannock War, a Crow scout known as "Frenchy" Bethune, also called "Little Rock" or "Big Pipe" by the Indians, met his demise at the hands of U.S. soldiers[69]. His death occurred after he was caught claiming spoils from the Bannocks, who had nearly been decimated in an engagement involving troops and scouts from Fort Custer.

The Bannock War of 1878 was fueled by multiple grievances against the U.S. and its citizens. Key among these was the failure of the U.S. to provide sufficient subsistence as promised in the Fort Bridger Treaty of 1868, compelling the Bannock to leave their reservation annually to hunt for food. This necessity clashed with their desire to engage in farming, a pursuit

---

[65] Dee Brown, *Bury My Heart at Wounded Knee: An Indian History of the American West* (New York: Macmillan, 2007), 370-387.
[66] Ibid., 275.
[67] Madsen, *The Bannock of Idaho*, 220.
[68] John Carrey and Cort Conley, *The Middle Fork: A Guide* (Boise: Backeddy Books, 1992), 302.
[69] Leforge, *Memoirs of a White Crow Indian*, 152.

hampered by the lack of resources to sustain them during the initial agricultural stages[70]. Additionally, white settlers' encroachment and the consequent depletion of game exacerbated the tribe's struggles for self-sufficiency. Another significant point of contention was the U.S. government's unfulfilled promise to reserve reasonable portions of the "Port Neuf and Kansas prairie" country, specifically the Camas Prairie, for the Bannock, an area vital for its camas plants, a principal food source. The whites' practice of driving hogs and cattle on the Camas Prairie deepened the Bannocks' resentment.

Tensions were also heightened in 1877 during the Nez Perce conflict, leading to the Bannocks' confinement at Fort Hall, where they faced forced famine due to reduced game and restricted access to rations[71]. Agent Danilson's favoritism towards the Shoshone, who received most of the government supplies, including those meant for the Bannock, further inflamed the situation. The confiscation of the Bannocks' horses and guns after two Bannock men retaliated against the rape of their sister by white men only worsened matters, leading to a cycle of violence and retribution that included the killing of a white man by a Bannock, resulting in severe punitive actions by the authorities.

The Bannock War distinguishes itself as a legitimate war within the historical context of the American West, in contrast to other conflicts like the 1863 Bear River Massacre (originally called the Bear River Battle), the 1877 Nez Perce War, and the 1879 Sheepeater War, which were characterized as one-sided surprise attack and massacre, forced flights, and punitive expeditions rather than organized military engagements. In preparing for the Bannock War, the Bannock meticulously orchestrated a campaign, appointed Buffalo Horn as War Chief, actively sought alliances with other tribes and executed a series of coordinated attacks and raids. This organized resistance, marked by strategic planning and collective action, sets the Bannock War apart as a true war, driven by a deep-seated need for justice and sovereignty. Given the historical injustices and the encroachment on their lands, the Bannock's decision to wage war represents a rational

---

[70] Madsen, *The Bannock of Idaho*, 227.
[71] Ibid., 229.

and understandable response to the cumulative grievances they faced.

In the aftermath of Chief Buffalo Horn's death, Chief Egan assumed leadership of the Bannock's warring faction. Tragically, Egan and several of his subchiefs fell victim to deceit by the Umatilla and were killed, leaving the Bannock and their Paiute allies without leadership. This disarray led to the dispersion of the Bannock and their Paiute allies, marking a turning point that effectively concluded the Bannock War of 1878. The war's end saw the remaining Bannock and Paiute warriors either being hunted down or succumbing to their wounds on the trail. As it relates to Wyoming, one of the final conflicts of the Bannock War of 1878 occurred near Heart Mountain on Clarks Fork[72]. Here General Miles and some 75 Crow Scouts "nearly exterminated the Bannocks".[73] The troops used a cannon in the engagement and a frontiersman named Finn Burnett described the battle scene as follows.

> The thickets had been blown to bits by cannon shots, and the dead bodies of squaws and papooses lay with the remains of Bannock warriors amid the wreckage....The path along which the Bannock had fled, was still slippery with blood.[74]

A week later, Second Lieutenant Hoel S. Bishop captured part of the Bannock who escaped in the Miles fight[75]. The remaining survivors of the battle were encountered by Lieutenant Bishop at Dry Fork, a tributary of the Snake River in Wyoming, on September 12. Thomas H. Leforge, the man who served with Buffalo Horn under Major Brisban, observed this engagement.

> The Bannock decided to surrender to the troops, and they moved in a peaceful manner to do so. Nevertheless, volleys of gun-fire were poured into them and several of them were killed. I remember that one woman had a thigh broken by a bullet. She hid out with her baby, but she was discovered,

---

[72] Madsen, The Bannock of Idaho, 224.
[73] P.W. Norris, Superintendent, "Report upon the Yellowstone National Park to the Secretary of the Interior," for the year 1878, 981.
[74] Robert Beebe David, *Finn Burnett, Frontiersman* (Glendale, Calif.: Arthur H. Clark Company, 1937), 354-55.
[75] Madsen, *The Bannock of Idaho*, 225.

brought in to the agency, and cared for until her recovery. It seemed to me that killing of these Indians when it was plainly evident they were trying to surrender was a violation of the humanities. They did not respond to the fire.[76]

What is probably not well known or understood, was that the Bannock women and children accompanied their husbands, brothers, fathers, and grandfathers during conflicts. Sadly, they suffered the same hardships and risks, and many were killed. The last of the warring Bannocks and Paiutes were finally captured by October of 1878 and the war was over[77]. After the war, some 349 Bannock Indians were unaccounted for and most probably died from wounds along the trail[78]. Willie George related an account of his mother, Weetowatsi, who was with the Bannock during the war.

> "they had gone through some bad times before, but the trip through Montana was the worst yet. Many of their people were sick; wounds received in earlier battles began to fester and turn black because they didn't have time to take proper care of them. The sick and wounded had to be carried and were slowing the progress of the camp. They asked to be left behind. Their friends and relatives placed them among rocks or willows and gave them a little food and water. If they got well before their food ran out, they could try to rejoin the camp. Most of them died; the old people said they supposed enemy Indians found some and killed them. Mother, when telling about this, would shake her head sadly and say, "we had to leave so many!"[79].

The Bannocks, who suffered casualties or were apprehended in Wyoming, were attempting, similar to the Nez Perce the previous year, to reach Canada in hopes of joining Chief Sitting Bull, who had himself been exiled from the U.S.[80]

Throughout the late 19th century, the collision between Euro-Americans and American Indians culminated in systematic

---

[76] Leforge, *Memoirs of a White Crow Indian*, 131.
[77] Madsen, *The Bannock of Idaho*, 226.
[78] Ibid., 226.
[79] Willie George as told to Jack F. Contor, "Two Trails," *True West Magazine*, February 1963, 58.
[80] Ibid., 223.

violence and the deliberate erasure of Indian populations. By the early 20th century, the American Indian population had dwindled dramatically to an estimated 237,196[81], a stark testament to the severity of these policies. The Shoshone, Bannock, and Nez Perce Tribes were the last Indian tribes to enter peace treaties with the U.S. However, the historical trajectory of Indian suffering began over four centuries ago with the introduction of European diseases, unlimited warfare, and the loss of vital food sources, leading to famine and the near extinction many tribes[82].

Specifically, the Bannock people endured a catastrophic smallpox outbreak in 1853, as noted by emigrant Harriet Ward, which nearly wiped them out[83]. This pattern of disease-induced mortality and warfare against the Bannock and Shoshone represents one of the final waves of the "Great Dying"—a term encapsulating the mass fatalities among Indian groups due to European colonization. This era of American death and suffering serves as a poignant reminder of the profound and lasting impacts of colonization on Indian populations, illustrated by the drastic demographic shifts experienced by American Indians in the contiguous U.S. (*Figure 5*).

---

[81] Department of Commerce, Bureau of the Census, "Indian Population in the United States and Alaska," Sam. L. Rodgers, Director, Bureau of the Census Library (Washington: Government Printing Office, 1910), 10.
[82] Roxanne Dunbar-Ortiz, *An Indigenous Peoples' History of the United States* (Boston, Massachusetts: Beacon Press, 2014), 39-42.
[83] Madsen, *The Shoshoni Frontier and the Bear River Massacre*, 13.

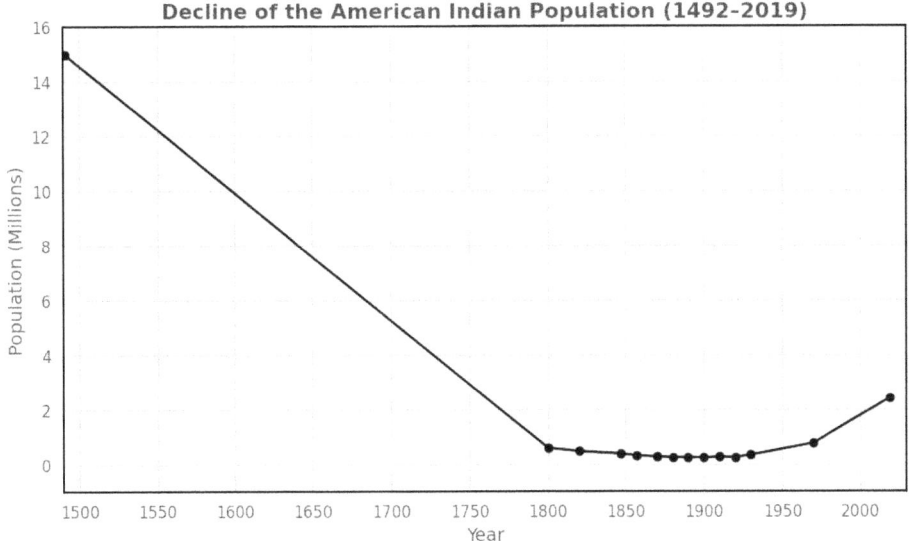

Figure 5. Graphical representation of the severe demographic changes among American Indian populations in the contiguous United States due to colonization. This chart highlights the significant reduction in American Indian populations over time, with the vertical axis indicating population numbers and the horizontal axis representing chronological progression in years.[84].

Like various wildlife species such as wolves, grizzly bears, bighorn sheep, buffalo, and later salmon, Indian populations experienced significant declines as a result of colonization. Life on reservations for many Indians paralleled the challenges faced by these animals, including the loss of enough land area to sustain oneself, susceptibility to diseases, and exposure to violence. It has been estimated that 90% of the pre-Columbian population in the

---

[84] Dunbar-Ortiz, *An Indigenous Peoples' History of the United States*, 10; Michael R. Haines and Richard H. Steckel, A Population History of North America (Cambridge, UK: Cambridge University Press, 2000), 24; Department of Commerce, Bureau of the Census, *Indian Population in the United States and Alaska 1910* (Washington: Government Printing Office, 1915), 13; Cleve Davis, "Treaty and Trust Responsibility Funding Trends in Indian Country: Focus on the Indian Health Service," *Journal of Native Sciences* 1, no. 1 (January 2020): 4; U.S. Department of Commerce, Bureau of the Census, *The Indian Population of the United States and Alaska* (Washington: United States Government Printing Office, 1937), 2; U.S. Bureau of the Census, *Census of Population: 1970 Subject Reports Final Report PC(2)-1F American Indians* (Washington, D.C.: U.S. Government Printing Office, 1973), 1.

Western Hemisphere died because of European colonization[85]. To put this into perspective, some 54.4 million souls were lost during the Great Dying. As the most densely populated areas in the Western Hemisphere were mostly agrarian, some scientists have linked secondary plant succession of Indigenous croplands that resulted from the Great Dying to global climate cooling[86]. In other words, The Great Dying in the Americas was so extensive and sudden that it is now believed to have been one of the first human-caused global impacts prior to the Industrial Revolution[87]. However, unlike the global warming we are seeing today, the Great Dying caused Earth system cooling. Although we will never know for certain, it is probably safe to assume that at least 50% of the Shoshone and perhaps a higher rate of mortality for the Bannock resulted from disease spread, not to mention the tremendous losses through local massacres and unlimited warfare.

These staggering losses—of land, life, and self-sufficiency—were not just physical, but cultural. As Indian populations declined and became increasingly confined to reservations, U.S. policy shifted toward eradicating what remained of Indian identity through forced assimilation. This new phase of cultural destruction targeted the youngest and most vulnerable members of tribal communities: the children.

The establishment of the U.S. boarding school system at Fort Hall in 1880[88] marks a dark chapter in American history—one in which Shoshone and Bannock children were systematically taken from their families in an effort to erase their culture, language, and way of life. The government, claiming the need to liberate these children from the backward and debilitating influences of their parents, mandated their enrollment in institutions like the one overseen by the Methodist Episcopal Church at Fort Hall. The conditions these children endured were abysmal—a grim testament to an egregious neglect of human rights. An 1886 investigation into the conditions at Lincoln Creek school revealed a harrowing environment that gravely endangered

---

[85] Alexander Koch, Chris Brierley, Mark M. Maslin, and Simon L. Lewis, "Earth System Impacts of the European Arrival and Great Dying in the Americas after 1492," *Quaternary Science Reviews* 207 (2019): 13.
[86] Ibid., 30.
[87] Ibid., 30.
[88] Madsen, *The Northern Shoshoni*, 182.

the health and survival of the children confined there. The investigation uncovered that the children were forced to consume drinking water contaminated by dead cattle. Additionally, they endured harsh conditions in a boarding school plagued by windows missing panes and woefully inadequate clothing and equipment. To compound their misery, they were locked up at night in the dilapidated facilities where, during the winter months, the lack of sufficient bedding left them freezing and at serious risk of hypothermia.

The forced attendance at these schools, as recounted by Indian Agent Gallagher in 1888, was predicated on a ruthless ideology:

> The Indians must conform to 'the white man's ways,' peaceably if they will, forcibly if they must. They must adjust themselves to their environment, and conform their mode of living substantially to our civilization. This civilization may not be the best possible, but it is the best the Indians can get. They can not escape it, and must either conform to it or be crushed by it.[89]

Gallagher's stark mandate highlights the coercive methods used to strip these children of their cultural identity. Unsurprisingly, an overwhelming majority of the Indians staunchly opposed these measures, especially the mothers and Indian medicine men. The medicine men harbored grave concerns, foreseeing that attending these schools would lead to the children's deaths.[90] Indeed, their fears were realized when, in 1891, scarlet fever ravaged through the children, killing ten—a tragic outcome that Indian Agent Fisher lamented, who had noted the higher mortality rate among those who attended school compared to those who stayed with their families in teepees.

Despite this, the push for increased enrollment continued unabated, with some resistance from Indian policemen who had to carry out the orders and strong opposition from the community. When families collectively resisted, the Indian agents called in the U.S. military. In 1894, Captain Van Orsdale sanctioned the use of "reasonable coercive measures"[91] leading to a forcible increase in

---

[89] Ibid., 184.
[90] Ibid., 183.
[91] Ibid., 186.

school enrollments through military intervention. Following the military's subjugation of the Indians, the responsibility for enrollment was transferred to Agent Thomas B. Teter the following year. Known for his ruthless enforcement tactics, Teter frequently engaged in confrontations with parents and was notorious for forcibly dragging children from their homes to ensure their attendance at school. The registration process described by the Pocatello Tribune in 1902 paints a harrowing picture and shows the ethnocentrism of the surrounding border towns.

> The agency officials and the reservation police go out with a wagon, run down the youngsters and haul them to school...Their parents hide them in the sage brush, in the willows, under piles of dirty skins and when they are found the squaws fight like old cats to prevent their being taken away. Sometimes the braves join the fight...After the youngsters are taken and loaded into the wagons they are hauled off squealing like young pigs while the squaws set up a howl besides which the yelping of a pack of coyotes is musical.[92]

Special Indian Agent Lane also vividly described the profound alienation and silent protest of the Indian families when visiting them in their teepees:

> they will all big, little, old and young wrap themselves up in their blankets, head and body and lay there like a dead person and give no sign of your presence.[93]

In a notable episode, Indian police attempted to take a 14-year-old girl, already married, to school against her and her husband's wishes. Her husband, with the help of friends, managed to rescue her, overpowering the police and seizing their weapons in the process.[94] Following this event, many of the older Indian women, who were consistently against the schooling mandates, collaborated with young Indian men. Together, they declared that nearly every young girl on the reservation was married, thereby assisting them in evading capture by the police.

---

[92] Ibid., 190.
[93] Ibid., 185.
[94] Ibid., 186.

Military intervention was deployed once more to enforce school attendance, restoring it through force. Once back in school, numerous children attempted to flee to their traditional camp lives, only to be recaptured and compelled to return. Overwhelmed by the severe culture shock, some students tragically resorted to suicide, with a few consuming Western hemlock as a means of escape from their unbearable circumstances[95]. To curb the alarming rate of deaths, a selective measure was implemented during the autumn enrollment period, where only children "in the best possible physical condition were taken".[96] Deplorable conditions and cruel treatment can only be described as profound neglect and dire circumstances imposed upon the young lives of children.

While the Indian youth were being subjugated, the U.S. was also focusing its attention on the acculturation of the older Indian people. To compel the adults into submission, traditional ceremonies such as the annual Sundance were forbidden. For example, in 1901 the Indian Agent A. F. Caldwell announced he would provide new farm wagons for those interested in farming, but the recipient was required to cut their hair. The destroying of cultural habits and customs of the Indian and supplanting them with white man's ways went on with vengeance. No rations were provided to able-bodied nonworking Indians and confinement in the guardhouse at hard labor was used to enforce the wearing of short hair and the prohibition of traditional dances.

This period of U.S. History was marked by a systematic cultural assault, where traditional ceremonies and lifestyles were banned to reshape American Indians into replicas of white Americans. The campaign of cultural eradication not only suppressed native ceremonies, such as the Sundance, but also enforced Western dress codes, illustrating a complete disregard for traditional ways of life. Moreover, economic repression was evident as even the use of paints and the sale of beads—crucial for artistic expression and economic survival—were prohibited[97]. This era's policies reflected not only a profound disregard for the cultural and human rights of the Shoshone-Bannock community but also highlighted the systemic failures of institutions like the Methodist

---

[95] Ibid., 187.
[96] Ibid., 187.
[97] Ibid., 182.

Episcopal Church and Indian Agency at Fort Hall, which was tasked with the education and care of the Shoshone and Bannock. The church's neglect, combined with the government's failure to provide adequate food, forced families to leave the reservation to hunt, further illustrating the dire circumstances and systemic neglect faced by these communities. Ominously, the harsh realities of the U.S. Indian boarding school policy in Fort Hall have mostly been overlooked and omitted from mainstream historical educational narratives.

  The narrative of anguish extended beyond Fort Hall, similar events occurred on many reservations across the U.S. In fact, during latter part of the 19th and throughout the 20th centuries, there were more than 523 government-funded, often church-run, Indian boarding schools[98]. Like Fort Hall, the Indian Agents would systematically remove children from their families and place them in these boarding schools, which could be located hundreds of miles away from their families. At these institutions, the children faced brutal punishments, such as beatings and starvation, for speaking their native languages. Some children sexually molestation and most, if not all, were forced to cut their hair to mimic hairstyles of white Americans as a tactic to further strip them of their cultural identity. This harsh treatment and the systematic destruction of traditions, values, and language is the primary reason why many Tribal Nations, including the Shoshone-Bannock Tribes, are struggling to maintain their heritage languages and culture.

  As I conclude this chapter, my reflections on the historical treatment of the American Indian within the U.S. bring me to a deeply personal and yet broadly contested question: did genocide occur here? While it is evident to me that the genocide of the American Indian is deeply embedded in U.S. history, the academic discourse on this subject remains divided[99]. Some scholars argue that while European and U.S. actions were undeniably cruel and unjust, they do not meet the criteria of genocide[100]. This

---

[98] "U.S. Indian Boarding School History." National Native American Boarding School Healing Coalition. Accessed April 27, 2024. https://boardingschoolhealing.org/education/us-indian-boarding-school-history/.
[99] Ostler, Jeffrey. "Genocide and American Indian History." In *Oxford Research Encyclopedia of American History*. 2015, 1.
[100] Ibid., 1.

perspective is frustratingly narrow to me, particularly with scholars who sympathize to U.S. colonialism and overlook significant events such as the Bear River Massacre—the deadliest in U.S. history. The complexity of American Indian history often leads scholars to shy away from a definitive answer, yet the debate essentially hinges on the definition of genocide.

The term genocide was first defined by Polish lawyer Raphäel Lemkin in 1944 during his work on Axis Rule in Occupied Europe. Lemkin coined the term genocide combining 'genos', meaning race or tribe, with 'cide', meaning killing. His intention was not only to describe the atrocities of the Holocaust but also to acknowledge historical instances of targeted destruction against specific groups. Lemkin's book culminated in genocide being recognized as an international crime by the United Nations General Assembly in 1946, and later codified in the 1948 Genocide Convention. According to the Convention, genocide involves acts committed with the intent to destroy, in whole or in part, a national, ethnical, racial, or religious group, including killing members of the group, causing them serious bodily or mental harm, inflicting conditions calculated to bring about their physical destruction, imposing measures to prevent births, and forcibly transferring children to another group.

However, it is ultimately up to the reader to determine whether the actions of the U.S. were intended to destroy, in whole or in part, Tribal nations, thereby bringing about their physical destruction. Additionally, readers must consider whether the forcible transfer of children to boarding schools qualifies as part of these genocidal actions. On the topic of imposing measures to prevent births—a crucial element of genocide as defined internationally—I must point out a significant, albeit lesser-known, aspect of this policy. The U.S. government continued to perform sterilizations on Indian women well into the 1970s, with these procedures conducted by physicians employed by the federal Indian Health Service[101]. While the sterilization of Indian women has been documented to some extent[102], it is less widely known

---

[101] Reilly, Philip R. "Eugenics and involuntary sterilization: 1907–2015." *Annual review of genomics and human genetics* 16 (2015): 360.
[102] Pegoraro, Leonardo. "Second-rate victims: The forced sterilization of Indigenous peoples in the USA and Canada." Settler Colonial Studies 5, no. 2 (2015): 161.

that Indian men, at least Indian men from Fort Hall were also subjected to sterilization. This fact became painfully clear to me during a conversation with my wife, who is a member of the Shoshone-Bannock Tribes. She disclosed that two of her male relatives were sterilized, likely during the 1970s. Her revelation was a stark and personal reminder that the policies of genocide were not just historical events, but actions that occurred within my own lifetime.

Moreover, it is illuminating—and profoundly disturbing—to realize that Nazi Germany, in the 1920s and 1930s, studied U.S. federal Indian law and policies as models for its own horrendous racial policies[103]. This shocking fact leads me to ponder: if the actions and policies that influenced Nazi ideology can be defined as genocidal, what does that imply about its original implementation in the U.S.? Ultimately, this is not just an academic exercise but a call for a deeper introspection about our history. As readers, as participants in this shared history, we must ask ourselves: if the foundation of such devastating ideologies was laid here, on this soil, can we truly deny the existence of genocide in America? The answer to this question is not just important for historical accuracy but is crucial in shaping our understanding of the present and our approach to the future.

---

[103] Whitman, James Q. *Hitler's American model: The United States and the making of Nazi race law.* Princeton University Press, 2017.

Chapter 5 – Bibliography

Ambrose, Stephen E. Undaunted Courage. New York: Simon & Schuster Paperbacks, 1996.

Augur, C. C. Transcript of Fort Bridger Treaty Negotiations, October 4, 1868. Reproduced at the National Archives.

Barber, Floyd R., and Dan W. Martin. Idaho in the Pacific Northwest. Caldwell, Idaho: The Caxton Printers, Ltd., 1956.

The Editors of Encyclopedia Britannica. "Louisiana Purchase." Encyclopedia Britannica. Last modified December 26, 2023. https://www.britannica.com/event/Louisiana-Purchase.

The Editors of Encyclopedia Britannica. "Washakie." Encyclopedia Britannica. February 16, 2023. https://www.britannica.com/biography/Washakie.

Brown, Dee. Bury My Heart at Wounded Knee: An Indian History of the American West. New York: Macmillan, 2007.

Carrey, John, and Cort Conley. The Middle Fork: A Guide. Boise: Backeddy Books, 1992.

Davis, Cleve. "Treaty and Trust Responsibility Funding Trends in Indian Country: Focus on the Indian Health Service." Journal of Native Sciences 1, no. 1 (January 2020): 4.

Danilson, W. H. "Report of Agents in Idaho, Fort Hall Indian Agency." In Annual Report of the Commissioner of Indian Affairs to the Secretary of the Interior for the Year 1876. Washington: Government Printing Office, 1876.

David, Robert Beebe. Finn Burnett, Frontiersman. Glendale, Calif.: Arthur H. Clark Company, 1937.

Dunbar-Ortiz, Roxanne. An Indigenous Peoples' History of the United States. Boston, Massachusetts: Beacon Press, 2014.

Executive Order, February 12, 1875. 1 Kappler 839.

Executive Order, "Fort Hall and Coeur d'Alene Reservations," June 14, 1867.

Howard, O. O. Nez Perce Joseph. Boston, 1881.

Haines, Michael R., and Richard H. Steckel. A Population History of North America. Cambridge, UK: Cambridge University Press, 2000.

Hopkins, Sarah Winnemucca. Life among the Piutes: Their Wrongs and Claims. New York: G.P. Putnam's Sons, 1883.

"Treaty with the Eastern Band Shoshoni and Bannock," July 3, 1868. 15 Stat. 673.

Koch, Alexander, Chris Brierley, Mark M. Maslin, and Simon L. Lewis. "Earth System Impacts of the European Arrival and Great Dying in the Americas after 1492." Quaternary Science Reviews 207 (2019): 13–30.

Lamarine, Roland J. "Alcohol Abuse Among Native Americans." Journal of Community Health 13, no. 3 (1988): 143–152.

Leforge, Thomas H. Memoirs of a White Crow Indian, vol. 584. Lincoln: University of Nebraska Press, 1974.

Madsen, Brigham D. The Bannock of Idaho. Moscow: University of Idaho Press, 1996.

Madsen, Brigham D. The Northern Shoshoni. Caldwell, Idaho: Caxton Press, 2007.

Madsen, Brigham D. The Shoshoni Frontier and the Bear River Massacre. Salt Lake City, UT: University of Utah Press, 1985.

Madsen, Brigham D. Chief Pocatello: The "White Plume". Salt Lake City: University of Utah Press, 1985.

National Native American Boarding School Healing Coalition. "US Indian Boarding School History." Accessed April 27, 2024. https://boardingschoolhealing.org/education/us-indian-boarding-school-history/.

Miller, Robert J. "Nazi Germany's Race Laws, The United States, And American Indians." St. John's Law Review 94 (2020): 751.

Moulton, Gary E., ed. The Definitive Journals of Lewis & Clark: Through the Rockies to the Cascades. Lincoln: University of Nebraska Press, 1988.

Northwestern Band of Shoshone Nation. "History." Accessed February 13, 2024. https://www.nwbshoshone.com/history/.

Norris, P.W., Superintendent. "Report upon the Yellowstone National Park to the Secretary of the Interior," for the year 1878.

U.S. Department of Commerce, Bureau of the Census. The Indian Population of the United States and Alaska. Washington: United States Government Printing Office, 1937.

Parry, Darren. The Bear River Massacre: A Shoshone History. Salt Lake City, Utah: By Common Consent Press, 2019.

Pegoraro, Leonardo. "Second-rate victims: The forced sterilization of Indigenous peoples in the USA and Canada." Settler Colonial Studies 5, no. 2 (2015): 161–185.

Reilly, Philip R. "Eugenics and involuntary sterilization: 1907–2015." Annual Review of Genomics and Human Genetics 16 (2015): 351–368.

Department of Commerce, Bureau of the Census. "Indian Population in the United States and Alaska." Sam. L. Rodgers, Director. Washington: Government Printing Office, 1910.

U.S. War Department. Annual Report of the Secretary of War, 1878, Vol. 1, pt. 2. U.S. Congressional Serial Set (1878): 151.

US Bureau of the Census. Census of Population: 1970 Subject Reports Final Report PC(2)-1F American Indians. Washington, D.C.: US Government Printing Office, 1973.

Whitman, James Q. Hitler's American Model: The United States and the Making of Nazi Race Law. Princeton: Princeton University Press, 2017.

Williamson, Darcy. River Tales of Idaho. Caldwell, Idaho: The Caxton Printers, Ltd.

George, Willie as told to Jack F. Contor. "Two Trails." True West Magazine, February 1963.

Chapter 6 - The Jackson Hole Conspiracy

The Greater Yellowstone area, with its vast herds of elk, bison, deer, antelope, and mountain sheep—and its rivers rich with trout—has long been a hunting ground for *Newe* people. They knew the region's value not only for its abundance of game and fish, but for its spiritual power and natural wonder. Non-Native newcomers later came to appreciate what the *Newe* had always understood: this land was extraordinary. On March 1, 1872, the U.S. government designated the area as Yellowstone National Park, the nation's first, centered on the active volcanic caldera at its heart. Although this designation made history and the area is now a World Heritage Site and Biosphere Reserve, the designation resulted in forced removal of its Indian inhabitants the *Dukudeka* to the Fort Hall, Wind River, and Lemhi reservations. No longer would the original inhabitants be able to hunt and steward this landscape as they had been doing for a time out of mind.

Originally, the promoters of Yellowstone National Park envisioned it operating without government expense[1]. Nathaniel P. Langford, a member of the Washburn Expedition and an advocate for the Yellowstone National Park Act, was appointed as the unpaid superintendent. Despite limited resources, including the lack of laws for wildlife protection and insufficient funds for infrastructure and law enforcement, Langford made efforts to manage the park best he could.[2] However, political pressure led to Langford's removal in 1877, and Philetus W. Norris was appointed the second superintendent. Under Norris's administration, and with congressional appropriations starting in 1878 "to protect, preserve, and improve the Park,"[3] significant developments occurred. Norris built roads, established a park headquarters at Mammoth Hot Springs, appointed the first "gamekeeper", and campaigned against hunters and vandals.[4]

---

[1] National Park Service, "Birth of a National Park," Last updated February 5, 2020, https://www.nps.gov/yell/learn/historyculture/yellowstoneestablishment.htm.
[2] Ibid.
[3] Ibid.
[4] Ibid.

During Norris's service, the U.S. was actively engaged in warfare with many American Indian tribes, including the Bannock War of 1878. To alleviate public fears about these conflicts, Norris propagated a myth that American Indians avoided Yellowstone due to a fear of hydrothermal features, particularly the geysers—a narrative that was a complete lie but nonetheless endures.[5] Political machinations led to Norris's dismissal in 1882. His successors, three superintendents who followed, struggled to protect the park effectively. Even the appointment of ten assistant superintendents as police could not halt the rampant poaching, squatting, woodcutting, and vandalism. In the eyes of many, the park was under siege, with its wildlife and natural resources suffering immensely.

In 1882, General Philip Sheridan undertook an expedition into the park and witnessed flagrant violations of park regulations and a lack of concern for the area's resources. He was convinced that it needed protection by troops, and he began a massive campaign to do just that when he returned to the east.[6] His efforts caught the attention of the Secretary of Interior, who called upon the Secretary of War to provide troops should congress fail to appropriate funds for the management of Yellowstone. In 1886, Congress failed to make any provision for the pay of the Superintendent or for the protection of the Park and the Secretary of the Interior took action. He requested assistance from the Secretary of War, leading to a deployment of military personnel for the Park's protection. Consequently, Captain Moses Harris and Troop M of the First U.S. Cavalry were dispatched and arrived in the Park on August 17th.[7] Captain Harris became the first acting superintendent of the period that would later become known as the Park's "Army Era", and he served from 1886 through 1889.[8]

---

[5] Ibid.
[6] Amanda Shaw, "The Superintendents -- Captain Moses Harris," National Park Service, June 24, 2016, https://www.nps.gov/yell/blogs/the-superintendents-captain-moses-harris.htm.
[7] D.W. Wear, "Report of the Superintendent of the Yellowstone National Park to the Secretary of the Interior," August 20th, 1886.
[8]Shaw, "The Superintendents -- Captain Moses Harris," NPS, June 24, 2016, https://www.nps.gov/yell/blogs/the-superintendents-captain-moses-harris.htm.

As for the Indians, they were now compelled to live on the Fort Hall Indian Reservation and reliant upon scant government rations and clothing which led to regular starvation and suffering. Each year when starvation reached a climax, the Indian agent at Fort Hall would issue passes to the Bannocks, who were more willing than the Shoshone, to leave the reservation and provide for themselves. They typically left to their hunting grounds in Wyoming and southern Montana, where game was more readily available.[9] Despite their necessity, these hunting expeditions by the Bannocks were met with much complaint from local and distant whites, particularly regarding their alleged use of fire as a hunting method.[10] Captain Harris was loud in opposing Indian hunting in Wyoming. He frequently wrote to various federal officials managing Indian affairs, expressing his concerns about Indians nearing Yellowstone Park boundaries, starting fires, overhunting, and scaring tourists. However, in reviewing numerous letters from Harris and others, there seems to be no concrete evidence or specific instances of verified kills by Indians from the Fort Hall, Lemhi, or Wind River reservations within Yellowstone Park.

Correspondence to the Editor of Forest and Stream, A Weekly Journal of Rod and Gun, indicated that after Yellowstone's designation as a national park, the Indians' preferred hunting areas included the headwaters of the Gallatin and Madison rivers, northwest of Yellowstone National Park. They also frequented the headwaters of the Snake River, south of the park in the area now known as the John D. Rockefeller Jr. Memorial Parkway, near Jackson's Lake in what is now Grand Teton National Park, the Teton Wilderness, and the Falls River Basin of the Caribou-Targhee National Forest. Additionally, they hunted in the mountains eastward of the park, a region where the Wind River Shoshone[11] would exercise their off-reservation treaty hunting rights.

---

[9] James Irwin, Shoshone Agency, letter to the Commissioner of Indian Affairs, September 22, 1883.
[10] Joel C. Janetski, *Indians in Yellowstone National Park*, revised ed. (Salt Lake City: University of Utah Press, 2002), 112.
[11] "Letters to the Editor," *Forest and Stream: A Journal of the Rod and Gun*, vol. XXXII, no. 12 (April 11, 1889): 233-234; Harris, "Report of the Superintendent of the Yellowstone National Park to the Secretary of the Interior," 1889, 16-19.

It was hardly surprising that white authorities and sportsmen, including Indian Agents, collectively opposed the presence of Indians within or close to the boundaries of Yellowstone Park. The public perception of Indians at the time, which persists to some degree today, was often negative and stereotypical. The sentiment was reflected in a letter to the editor, which stated,

> [t]hese Indians have large reservations on which they are supposed to stay, where they are fed and clothed at the expense of the Government; reservations from which a white man is expelled if there without a permit".[12]

Despite this general view, the Bannock tribe, in particular, faced criticism for their hunting practices, often accused of hunting solely for hides and setting fires. Yet, a contrasting perspective was offered in another complaint letter to the Editor of Forest and Stream, which acknowledged, "I will give them credit for not wasting much, for they dry hides, meat, paunch and some of the intestines for winter use".[13]

The exchange of letters between Captain Harris and various officials responsible for Indian affairs often followed a consistent pattern. Harris frequently sent letters leveling accusations against the Indians for trespassing near park boundaries, excessive hunting, and initiating fires. Reacting to these charges, the Commissioner of Indian Affairs would direct U.S. Agents to bar the Indians from entering and even going near Yellowstone National Park. The Indian Agents, in turn, would communicate back to both Harris and the Commissioner, affirming that they had repeatedly advised the Indians to avoid Yellowstone as well as the Lost River Country in Idaho. Interestingly, Indian hunting in Idaho's Lost River Valley was also subject to disapproval, even though it has never been part of a national park. Yet, amidst these exchanges, some Indian Agents expressed skepticism about the validity of the accusations levied against their charges. In their responses to the Commissioner, they conveyed doubts about the Indians' alleged transgressions, suggesting that they did not fully

---

[12] Janetski, *Indians in Yellowstone National Park*, 234.
[13] Ibid., 234.

believe the Indians were guilty as Harris had claimed[14]. P. Gallagher the U.S. Indian Agent at the Fort Hall Agency wrote.

> these Indians stoutly deny having gone into the Park, much less near there, and that the charges of burning and laying waste does not properly lie at their door. This is just as they stated things some two months ago, and have continued in disclaiming. But a short time now till they could be 'rounded up', if guilty of the charges alleged, & if desired that a thorough investigation be made as to these and the Lemhi Indians, (for they disclaim also I am informed,) I will proceed at an early day to do so[15].

For three years, Captain Harris and local whites sent written complaints to the three Indian Agents of the Bannock and Shoshone who signed the 1868 Fort Bridger Treaty, as well the Secretary of the Interior, expressing their unease about the Indians' hunting and spear fishing[16]. Harris' sentiment was also echoed by the third governor of Wyoming, John Eugene Osborne, where he wrote a letter to Hoke Smith the Secretary of Interior in 1894.

> I am reliably informed that a considerable number of Indians from the Shoshone reservation in this state, and the Fort Hall reservation in Idaho, are now off their reservations, and in the vicinity of the National Park are setting destructive forest fires, and wantonly killing game for hides. These depredations have been going on for some time. In fact we have this same trouble with the government wards, every year. Our people would consider it a special favor if you will notify the Indian agents of the respective reservations, to at once order their Indians back to their reservations, where they belong.[17]

---

[14] P. Gallagher, Fort Hall U.S. Indian Agent, letter to J.D.C. Atkins, Commissioner of Indian Affairs, June 16, 1888; P. Gallagher, Fort Hall U.S. Indian Agent, letter to A.B. Upshaw, Acting Commissioner of Indian Affairs, September 25, 1888.
[15] P. Gallagher, U.S. Indian Agent, Fort Hall Idaho Agency, letter to the Commissioner of Indian Affairs, August 13, 1888.
[16] J. Sargent, letter to Assistant Secretary, August 29, 1890.
[17] John Eugene Osborne, Governor of Wyoming, letter to Hoke Smith, Secretary of the Interior, September 5, 1894.

One striking aspect of Osborne's letter is his use of "off their reservations." This phrase echoes the colloquial English expression "off the reservation" to describe improper behavior. The frequent use of such language by authoritative figures likely cemented this colonial phrase into American English, where it persists even today[18]. In retrospect, the complaints against the Indians drew parallels to wolves, which, like them, faced persecution and near-eradication from the lower 48 states, barring parts of northeast Minnesota, until their reintroduction in 1995 to central Idaho and Yellowstone National Park[19]. The Forest and Stream Journal wrote the following about the Bannock and Shoshone from the Fort Hall, Lemhi, and Wind River Reservations, "[t]he destruction of the deer and elk killed by these Indians is in itself a serious matter, but it does not compare in the importance with the damage done by the forest fires".[20]

While it's indisputable that American Indians historically utilized fire for ecological management and hunting game, the use of similar practices in the Greater Yellowstone region by the Bannock and Shoshone during late 1800s is likely but not known for certain. The possibility that fire was used as a hunting tool by the *Newe* exists, but such claims during this time were probably exaggerated greatly,[21] and more likely used as a pretext for their displacement by the U.S. government and its citizens. At that time, the Park was also encircled by white "frontiersmen", hunters, trappers, and "squaw-men" who were also suspected as starting the fires[22]. As game dwindled outside the park, these individuals would set fires at the park's edges to drive game out, reinforcing the Park officials' prevailing belief that fire was detrimental.

---

[18] Cleve Davis, "Racists and Colonizing Metaphors," *Indian Country Today*, 2017, https://ictnews.org/archive/racists-colonizing-metaphors.
[19] U.S. Fish & Wildlife Service, "Gray Wolf (Canis lupus)," accessed January 14, 2024, https://www.fws.gov/species/gray-wolf-canis-lupus.
[20] "Forest and Stream: A Weekly Journal of the Rod and Gun," vol. XXXII, no. 11 (April 4, 1889): 1.
[21] Robert Woodbridge, U.S. Indian Agent, Lemhi Agency, Idaho, letter to John Atkins, Commissioner of Indian Affairs, September 15, 1886, 2.
[22] "Report of the Superintendent of the Yellowstone National Park to the Secretary of the Interior," 1886. Washington: Government Printing Office, 7.

Ironically, in modern ecological understanding and practice, prescribed burns are acknowledged as beneficial.[23] Many ecologists and federal land management organizations, like the National Park Service, now recognize that controlled or prescribed fires can positively impact forest health and public safety.[24] In fact, the Yellowstone Fires of 1988 have been attributed to fire suppression policy of the U.S. from 1872 to 1972 leading to abnormal fuel conditions[25]. Today's understanding of fire in land management showcases a dramatic shift from late 19th-century perceptions. Contemporary strategies use fires intentionally for ecosystem management, aiding in biodiversity preservation, mitigating underbrush to prevent larger wildfires, and fostering the health and growth of diverse plant species. This modern approach, in stark contrast to the past misconceptions and fears, recognizes the strategic use of fire as a vital tool.

This evolution is evident in what is now known as "Indigenous Fire Stewardship"[26]. Historically, Indian communities used fire for various purposes, including adapting fire regimes to changing climates and environmental conditions. These practices were aimed at shaping landscapes and ecosystems, enhancing preferred species' presence, and increasing access to essential resources. They also played a vital role in preserving traditional ecological knowledge systems and supporting ceremonial, subsistence, and economic activities. While some *Newe* elders may still retain this knowledge, the modern integration of traditional Indian fire practices into contemporary fire management strategies may be seen as too little, too late. Nonetheless, it highlights a critical point: U.S. assimilation policies and its genocide against Indian peoples have contributed to the erosion of valuable

---

[23] Marcos Francos and Xavier Úbeda, "Prescribed fire management," Current Opinion in Environmental Science & Health 21 (2021): 100250, https://doi.org/10.1016/j.coesh.2021.100250.
[24] National Park Service, "Wildfire Fire: What is a Prescribed Fire?" accessed January 14, 2024, https://www.nps.gov/articles/what-is-a-prescribed-fire.htm.
[25] William H. Romme and Don G. Despain. "Historical Perspective on the Yellowstone Fires of 1988," *BioScience* 39, no. 10 (1989): 695–99. https://doi.org/10.2307/1311000.
[26] F.K. Lake and A.C. Christianson, "Indigenous Fire Stewardship," in *Encyclopedia of Wildfires and Wildland-Urban Interface (WUI) Fires*, edited by S.L. Manzello (Cham: Springer, 2020), https://doi.org/10.1007/978-3-319-52090-2_225.

knowledge systems and poor management of the ecosystem. These traditional Indian practices, if preserved and applied, could have been instrumental in addressing current challenges with wildfires in forested ecosystems, showcasing a lost opportunity to benefit from Indian ecological wisdom.

For instance, a letter to the Editor of Forest and Stream, criticizing the Bannock Indians for forest burning, ignorantly attempted to portray the Indians as reckless and unwise. The author noted:

> "A great portion of the southern part of the Park, and nearly all the country to the south of it which has been frequented by Indian hunting parties, has been burned over within comparatively a few years. What little green timber there is is small second growth, or timber so favorably located that fires could not spread in it."[27]

This view overlooks how such fire practices could contribute positively to forest health. Ironically, these conditions – lower intensity fires and reduced fuel loads – are what many forest managers in the West now aim for to prevent dangerous high-intensity wildfires. Nonetheless, these ethnocentric complaints, although ignorant, were made to support Captain Harris' claims with affidavits and reports of Indian hunting activities both in and near Yellowstone Park[28].

Although Harris regarded the use of Yellowstone's game by the Indians as a severe issue and sought local support to address it, probably to his frustration, his attempts to garner assistance from Indian agents were not addressed to his liking.[29] The Indian agent at Fort Hall was acutely aware of the dire conditions and lack of food on the reservation and they also knew the Indians had reserved the right to hunt on unoccupied U.S. lands, a right

---

[27] "Letters to the Editor," Forest and Stream, April 11, 1889, 234.

[28] Ibid., 112.
[29] Janetski, *Indians in Yellowstone National Park*, 113.

enshrined under Article IV of the Fort Bridger Treaty of 1868 where it says.

> The Indians herein named agree, when the agency house and other buildings shall be constructed on their reservations named, they will make said reservations their permanent home, and they will make no permanent settlement elsewhere; but they shall have the right to hunt on the unoccupied lands of the United States so long as game may be found thereon, and so long as peace subsists among the whites and Indians on the borders of the hunting districts.[30]

In 1889, the Boone and Crockett Club of New York City, addressing concerns over Indian hunting practices, criticized the Indians for hunting only for hides and outside the designated hunting seasons.[31] Theodore Roosevelt, who at that time was the President of the Boone and Crockette Club[32] and who would later become President of the U.S., expressed his disapproval of the Bannock and Shoshone Indians' hunting and their role in starting forest fires. Roosevelt even asserted that the Indians' burning of forests could disrupt the water supply in the plains below the Rocky Mountains. He strongly opined that "they should never be allowed off the reservation unless a responsible white man is with them."[33] The collective stance led to a decisive action by the Boone and Crockett Club, culminating in a resolution that was unanimously adopted at a meeting held at the Knickerbocker Club in New York City. The resolution reflected the club's position and Roosevelt's views on the matter, signifying a significant moment in the ongoing debate over Indian hunting rights and conservation practices in Wyoming.

> *Whereas*, It has for some years been the custom for Indians from the Fort Hall and Lemhi agencies, and from Washaki [Wind River] and perhaps, the Crow agency, to spend the summer or a part of it on the borders of the Yellowstone

---

[30] "Treaty with the Eastern Band Shoshoni and Bannock," July 3, 1868, 15 Stat. 673.
[31] Janetski, *Indians in Yellowstone National Park*, 113.
[32] Boone and Crockett Club, letter to the Secretary of the Interior, April 12, 1889.
[33] "Forest and Stream: A Journal of Outdoor Life, Travel, Nature Study, Shooting, Fishing, Yachting," vol. 32, no. 12 (April 11, 1889): 235.

National Park hunting and collecting dried meat and hides of game, and

Whereas, These hunting parties destroy great quantities of game without regard to the game laws in force in the Territories where their hunting is done, and

Whereas, In addition to this destruction of game, they cause incalculable damage to the forests of the continental watershed by the fires which they start, either through carelessness or intentionally, as adjuncts to their hunting, and

Whereas, The acting superintendent of the Yellowstone National Park has repeatedly brought this matter to the attention of the Interior Department, and has fortified his reports by affidavits from intelligent and trustworthy men, most of whom are well known to many members of the Boone and Crockette Club, and

Whereas, The destruction of forests and game caused by these Indian hunting parties is a serious evil and ought at once to cease, therefore be it

Resolved, That the Indians of the Fort Hall, Lemhi, Washaki [Wind River] and Crow agencies should not be permitted to leave their reservations in large parties, except when in charge of some reliable white man who can be held responsible for the conduct of the Indians whom he accompanies, and that under no circumstances should these Indians be permitted to approach within twenty-five miles of the borders of the Yellowstone National Park, and

Resolved, That the Secretary of the Interior be respectfully requested to call this matter to the attention of the Commissioner of Indian Affairs, and to instruct him to direct the agents in charge of the above named tribes to keep their people on the reservation.[34]

The predominantly white residents of Wyoming also perceived the off-reservation treaty hunting rights of the Tribes as being at odds with the nascent state's hunting regulations, which did not permit year-round hunting. This perception and political

---

[34] "Letters to the Editor," Forest and Stream, April 11, 1889, 234.

pressure led the Commissioner of Indian Affairs to issue a directive to agencies surrounding Yellowstone, including those at Fort Hall, Lemhi, Wind River, and Crow. The directive placed restrictions on hunting game without utilizing the meat and warned of confining Indians to reservations if they hunted without proper permits.[35] In response to this directive, J. T. Van Orsdale, the agent at Fort Hall, pointed out the treaty-guaranteed rights of the Indians to hunt on federal lands to the Secretary of Interior.[36] He criticized the double standards in play, highlighting how Jackson Hole guides permitted their wealthy clients from the eastern U.S. and abroad to hunt solely for horns and ivory eye teeth. Van Orsdale also emphasized the importance of elk to the Indian economy. He noted that the Indians used elk hides to make gloves, moccasins, and other items for trade, emphasizing their resourcefulness and the economic value of their traditional practices.

    The agent for the Shoshone Agency noted that "hordes of white hunters infested the country entirely unmolested"[37], a situation of which Harris was cognizant, particularly regarding the hunting activities of non-Indians along the Park's boundary. White poachers, notably those hunting buffalo near Henry's Lake in Idaho, were in breach of the newly enacted Lacey Act. In other words, it seems that the white hunters were the ones doing the actual poaching. Nonetheless in 1893, approximately 25 hunting guides, colloquially referred to as "dudes", who profited from the influx of tourists into the mountainous terrains of Jackson Hole, collectively decided against the presence of Indians in the area. They expressed grievances, asserting that the Indians excessively killed game, rustled livestock, and that they feared for their lives. An illuminating correspondence from the U.S. Indian Service's Fort Hall Agency articulated their underlying motives: "by keeping the Indians out of this Country, these people realize large sums as guides for tourists and hunting".[38] The settlers in Wyoming became so fervent in their wish to expel the Indian populations

---

[35] Janetski, *Indians in Yellowstone National Park*, 113.
[36] Ibid., 113.
[37] Report of the Commissioner of Indian Affairs, "Disturbances in Jackson's Hole Country Wyoming," Executive Document No. 5, 54th Congress, 1st Session (1896): 62.
[38] United States Indian Service, Fort Hall Agency, Idaho, "Letter to Secretary of Interior," October 6, 1895, Fort Hall, National Archives, 6.

that by 1894, it emerged as the dominant political issue.[39] Further escalating the situation, the Fort Hall Agency appointed a new Indian Agent, Thomas B. Teter[40] in 1895.

From their initial encounters with white settlers to the dawn of the 20th century, the Bannock were perceived as warlike and unrestrained.[41] Following the 1868 Fort Bridger Treaty, both the Bannock and Shoshone of Fort Hall were transitioning to life on the reservation. Despite their lesser tendency to adapt to reservation norms compared to the Shoshone, the Bannock, particularly after their defeat in the Bannock War of 1878 and under the stringent oversight of Indian Agents, maintained a low profile while hunting off-reservation. They generally kept to themselves and steered clear of conflicts during these excursions.[42] Unlike the Shoshone, who were more inclined to depend on the U.S.-provided rations, the Bannock were more likely to leave the reservation for hunting. This tendency led some Shoshone to even refer to the Yellowstone area as *Bannaite' Doya'* or the "Bannock Mountains". This situation prompted high-ranking officials, including Governor William A. Richards and Frank C. Armstrong, the acting Commissioner of Indian Affairs, to advocate for measures that restricted Bannock hunting in western Wyoming, reflecting the growing tensions, and differing responses of the two tribes to reservation life.

Bolstered by the Governor's support, Constable William Manning of Marysvale assembled a posse, predominantly consisting of the hunting guides, to deter the Bannock hunters from entering Wyoming. Strategically, they aimed to leverage the nascent Wyoming fish and game regulations as a pretext to penalize and, in some instances, commit violent acts against the Bannock. Their rationale was that by instigating a violent confrontation, the judicial system would rule in their favor. Although the Bannock and Shoshone had reserved off-reservation treaty rights to hunt on unoccupied lands, the Department of Interior Office of Indian Affairs, also supported Wyoming in not

---

[39] U.S. District Attorney, "Letter to Secretary of the Interior on report concerning outrages on the Indians," August 30, 1895, National Archives.
[40] Janetski, *Indians in Yellowstone National Park*, 114.
[41] Brigham D. Madsen, *The Bannock of Idaho* (Moscow: University of Idaho Press, 1996), 249.
[42] Ibid., 253.

allowing the Indians to hunt. The acting Commissioner of Indian Affairs wrote to the Indian Agents the following.

> This office has recently received a great many complaints to the effect that numerous parties of Indians are continually leaving their reservations with passes from their Agents to make social visits to other reservations; that they slaughter game in large quantities merely for the sake of killing and for the hides...Upon receipt of this letter you will call a council of your Indians...and tell them that the restrictions as to hunting contained therein must be strictly complied with...Further, that they will be liable to arrest and punishment by state officers for violating the game laws of the state of territory in which they may be found hunting.[43]

In other words, the top government official who was supposed to represent the Indian interests as a trustee, compelled the Indians to not exercise their treaty rights and obviously supported the authority of the state of Wyoming over hunting.

In Jackson Hole, the settlers did not know or care that the Bannock were only permitted to venture outside the reservation during times when the government rations were insufficient. Presented below is a transcribed letter, originally handwritten, penned by representatives of the Fort Hall Indian community to the U.S. President in 1895, detailing their circumstances on the Fort Hall Reservation and disfavor of their new Indian Agent Teter.

> We the undersigned Bannock and Shoshone Indians of the Fort Hall reservation having met in Councils have decided to ask our Father in Washington for a new Agent, our present Agent Mr Teters is afraid of us and we want no one that is afraid for he can do us no good. He carries a Pistol and shot himself when he first came here. If he had been away from the Agency and killed himself no Indians would have been accused of killing him. We cannot believe him he tells us so many lies, he told us this spring to plough as much land as we could and he would give us seed and when we did and went to him for the seed he said he had none. Some of the Indians got mad and went hunting and

---

[43] Frank C. Armstrong, Acting Commissioner, Department of the Interior, Office of Indian Affairs, letter, May 22, 1894.

got into trouble he tells us to do something this week and tells us not to do it next week. What we want is an Agent who is not afraid, who will tell us the truth and talk to us and for us. One we can depend on to look out for the interest of the Indian one to be Agent for the Indians and not the Whites. The whites have taken our water and our crops of seed.[44]

Thomas B. Teter, the designated Fort Hall Indian Agent, was entrusted with upholding the interests of the Fort Hall Indians in related affairs. Contrarily, his actions conveyed a stark deviation from his expected duties. Teter not only turned a blind eye to the appropriation of resources from the Fort Hall Indians by white settlers but also subsequently penned a letter to Washington D.C., advocating for the establishment of a commission to revoke the off-reservation hunting rights of the Bannock and Shoshone. His correspondence culminated in a legislative bill that sought to regulate the hunting activities of the Fort Hall community, both within and outside the reservation, in alignment with state law.[45] However, this bill did not progress further and was shelved in the committee stage.

The phrase "got into trouble," as articulated in the Council's letter to the President, alludes to a series of arrests executed by Constable Manning and his posse of dudes. Despite being instructed to exclude the Indians at "all costs",[46] and having made several arrests in the summer of 1895, Manning faced a defiant group of fifteen Bannocks in June 1895. The Bannocks boldly told Manning and his posse to "go to hell as they were not afraid [of the soldiers]," leading Manning and his men to retreat.[47] Notably, on July 4, 1895, eight Bannocks were detained near Rock Creek, located at the Green River's source. Among them, six Bannock individuals were collectively fined and charged costs totaling $1,400.[48] To contextualize this figure for contemporary readers, the sum of $1,400 in 1895 would approximate a value of around

---

[44] Fort Hall Indian Council, "Letter 'To our Father in Washington'," October 7, 1895, Fort Hall, National Archives.
[45] U.S. House of Representatives, 54th Congress, 1st Session, H.R. 1705, "A Bill To prevent the unlawful killing of game by Indians, and for other purposes," December 16, 1895.
[46] *Report to the Commissioner of Indian Affairs for 1896*, 79.
[47] Madsen, *The Bannock of Idaho*, 257.
[48] Ibid., 256.

$53,000 in the 2024 economy.⁴⁹ Predictably, the financial burden was insurmountable for the Bannock Indians. Consequently, they were detained, pending guidance from county officials on their fate. Intriguingly, the anticipated directives never materialized, and the overseers subsequently allowed the Bannocks to escape.⁵⁰ The "escape" incident had political ramifications and intensified pressure on Manning and his posse, compelling them towards more aggressive tactics.

Emblematic of this heightened aggression, on July 13th, Manning, aided by 26 deputies, detained a group of Bannocks near the Fall River in Wyoming. The group, comprising 10 men and 13 women,⁵¹ and five infant children⁵² were confronted at gunpoint within their encampment. In a harrowing incident detailed by Acting Attorney General E.B. Whitney in an August 30, 1895, letter to the Secretary of the Interior, the aggressive detention and subsequent actions against the Bannock Indians under Constable Manning and his deputies culminated in tragic outcomes. Within Whitney's letter he also attached a report the U.S. District Attorney of Wyoming received regarding an investigation into the incident. The report in its entirety is reproduced here as follows.

> A careful investigation of the whole affair, will, I am certain, result in showing the correctness of the following statements, which are made after personally interviewing a number of the leading participants in the trouble, both among the Indians and the Jackson Hole settlers and by noting the exact condition of affairs in the region relative to the habits of the Indians, the settlers, etc.
>
> First. I desire to state that the reports made by settlers charging the Indians with wholesale slaughter of game for wantonness or for the purpose of securing the

---

⁴⁹ "$1,400 in 1895 → 2024 | Inflation Calculator," Official Inflation Data, Alioth Finance, January 5, 2024, https://www.officialdata.org/us/inflation/1895?amount=1400.
⁵⁰ Madsen, *The Bannock of Idaho*, 256.
⁵¹ E.B. Whitney, Acting Attorney General, letter with attachment (original letter from a government employee in Wyoming, page 3), August 30, 1895, File Number 11,928-1895, Department of Justice, Washington D.C., 5.
⁵² Madsen, *The Bannock of Idaho*, 256.

hides of the animals killed have been very much exaggerated. During my stay in Jackson Hole I visited many portions of the district and saw no evidence of such slaughter. Lieuts. Gardiner, Park and Jackson, of the Ninth U.S. Cavalry, who conducted scouting parties of troops through all portions of Jacksons Hole also found this to be the case. No carcasses, or remains of elk were found in quantities to justify such charges. On Aug. 12, I visited a camp of Bannock Indians who had been on a hunting trip in Jacksons Hole until ordered by the troops to return to their reservation. I found the Indian women of the party preparing the meat of seven or eight elk for winter use, drying and "jerking" it. Every particle of flesh had been taken from the bones, even the tough portions of the neck being preserved. The sinews and entrails were saved, the former making threads for making gloves and clothing and latter for casings. The hides were being prepared for tanning; the brains had been eaten; some of the bones had been broken and the marrow taken out and others were being kept to make whip handles and pack saddle crosstrees. In fact every part of the animal was being utilized either for future food supply or possible source of profit.

Second. In connection with the troubles between the Indians and the whites I spent some time inquiring into the causes for the unconcealed hostility of the Jackson's Hole people against the Indians. I found little or no complaint among the settlers of offensive manners on the part of the Indians. Except in rare instances they have kept away from the houses of the settlers and have not been in the habit of begging. In no instance has there ever been a well authenticated case where a settler has been molested by an Indian.

About twenty-five of the Jackson's Hole settlers are professional guides for tourists and hunting parties visiting the region from other states and from abroad. The business is very profitable, guides sometimes making sufficient money in the short hunting season to keep them through the remainder of the year. These guides, while most of them have small ranches, make stock raising or the cultivation of their places a secondary consideration and make the business of guiding tourists or "dudes" as they are called in the region, their principal occupation. The killing of game by the Indians and by the increasing number of "dude" hunters threatens to so deplete the region of big game, deer, elk, moose, etc., as to jeopardise the occupation of the guides. It was decided at the close of last season to keep the Indians out of the region this year and the events of this summer are the results of carefully prepared plans. Mr. Pettigrew, United States Commissioner at Marysvale, said: "At our last election the question of keeping out the Indians was the most important one we had to deal with and the township officers elected, Constable and Justice of the Peace, were selected because we knew they would take decided steps to help us keep the Indians out." Constable Manning said: "We knew very well when we started in on this thing that we would bring matters to a head We knew some one was going to be killed, perhaps some on both sides, and we decided the sooner it was done the better so that we could get the matter before the courts."

Third. If a full investigation of the Jackson's Hole affair should be had the fact will be established that when Constable Manning and his posse of 26 settlers arrested a party of Indians on July 13, and started with them for Marysvale, he and his men did all they could to tempt the Indians to try to escape in order that there might be a basis of justification for killing some of them. On July 4, a party of eight Bannocks was arrested on Rock Creek near the head of Green River and taken to Marysvale where six of the party were fined $75 each and costs, the total amount of fines and costs being about $1400. This the Indians were unable to pay and they were placed under guard to await instructions as to their disposal. The county authorities from whom the information was asked failed to reply to the inquiries of the Jackson's Hole officers, who, at once relaxed guard duty over the Indians who escaped from custody. The next arrest of Indians was made July 13. Constable Manning and 26 deputies surrounded a camp of 10 bucks and 13 squaws at night and early in the morning with guns leveled at the Indians made the arrest, the Indians offering no resistance. The arrest was made on Fall River, 55 miles from Marsvale[sic]. The warrant was for

Bannock and Shoshone Indians, the names and number of the Indians to be arrested not being stated. After the arrest was made, the arms, meat, and other articles in the possession of the Indians were taken from them. Constable Manning also took their passes, ration checks, etc. These papers gave the name and residence of most of the Indians. From an interview with Nemits, an Indian boy, who was one of the party of Indians arrested an[sic] shot, and from interviews with several of Mr. Manning's posse I learned that the Constable and his men told the Indians some of them would be hung and some would be sent to jail and that this was believed by the Indians. The Constable also said in the hearing of the Indians, some of whom understood English, that if the Indians attempted to escape the men should shoot their horses. If the truth of the matter can be reached it will be found that the captors did not care particularly about getting their prisoners safely to Marsvale[sic] where they same formality of fining them and then having to let them escape would result as the previous case, but on the contrary tempted the Indians to try to escape, first by making them believe they were to be sent to jail or hunt and then by leading them to believe if they tried to escape their horses only, and not they, would be shot. The Indians are in many respects like children and are very credulous. They believed the threats of being sent to jail and of being hunt were true and they saw no trick in Manning's instructions given in their hearing to shoot their horses if they tried to get away.

    In an interview with Constable Manning he was asked why he did not tie the Indians on their horses and thus effectively prevent their escape. He said in reply: "The trail was a dangerous one and if a horse fell the Indian tied on might get hurt and I would have been censured." Asked why it was necessary to kill the escaping prisoners when he knew their names and addresses and could have subsequently obtained his prisoners by going to the Fort Hall agency for them, he said: "The Agent would probably refuse to give up the Indians if any demand were made for them."

    From Mr. Manning I learned that none of the horses of the escaping party of Indians were shot, notwithstanding his order, but that at least six Indians were hit by bullets. Of these, Timega, an old man was killed, Nimits, a boy of about 20, was wounded so that he could not escape and the others got away. Constable Manning said to me: "The old Indian was killed about 200 yards from the trail. He was shot in the back and bled to death. He would have been acquitted had he come in and stood his trial for he was an old man, almost blind and his gun was not fit to kill anything."

When the body of this old, sick, blind man was found after lying unburied in the woods for about twenty days it was found he had been shot four times in the back. They boy, Nemits, who was wounded, was shot through the body and arm. He was left on the ground where the shooting occurred and remained there living on some dried meat for ten days. He crawled for three nights to reach a ranch of a man friendly to Indians and was seventeen days without medical attendance.

The whole affair was, I believe, a premeditated amd[sic] prearranged plan to kill some Indians and thus stir up sufficient trouble to subsequently get United States troops into the region and ultimately have the Indians shut out from Jackson's Hole. The plan was successfully carried out and the desired results obtained. It would, however, be but an act of simple justice to bring the men who murdered the Indian, Timega, to trial. I would state, however, in this connection, that there are no officials in Jackson's Hole, county, stare[sic], or National, who would hold any of Manning's posse for trial. Either the anti-Indian proclivities of these officials or the fear of opposing the dominating sentiment of the community on this question would lead them to discharge all of these men should they be brought before them for a hearing.[53]

Something not mentioned in Whitney's letter was that two infants were jostled from the horses during the attack.[54] While one

---

[53] E.B. Whitney, Acting Attorney General, letter with attachment (original letter from a government employee in Wyoming, page 3), August 30, 1895, File Number 11,928-1895, Department of Justice, Washington D.C.
[54] Madsen, *The Bannock of Idaho*, 257.

was discovered and taken in by Mormon settlers, the fate of the other remains uncertain. It is assumed that the baby died or was taken by someone or something. It is not known if the Mormon settlers ever returned the other baby to the mother. Although the "Bad Men" Article or Article 1 of the 1868 Fort Bridger Treaty should have been in full force and effect, the Attorney General had this to say about the attack, "[t]here is, however, unfortunately no statute of the United States under which this Department can afford any assistance".[55] It is unclear whether the Bad Men clause was ignored or simply deemed irrelevant by the government. But the reader may judge for themselves whether it should have applied in this case. The clause reads:

> "If bad men among the whites, or among other people subject to the authority of the United States, shall commit any wrong upon the person or property of the Indians, the United States will, upon proof made to the agent and forwarded to the Commissioner of Indian Affairs, at Washington City, proceed at once to cause the offender to be arrested and punished according to the laws of the United States, and also re-imburse the injured person for the loss sustained."[56]

The Bannock Indian men involved were identified as Ta ne ga, Ben Senowin, Nemuts (Nemits), We-ha-she-go, Ya-ps-ojo, Poo-dat, Pah-goh-zite, Mah-mout, Ze-we-agat, and Boo-wah-go.[57] However, the records did not specify the names of the women and children present. The white perpetrators involved were J.O. Fisk, Ham Wort, Steve Adams, Joe Calhoun, William Crawford, Ed. Crawford, Martin Nelson, Joe Enfinger, J. Munger, Ed. Hunter, Frank Woods, Frank Peterson, Jack Shive, George Madison, Andrew Madison, M.V. Ciltner, Charles Estes, James Estes, Tom Estes, George Wilson, John Wilson, Ery Wilson, Victor Gustavae, Steve Leek, William Bellvue, John Cherrey, and William Manning.[58] The Commissioner of Indian Affairs concluded that the Bannocks "have, in the opinion of this office, been made the

---

[55] Whitney, Acting Attorney General, letter with attachment, August 30, 1895, DOJ, Washington D.C., 2.
[56] "Treaty with the Eastern Band Shoshoni and Bannock," July 3, 1868, 15 Stat. 673.
[57] Department of Justice, "Letter to Gibson Clarke Esq.," September 24, 1896, p. 1, National Archives, Washington D.C.
[58] Ibid., 1-2.

victims of a planned Indian outbreak by the lawless whites infesting the Jacksons Hole country with the idea of causing their extermination or their removal from that neighborhood".[59]

The posse rode under the color of law, but their genuine objective was the expulsion of the Indians from the state of Wyoming. Warrants for the arrest of any Bannock Indian hunting in Wyoming were authorized by Justice of the Peace, Frank H. Rhoads.[60] Concerned about potential repercussions from U.S. federal authorities, Rhoads sought assurances from Governor Richards of Wyoming. In a gesture of full support, Governor Richards advised Rhoads to uphold Wyoming's laws at all costs and to ensure the removal of the Indians from the state. The Governor further affirmed to Rhoads that he could depend upon him for protection and that he would "see him through".[61]

Although the Commissioner of Indian Affairs Daniel M. Browning did absolutely nothing to address the murders, the conspiracy got greatly bolstered when he directed his U.S. Indian Service Inspector, Province McCormick, to suggest to the Wyoming Governor that a precedent-setting case be instituted to determine the validity of the Indians' hunting rights in Wyoming.[62] The Commissioner's orchestrated strategy was delineated as follows.

> ...by having an Indian arrested by the State officials for hunting, and an application brought by the United States attorney for Wyoming for a writ of habeas corpus for the release of such prisoner, or in some other way, and that he shall agree that in case it shall be decided that the Indians have a right to hunt, and that the laws of Wyoming are in

---

[59] Douglas B.L. Endreson, Anne D. Noto, Frank S. Holleman IV, William F. Bacon (Counsel of Record), Monte Gray, Brief of Amicus Curiae Shoshone-Bannock Tribes of the Fort Hall Reservation in Support of Petitioner, No. 17-532, in the Supreme Court of the United States, Clayvin B. Herrera v. State of Wyoming (Washington, D.C.: Wilson-Epes Printing Co., Inc.), 10.
[60] Department of Justice, letter to Gibson Clarke Esq., September 24, 1896, 2.
[61] Ibid., 2.
[62] United States. Office of Indian Affairs, "Annual Report of the Commissioner of Indian Affairs, for the Year 1896," Washington, D.C.: Government Printing Office, 1896, 57, https://digital.library.wisc.edu/1711.dl/3YVW4ZRARQT7J8S.

no effect as against them, then in that event, he, Governor Richards, shall, by all the means in his power, protect the Indians in such right; and on the other hand, if it shall be decided by the courts that the Indians have no right to hunt, in violation of the State laws, or, in other words, that the State laws operate to abridge or defeat their said treaty rights, then this Department will recommend to Congress that an agreement be made with them for the relinquishment of the rights guaranteed to them by the treaty of 1868, and which they claim and believe are still in full force.[63]

In line with the Commissioner of Indian Affairs' strategy, Governor Richards swiftly concurred with the proposition for a precedent-setting case. Subsequently, Inspector McCormick journeyed to Fort Hall where he enlisted "two Indians suitable for the purposes of the test case".[64] In his interactions, McCormick convened a council with both the Bannocks and Shoshone headmen on ration distribution day. Therein, he assured them that "no effort would be spared to restore to them guaranteed rights and also the punishment of their murderers".[65] Following his address, McCormick individually consulted the tribal leaders, inquiring if they were amenable to the Department overseeing the issue, to which, he said they universally concurred. As detailed by McCormick he wrote.

I think I can safely say that I have discovered no disposition on the part of a single Indian to undertake for himself any revenge, but that he is relying implicitly upon the Government to right him in this matter. There seems to be none of the soreness or sullenness that one would ordinarily expect to see after the perpetration of such a dastardly, cowardly, preconcerted, outrageous crime as was inflicted upon these defenseless persons by the so-called law officers of Wyoming.[66]

In accordance with the strategy jointly formulated by the Commissioner of Indian Affairs and the Governor of Wyoming, Agent Teter identified two Indians to participate in the landmark

---

[63] Ibid., 57.
[64] Ibid., 58.
[65] Ibid., 58.
[66] Ibid., 59.

test case. On October 7, 1895, "Indians are in custody here for purpose of test case. Must have habeas corpus proceedings tried at once to avoid trouble by keeping them in custody. Please instruct U.S. attorney for Wyoming to proceed without delay".[67] The two selected Indians lacked proficiency in English, necessitating the acquisition of an interpreter. One was recognized as "Race Horse", more comprehensively known as John Race Horse Sr. or *Pohave*, my great-great grandfather (Figure 6). The other was Ben Sinowan, also spelled Sin-O-Win.[68] Ben Sinowan was identified among the Bannock Indians detained and subsequently attacked by Manning and his dude posse. Despite the execution of writs of habeas corpus by U.S. Marshal McDermott, Ben Sinowan's was subsequently released for unexplained reasons.[69] Consequently, Race Horse emerged as the lone representative of the Bannock Tribe in the test case, perhaps because he was not directly involved in the Manning murders. In other words, it is conceivable that the conspirators aimed to prevent any eyewitnesses from revealing that the so-called justice being pursued was not related to the murders at all, but instead focused exclusively on treaty hunting rights.

---

[67] Ibid., 59.
[68] *The Boomerang*, Vol. XV, No. 61, Laramie, Wyoming, October 10, 1895, 1.
[69] The Cheyenne Daily Sun-Leader, Vol. XXIX, No. 18, Cheyenne, Wyoming, October 9, 1895, 4.

Figure 6. A photograph of John Race Horse Sr., *Pohave*, was supplied by Nelson Racehorse. The identity of the photographer remains uncertain. It has been suggested, though not confirmed, that this image was taken as a booking photograph during his detainment for allegedly killing seven elk in Wyoming.

    In legal jargon, a writ of habeas corpus is a formal request made by an individual to a court for an immediate release from illegal detention or imprisonment that violates constitutional rights. This order compels the detainee's appearance before a judge to assess the legitimacy of their incarceration. However, the situation of John Race Horse Sr.'s supposed detention by the State of Wyoming raises questions about the appropriateness of using habeas corpus. It's unclear whether John Race Horse Sr. was fully cognizant of his arrest and the subsequent infringement on his liberty. This uncertainty is highlighted in a noteworthy letter from Agent Teter to the Commissioner of Indian Affairs, dated October 10, 1895, which sheds light on some of the ambiguity surrounding Race Horse's condition of detainment.

> I have the honor to inform you that I have this date returned from Evanston, Wyoming, where I left the Bannock Indians, whom I had taken to Evanston for the purpose of fulfilling the agreement entered into between the Interior Department and the Governor of Wyoming; the Indians, though in the custody of the Sheriff, are not aware of the fact of their arrest and, it is my intention to keep them in ignorance, owing to the bad effect it would have upon the Indians on the reservation.
>
> In order to keep the Indians now at Evanston in a good humor I promised them I would take them to Cheyenne, Wyoming, on the 26th instant, when their case is called before the Federal Court; I, therefore respectfully, request authority to escort the Bannock Indians now at Evanston, to Cheyenne, on or about the 20th of the present month; said authority to be telegraphed if granted. I am.[70]

The 1895 Uinta County jail records, dated October 14-15, list five Indians but notably exclude both John Race Horse and Ben Sinowan.[71] This omission is particularly striking considering the context: if Race Horse had been formally arrested, one would anticipate his detention to be recorded prior to October 10th. The absence of his name in these records raises questions about the procedural integrity surrounding his case, especially given its high political stakes in 1895. Such an oversight is unexpected, especially in a case significant enough to warrant habeas corpus

---

[70] Thomas B. Teter, U.S. Indian Agent, Fort Hall Agency, Idaho, letter to the Commissioner of Indian Affairs, Washington, D.C., October 10, 1895, Department of the Interior, U.S. Indian Service.
[71] 1895 Jail Record, Uinta County, Wyoming, Office of Louis J. Napoli, Sheriff.

proceedings. Furthermore, this anomaly aligns with the strategy of Governor Richards and is corroborated by Agent Teter's admission that he had only transferred two Bannock Indians to the sheriff's custody. His intention, as revealed in his correspondence dated October 10, 1895, was to keep the Indians unaware of their arrest to avoid negative repercussions on the reservation. This strategy, while politically motivated, adds another layer of ambiguity to the legal proceedings and the treatment of Race Horse and Sinowan.

Amidst these unfolding events, the charges leveled against Race Horse are particularly conspicuous. He faced accusations of illegally hunting and killing seven elk, purportedly beyond what was needed for immediate sustenance, thereby breaching state laws. This allegation, when juxtaposed with the lack of police or arrest records from that period, fuels speculation. The charges were likely completely fabricated for the test case and potentially part of a broader scheme intended to erode the treaty rights of the Bannock and Shoshone Indians. The circumstances imply a situation with deeper implications.

Court documents show Race Horse's admission to hunting these elk near Mount Hoback in Uinta County, around July 1, 1895.[72] Yet, this acknowledgment raises pertinent questions. Why is there an absence of police documentation or an arrest report corresponding to this alleged incident? The legitimacy of this charge becomes more questionable when one considers the possibility that it might have been a deliberate misrepresentation by government officials, aimed at challenging and potentially undermining the treaty. Despite these circumstances, the case proceeded and was initially heard by the Circuit Court of the District of Wyoming. This court concluded that the arrest of Race Horse was unwarranted, identifying the areas where he hunted as "unoccupied land of the United States", as identified in the 1868 Fort Bridger Treaty. Furthermore, the Circuit Court recognized the supremacy of the Treaty, declaring that Wyoming's state laws did not apply to the Bannock Indians, as highlighted in the habeas corpus proceedings of 1895.

However, the State of Wyoming challenged the Circuit Court decision, leading to its eventual reversal by the U.S. Supreme Court on May 25, 1896. In this pivotal ruling, Justice White,

---

[72] Ward v. Race Horse, 163 U.S. 504 (1896).

delivering the Supreme Court's opinion, disregarded the specifics of where the elk were killed. Instead, the Court scrutinized the continued validity of the Treaty following Wyoming's attainment of statehood. The Treaty's clause "so long as game may be found thereon" and the Bannock's original interpretation of the Treaty were deemed irrelevant or not even considered by the Supreme Court. The Court reasoned that since Wyoming's admission to the Union did not explicitly preserve Indian rights, the hunting rights granted by the Treaty ceased with Wyoming's statehood.

Furthermore, the Supreme Court determined that the provisions of the Fort Bridger Treaty of 1868 were incompatible with Wyoming's state laws, a decision that significantly undermined the rights of the Bannock and Shoshone Indians. This ruling effectively terminated the off-reservation hunting rights that had been guaranteed by the Treaty, concluding a brief period of 22 years during which these rights were known but not honored. The outcome not only marked the end of the Tribes' hunting rights in Wyoming but also set a precedent with long-lasting implications for Indian treaty hunting rights across the U.S. After the Supreme Court declared Race Horse guilty, Wyoming's attorney general persuasively argued that he should not be punished further. Ironically, Race Horse, who was supposedly detained, could not be immediately located as he had joined other Bannock and Shoshone on a hunting expedition in Jackson's Hole.[73] He was eventually found and brought back to appear before the judge. The ruling in the Race Horse case decisively terminated the off-reservation hunting rights in Wyoming, affecting every member of the Shoshone and Bannock tribes at Fort Hall and Wind River. This decision further diminished the tribes' capacity for self-sufficiency, as many relied on hunting not just for food, but also for materials like hides used to make moccasins, gloves, and other items.[74] Increasing reliance, often criticized by the non-Indian people to this very day, is a direct consequence of their collective actions over time, yet they almost always fail to acknowledge their role in creating the dependency.

---

[73] Janetski, *Indians in Yellowstone National Park*, 116.
[74] F. G. Irwin, Jr., "Reports of Fort Hall Agency, in Report of Agents in Idaho," in *Annual Report to the Commissioner of Indian Affairs*, (Washington: Government Printing Office, 1897).

The Wheatland World newspaper of Laramie County Wyoming captured what was well known at the time, that the whole affair was actually arranged.

> It will be remembered that the Bannocks entered Jackson Hole and wantonly slaughtered game, and that the settlers attempted to prevent them from continuing the work. Finally trouble ensued which called a troop of cavalry to the scene of the disturbance to prevent further bloodshed. When the warlike features of the affair subsided another phrase equally important arose. The government authorities claimed the Indians had a right under an old Bannock treaty to hunt and kill game in Wyoming at all seasons of the year, without regard to local laws or state regulations, and as the settlers who attempted to interfere with the Bannocks were in some measure acting under or in connection with state authority, a clash arose between the federal and state forces. To settle the dispute it was arranged that Race Horse, a Bannock, be arrested by Sheriff Ward, of Uinta county, and that a writ of habeas corpus be applied for before Judge Riner of the U.S. court. [75]

The Laramie Republican newspaper, in its July 21, 1896 edition, provided the following commentary on the verdict's conclusion.

> Many of the Indians are now employed on the irrigating canal near Fort Hall are earning good wages. Others are doing farming and other work and seem well satisfied with the changing conditions of things. Agent Teter is greatly pleased with their behavior and at the outcome of the test case which gives the state control over the Indians off the reservation. All parties seem to be pleased at the settlement made.
>
> Race Horse will now be taken to Evenston and delivered to the custody of Sheriff Ward, who will bring him into Judge Knight's court for final disposal of his case. Under the circumstances he will probably be released from the penalty of the law, and after being properly admonished to go and

---

[75] "The Bannock Indian Case," The Wheatland World, Vol. II, No. 32, Wheatland, Laramie County, Wyoming, May 29, 1896, 1.

sin no more will be free from the clutches of court, sheriff and lawyers.[76]

The reporting by The Laramie Republican in 1896, reflects a distinctly ethnocentric view of the situation surrounding Indian peoples at the time. The newspaper's portrayal of Indians engaging in canal digging and farming near Fort Hall as a positive development overlooks the broader context of forced assimilation policies imposed by the U.S. government. This perspective fails to acknowledge that such work might not have been a voluntary choice for Indian people but rather a part of the larger U.S. policy of assimilation, which often coerced them into abandoning their traditional ways of life, such as hunting for subsistence and moving with seasons.

This era was marked by a prevailing assimilationist ideology, epitomized by Captain Richard Henry Pratt's infamous philosophy: "Kill the Indian in him, and save the man." Pratt's speech laid the groundwork for the establishment of the Carlisle Indian School in 1879 and other similar boarding schools across the country. These institutions aimed to "civilize" and "Americanize" Indian children, often through harsh methods and the suppression of Indian cultures and languages. Consequently, numerous children died, and the repercussions of these policies were deeply traumatic, eroding cultural identities and heritages under the pretext of so-called assimilation and advancement.[77]

The actions of Constable Manning and his posse, and the subsequent indifference of the U.S. justice system, is not an isolated historical incident but part of a continuing pattern of injustice toward Indian communities. The harrowing events near the Fall River, marked by the loss of Bannock infants, the killing of an elder, the shooting of a boy, and the wounding of others, feature a profound disregard for the most vulnerable members of the community. This incident, a microcosm of the broader

---

[76] "THE RACE HORSE CASE," *The Laramie Republican*, Vol. VI, No. 288, July 21, 1896, 1.
[77] Kaitlyn Sebwenna-Painter. "Psychological Impacts of Historic Loss and Current Events Surrounding American Indian Boarding Schools." *American Indian and Alaska Native Mental Health Research* (Online) 30, no. 2 (2023): 1-21.; Ann Piccard, "Death by Boarding School: The Last Acceptable Racism and the United States' Genocide of Native Americans." *Gonzaga Law Review* 49 (2013): 137.

narrative, reflects a systemic failure to protect Indian rights and lives.

The blatant lack of justice for the murder of Indians, exemplified in the past, finds its echoes in contemporary issues, most notably in the movement of Missing and Murdered Indigenous Women (MMIW). This movement is helping to shine a light on a grim reality: Native women and girls in the U.S. and Canada are being abducted or murdered at alarming rates. The MMIW movement, driven by profound anger and sorrow within Indian communities, identifies a lasting crisis that extends beyond women and girls. Although the movement focuses on women and girls, it should also be mentioned that many Indian men are also murdered and missing. The widespread disappearances and murders leave families grappling with unending grief. These losses add layers upon layers of trauma to communities already bearing deep historical wounds, such as what happened in Wyoming in the latter part of 19th century.

The current ongoing crisis is a stark reminder of the failures of the U.S. justice system to adequately address the safety and rights of Indian peoples. It demonstrates a disturbing continuity from the era of Manning's impunity to the present, where Indian families still await answers and justice for their loved ones. This continuity of injustice serves as a painful reminder of the need for profound changes in how the legal system addresses crimes against Indian peoples, acknowledging their unique cultural and societal contexts, and ensuring their protection and rights are upheld.

Chapter 6 - Bibliography

Armstrong, Frank C. Letter, Acting Commissioner, Department of the Interior, Office of Indian Affairs, May 22, 1894.

Barrett, Amanda. "The Superintendents -- Captain Moses Harris." National Park Service, June 24, 2016. https://www.nps.gov/yell/blogs/the-superintendents-captain-moses-harris.htm.

Davis, Cleve. "Racists and Colonizing Metaphors." Indian Country Today, 2017. https://ictnews.org/archive/racists-colonizing-metaphors.

Endreson, Douglas B.L., et al. Brief of Amicus Curiae Shoshone-Bannock Tribes of the Fort Hall Reservation in Support of Petitioner, No. 17-532, in the Supreme Court of the United States, Clayvin B. Herrera v. State of Wyoming. Washington, D.C.: Wilson-Epes Printing Co., Inc.

Francos, Marcos, and Xavier Úbeda. "Prescribed Fire Management." Current Opinion in Environmental Science & Health 21 (2021): 100250. https://doi.org/10.1016/j.coesh.2021.100250.

Gallagher, P. Letters to J.D.C. Atkins, A.B. Upshaw, and the Commissioner of Indian Affairs, 1888.

Irwin, James. Letter to the Commissioner of Indian Affairs, September 22, 1883.

Irwin, F. G., Jr. "Reports of Fort Hall Agency, in Report of Agents in Idaho." In Annual Report to the Commissioner of Indian Affairs. Washington: Government Printing Office, 1897.

Janetski, Joel C. Indians in Yellowstone National Park. Revised ed. Salt Lake City: University of Utah Press, 2002.

Lake, F.K., and A.C. Christianson. "Indigenous Fire Stewardship." In Encyclopedia of Wildfires and Wildland-Urban Interface (WUI) Fires, edited by S.L. Manzello. Cham: Springer, 2020. https://doi.org/10.1007/978-3-319-52090-2_225.

Madsen, Brigham D. The Bannock of Idaho. Moscow: University of Idaho Press, 1996.

National Park Service. "Birth of a National Park." Last updated February 5, 2020. https://www.nps.gov/yell/learn/historyculture/yellowstoneestablishment.htm.

National Park Service. "Wildfire Fire: What is a Prescribed Fire?" Accessed January 14, 2024. https://www.nps.gov/articles/what-is-a-prescribed-fire.htm.

Osborne, John Eugene. Letter to Hoke Smith, Secretary of the Interior, September 5, 1894.

Piccard, Ann. "Death by Boarding School: The Last Acceptable Racism and the United States' Genocide of Native Americans." Gonzaga Law Review 49 (2013): 137.

Romme, William H., and Don G. Despain. "Historical Perspective on the Yellowstone Fires of 1988." BioScience 39, no. 10 (1989): 695–99. https://doi.org/10.2307/1311000.

Sebwenna-Painter, Kaitlyn. "Psychological Impacts of Historic Loss and Current Events Surrounding American Indian Boarding Schools." American Indian and Alaska Native Mental Health Research (Online) 30, no. 2 (2023): 1–21.

Shaw, Amanda. "The Superintendents -- Captain Moses Harris." National Park Service, June 24, 2016. https://www.nps.gov/yell/blogs/the-superintendents-captain-moses-harris.htm.

United States Fish and Wildlife Service. "Gray Wolf (Canis lupus)." Accessed January 14, 2024. https://www.fws.gov/species/gray-wolf-canis-lupus.

United States. Office of Indian Affairs. Annual Report of the Commissioner of Indian Affairs, for the Year 1896. Washington, D.C.: Government Printing Office, 1896. https://digital.library.wisc.edu/1711.dl/3YVW4ZRARQT7J8S.

Ward v. Race Horse, 163 U.S. 504 (1896).

Wear, D.W. "Report of the Superintendent of the Yellowstone National Park to the Secretary of the Interior." August 20, 1886.

Whitney, E.B. Letter with attachment, August 30, 1895. File Number 11,928-1895. Department of Justice, Washington, D.C.

"$1,400 in 1895 → 2024 | Inflation Calculator." Official Inflation Data, Alioth Finance, January 5, 2024. https://www.officialdata.org/us/inflation/1895?amount=1400.

Chapter 7 - In the Shadow of Race Horse

While earlier chapters explored the hunting history and the first legal battle over hunting rights involving the Fort Hall Bannock and Shoshone, the focus now turns to the contemporary legal challenges the Indians continue to face. The current legal landscape surrounding Indian hunting and fishing rights is complex, shaped over decades by legal battles waged by Tribes across the U.S. to defend and affirm their treaty-protected rights. In general, it has mostly been influenced by challenges of states and court interpretations of the language used in treaties. In the following chapters you will see the dynamic and evolving nature of federal Indian law as it relates to hunting and fishing. My goal is to make this complicated legal terrain more approachable—to break it down in a way that allows readers to follow the key court cases, legal principles, and treaty interpretations that have shaped Indian hunting and fishing rights. Through this legal journey, I hope readers gain a clearer understanding of the ongoing tension between Tribal sovereignty, federal authority, and state power.

As you can probably expect from the previous chapters, Tribes have always faced an uphill battle to exercise their reserved Treaty hunting and fishing rights. Court cases can have profound impacts upon not only the Tribe directly involved but potentially every federally recognized Tribe in the Nation. To begin with we will explore how the miscarriage of justice in the Ward v. Race Horse[1] verdict impacted the Crow Tribe's off-reservation treaty hunting in Wyoming. The legal saga concerning the Crow Tribe's hunting rights unfolded in the Big Horn National Forest of Wyoming. The linkage between the cases arose from the identical phrasing within Article IV of both the 1868 treaties—the Treaty with the Crows and the Fort Bridger Treaty involving the Eastern Shoshone and Bannock. Specifically, Article IV of the Treaty with the Crows reads,

> The Indians herein named agree, when the agency-house and other buildings shall be constructed on the reservation named, they will make said reservation their permanent home, and they will make no permanent settlement elsewhere, but they shall have the right to hunt on the unoccupied lands of the United States so long as game may

---

[1] *Ward v. Race Horse*, 163 U.S. 504 (1896).

be found thereon, and as long as peace subsists among the whites and Indians on the borders of the hunting districts.[2]

The struggle of the Crow within, what has been termed by Indian scholars, the "Courts of the Conqueror"[3] is a prime example of an enduring legal battle for recognition and exercise of off-reservation hunting rights on public lands in Wyoming.

In 1989, Thomas L. Ten Bears, a member of the Crow Tribe, was cited by Chuck Repsis, a game warden of the Wyoming Fish and Game Department, for killing an elk within the confines of the Big Horn National Forest in Wyoming. Drawing parallels to the predicament faced by John Race Horse Sr., the Crow Tribe, representing Ten Bears, contended that the Tribe held an unequivocal Treaty Right to hunt in the Big Horn National Forest and that the land Ten Bears killed the elk upon was "unoccupied lands of the United States"[4] pursuant to Article IV of the 1868 Treaty with the Crows. Advocating on behalf of Ten Bears' right to hunt, the Crow Tribe sought a legal declaration from the court confirming that the Crow held the right to hunt and fish on Wyoming's public lands.

However, the Wyoming District Court would do no such thing and ruled against Ten Bears and the Crow Tribe. The case is now known as Crow Tribe of Indians v. Repsis, 866 F. Supp. 520 (D. Wyo. 1994), commonly referred to as Repsis I.[5] Somewhat ironically, in that case the defendants—Chuck Repsis and Francis Petera of the Wyoming Department of Game and Fish—argued that "game no longer existed" in the area.[6] This appeared to be a strategic attempt to sidestep the Treaty language by claiming the absence of wildlife rendered the hunting rights void. While the Repsis court acknowledged that Race Horse had been criticized and largely abandoned by other courts, it nonetheless concluded

---

[2] *Treaty with the Crows*, May 7, 1868, 15 Stat. 649.
[3] Walter Echo-Hawk. *In the Courts of the Conqueror: The 10 Worst Indian Law Cases Ever Decided.* (Golden, CO: Fulcrum Publishing, 2018).
[4] *Treaty with the Crows*, 15 Stat. 649.
[5] *Crow Tribe of Indians v. Repsis*, 866 F. Supp. 520 (D. Wyo. 1994).
[6] Ibid., 522–23.

that Race Horse remained binding precedent and dismissed the Tribe's claim.[7]

Nonetheless, the Repsis I court ruled that the Race Horse case had not been expressly rejected or overruled. It also stated that it disagreed with the decision or logic used in the Race Horse case, but that it still had to follow the precedent because it was a controlling decision. The Repsis I court went on further to state that unless a higher court, like the Tenth Circuit Court of Appeals or the Supreme Court of the U.S., explicitly states that the Race Horse case is no longer a valid precedent, it was obligated to apply it. As a result, the court approved the defendants' request to dismiss the Crow's lawsuit seeking a declaration that they have a treaty-based right to hunt and fish freely on lands within the Big Horn National Forest in Wyoming, as established in the 1868 Treaty with the Crows.

Unyielding, the Crow Tribe appealed the Repsis I decision and the appeal became known as Crow Tribe of Indians v. Repsis, 73 F.3d 982 (10th Cir. 1995), also known as Repsis II[8]. The appeal encountered significant resistance with Senior Circuit Judge Barrett, presiding over the Tenth Circuit of the U.S. Court of Appeals. Barrett was unmoved by the arguments presented by the Crow Tribe. Barrett's final decision emphasized that both cases centered around interpreting identical treaty language, notably the reference to the "unoccupied lands of the United States so long as game may be found thereon, and so long as peace subsists among the whites and Indians on the borders of the hunting districts."[9] His decision articulated several key points:

1. The 1868 treaty reserved only a temporary right to hunt on "unoccupied lands of the United States, which was repealed with Wyoming's admission into the Union.
2. The land of Big Horn National Forest had been "occupied" since 1887 when they became a national forest.
3. The Crow Tribe and its members were subject to Wyoming game laws.

---

[7] Ibid., 523–24. See also *Idaho v. Tinno*, 94 Idaho 759, 497 P.2d 1386, 1392 (1972) (declining to follow Race Horse).
[8] *Crow Tribe of Indians v. Repsis*, 73 F.3d 982 (10th Cir. 1995).
[9] *Treaty with the Crows*, 15 Stat. 649.

4. The Crow Tribe, as private party, lacked standing to bring suit under the Unlawful Inclosures (UIA) of Public Lands Act.

Pertaining to the UIA, the Crow Tribe tried force the state of Wyoming to dismantle a seven mile long "elk-proof fence" erected by the Wyoming Game and Fish Department, which stood as a barrier between the state's boundary and the Tribal reservation. Apparently, the state of Wyoming did not want any of their non-existent elk to migrate upon the Crow Reservation.

Barrett's decision delivered a heavy blow to the chin of the Crow Tribe, and even lambasted the lower court's decision by stating,

> Unlike the district court's apologetic interpretation of and reluctant reliance upon Ward v. Race Horse, we view Race Horse as compelling, well-reasoned, and persuasive. Also, contrary to the Tribe's views, there is nothing to indicate that Race Horse has been "overruled, repudiated or disclaimed;" Race Horse is alive and well.[10]

Barrett also ruled that the right to hunt on "all unoccupied lands of the United States as long as game may be found thereon"[11] was a temporary right that ceased with Wyoming's statehood. Moreover, even though the 1868 Treaty with the Crows granted a right to hunt on "unoccupied lands," the Big Horn National Forest lands have been considered "occupied" since 1887.[12]

This decision must have been challenging for the Crow, especially when considering the foundational purpose of creating a forest reserve was to safeguard its status as unoccupied and to ensure its preservation. The court's interpretation of these lands as "occupied" was confusing as the purpose of the designation was to prevent occupation and preserve natural habitats. The Repsis II decision also clearly neglected any notion of historical and intended spirit of the hunting treaty right. The Barrett court's interpretation would have also likely confounded the original Indian chiefs who signed the 1868 Treaty, as their understanding of "unoccupied" would likely align with lands free from settlement

---

[10] Crow Tribe, 73 F.3d at 985.
[11] Ibid.
[12] Ibid.

or development and supporting game — a perspective fundamentally at odds with Barrett's ruling.

Since the Race Horse decision, the Supreme Court of the U.S. had provided guidance on how courts should interpret treaties, particularly Jones v. Meehan[13] and U.S. v. Winans[14]. These decisions emphasized interpreting treaties in a manner consistent with the Indian's understandings at the time of signing. In the case of Jones v. Meehan, the Supreme Court established that treaties between the U.S. and Indian tribes should not be interpreted based on the technical meaning as understood by lawyers, but rather in the way the language would have been understood by Indians. The Jones v. Meehan court also recognized that a treaty could effectively grant specific land rights to individuals within a tribe without requiring additional formalities like an act of Congress or a patent from the U.S. Executive.

Central to the Jones v. Meehan case was the Treaty of 1863 with the Red Lake and Pembina bands of Chippewa Indians[15]. This treaty reserved land near the Thief River for Chief Moose Dung and the Jones v. Meehan court determined that the Treaty of 1863 granted Chief Moose Dung an alienable title in fee to the specified land. Furthermore, when such a treaty-based title is granted, the inheritance rights pertaining to that land are guided by tribal customs and not by state law or decisions of the Secretary of the Interior. Lastly, the court emphasized that the interpretation of treaties primarily lies within the judiciary's domain, and Congress doesn't hold the power to change rights established by treaties unless in cases of a political nature.

The Repsis I & II decisions also failed to follow precedents established in the U.S. v. Winans case, which involved interpretation of a Stevens Treaty made with the Yakama Indians. To understand why this particular court case could have been particularly relevant to the Crow's plight, the U.S. v. Winans case found that while negotiating the Treaty with the Yakama in 1855[16] the U.S. negotiators promised, and more importantly the Indians understood, that the Yakamas would forever be able to continue

---

[13] *Jones v. Meehan*, 175 U.S. 1 (1899).
[14] *United States v. Winans*, 198 U.S. 371 (1905).
[15] *Treaty with the Red Lake and Pembina Bands of Chippewa Indians*, October 2, 1863, 13 Stat. 667.
[16] *Treaty with the Yakama*, June 9, 1855, 12 Stat. 951.

the same off-reservation food gathering and fishing practices as to time, place, method, species, and extent as they had or were exercising at the time of treaty making. The Winans decision also recognized that a,

> Treaty between the United States and the Indians... is not a grant of rights to the Indians, but a grant of rights from them—a reservation of those granted.[17]

The pivotal decision of U.S. v. Winans introduced what is now known as the "reserved rights" doctrine of federal Indian law. In making its determination, the Court acknowledged the longstanding cultural and historical significance of hunting and fishing to Indian communities. It recognized these rights as integral elements of a broader set of rights safeguarded by the Treaty. Nonetheless, the Repsis II decision did not apply the Jones v. Meehan and U.S. v. Winans precedents, and judge Barrett instead applied the precedent established by the Race Horse decision, which not only has been criticized and rejected by other courts, but more importantly based upon a conspiracy and murder of Bannock Indians back in the late 1890s to guide his decision in Repsis II. More specifically, it leaned on the contrasting perspectives of the Race Horse ruling, which articulated:

> Doubtless the rule that treaties should be so construed as to uphold the sanctity of the public faith ought not to be departed from. But that salutary rule should not be made an instrument for violating the public faith by distorting the words of a treaty, in order to imply that it conveyed rights wholly inconsistent with its language and in conflict with an act of Congress, and also destructive of the rights of one of the States.[18]

Although the Repsis II decision did acknowledge the importance of interpreting treaties in a way that respects the spirit and intent. The court completely overlooked the phrase "so long as game may be found thereon" which unmistakably suggests that a specific condition or situation will persist as long as wildlife or game exists for hunting or observation on a given tract of land or region, not to mention how the Indians themselves would have interpreted the meaning. In defense of the state of Wyoming, it

---

[17] *Winans*, 198 U.S. 371.
[18] *Race Horse*, 163 U.S. 504.

should also be noted that the Wyoming Department of Game and Fish did in fact argue that "game no longer existed...", apparently Ten Bears killed the last elk in the Bighorn National Forest. Like the verdict in Ward v. Race Horse, the Repsis II decision revealed a deep unwillingness to interpret treaties in a way that might constrain state power—driven less by legal reasoning than by a persistent, discriminatory bias against Indian rights.

Much like the Race Horse verdict, the decision in Repsis II appears to reflect regional political sentiment more than a principled effort to reconcile state authority with federal treaty obligations. Since Race Horse, numerous states have shown that state regulations can, in fact, coexist with treaty-guaranteed hunting rights—Idaho being a notable example. [19]

The claim in *Race Horse* that the treaty may imply "rights wholly inconsistent with its language"[20] is, at best, a legal paradox. The language in question— "so long as game may be found thereon"—is unambiguous and strongly suggests a right meant to persist as long as the resource exists, not one easily extinguished by shifting state priorities. This is a clear instance of how legal professionals can interpret plain treaty text in ways that defy its ordinary meaning. Sometimes I wonder if judges already know the outcome they want—like taking rights away from Indian people—and then just twist the law around to make it sound legal. They use complicated words and legal tricks to cover what they're really doing.

As it relates to hunting and fishing in conservative Idaho, even the Idaho Supreme Court, in Idaho v. Tinno,[21] prioritized understanding the treaty language from the perspective of the Indians. This particular case began when in 1968, Gerald Cleo Tinno, a member of the Shoshone-Bannock Tribes who lived on the Fort Hall Reservation, was charged with using a traditional spearfishing technique to catch a Chinook salmon in the Yankee Fork of the Salmon River in Custer County. While Tinno acknowledged his actions, he argued that Article IV of the Fort Bridger Treaty granted him a distinct right, making him exempt from state fishing rules. To strengthen his argument, he sought

---

[19] Idaho v. Tinno, 94 Idaho 759, 497 P.2d 1386 (1972).
[20] *Race Horse*, 163 U.S. 504.
[21] *Tinno*, 94 Idaho at 759

the expertise of Dr. Sven S. Liljeblad, an esteemed professor of anthropology and linguistics at Idaho State University.

Dr. Liljeblad provided expert testimony on the linguistic complexities of the Shoshone and Bannock languages, and noted the absence of exact matches in the Shoshone and Bannock languages for certain English legal terms present in the Fort Bridger Treaty, suggesting a likely discrepancy during treaty discussions. Dr. Liljeblad pointed out that the languages:

> did not employ separate verbs to distinguish between hunting and fishing but rather used a general term for hunting and coupled with the noun corresponding to the object (either animal or vegetable) sought. The Shoshone verb was 'tygi' while the corresponding Bannock term was 'hoawai'; both were defined as meaning 'to obtain wild food'[22].

In 1974, the Idaho Supreme Court's decision in Tinno highlighted that the Shoshone-Bannock Indians, who were part of the 1868 Fort Bridger Treaty discussions, integrated fishing into their subsistence practices. Notably, their languages utilized a unified term for hunting, which did not distinctly set apart hunting and fishing activities. Consequently, even without an explicit reference to fishing rights in the Treaty, the court interpreted it as encompassing such rights. It's important to note, however, that the Tinno ruling had no influence or relevance in the state of Wyoming and is only applicable in Idaho.

Despite the significant setback in Repsis I & II. Indian prayers and justice may yet prevail over evil. In 2019, the U.S. witnessed a landmark decision that may restore the vitality of off-reservation treaty hunting rights for the Crow Tribe in Wyoming and possibly the Shoshone-Bannock and Eastern Shoshone Tribes. This case began five years earlier when, in 2014, Clayvin Herrera and other Tribal members tracked a herd of elk beyond the confines of the reservation, leading them into Wyoming's Bighorn National Forest. It is unclear if these Crows knew they were in the state of Wyoming or not, at least this was implied from the case law. After the hunt, Herrera shared a photograph of the kill on social media and a Wyoming Game Warden investigated the

---

[22] *Tinno*, 94 Idaho at 759

kill site and confirmed it was within the Bighorn National Forest of Wyoming.

As a result, the State of Wyoming prosecuted Herrera on several counts: hunting elk outside the designated season, engaging in hunting activities without a valid state license, and acting as an accomplice to the aforementioned transgressions. Making the same appeal as Race Horse and Ten Bears, Herrera defended his actions, invoking the Crow Treaty of 1868 as the foundation of his right to hunt in Bighorn National Forest outside of the reservation's boundary. To no surprise, Wyoming judiciary found Herrera guilty as charged, prompting him to seek redress at the U.S. Court of Appeals for the Tenth Circuit. However, his hopes were dashed when the Tenth Circuit declined to entertain the appeal, grounding its stance on the Repsis I decision, which contended that with Wyoming's ascension to statehood, the Crow Tribe's off-reservation hunting privileges were terminated.

Determined, Herrera was able to successfully escalate his case to the Supreme Court. He posited that the court's prior ruling in Minnesota v. Mille Lacs Band of Chippewa Indians[23], overturned the precedents set by Race Horse, thereby rendering the conclusions drawn in Repsis I & II decisions null and void. The ensuing legal deliberations and subsequent Supreme Court judgment would come to have a profound implication for treaty rights interpretations, key to the decision rested upon a prior ruling in Minnesota v. Mille Lacs Band of Chippewa Indians.

In this case, also known simply as Mille Lacs, the Mille Lacs Band of Chippewa Indians made the argument that "usufructuary rights", which encompass activities like hunting, fishing, and gathering, remained intact even after the state of Minnesota joined the U.S. In 1999, the Supreme Court agreed, and the judgment effectively overruled the 1896 Ward v. Race Horse case. Additionally, the Mille Lacs decision recognized the legal principle of taking a favorable interpretation of the written text used in the Treaty for Indian Tribes, as established by the Meehan and Winans decisions. In other words, ambiguities within treaties should be resolved in favor of the Indians, or the terms are interpreted in a manner consistent with the Indians'

---

[23] *Minnesota v. Mille Lacs Band of Chippewa Indians*, 526 U.S. 172 (1999).

understanding at the time of signing. For some, this approach to treaty interpretation might appear counterintuitive. However, when considering the historical context, it becomes clear why such an interpretive lens is necessary. Many Indian leaders during the time when treaties were struck between Nations, likely had limited, if any, proficiency in the English language. Thus, they were at a distinct disadvantage when negotiating with adept federal treaty drafters' intent on abrogating Indian rights. Another way of saying this is that the Indian leaders faced a considerable challenge when pitted against the well-educated and often manipulative federal negotiators, who had a deep understanding of legal frameworks, property rights, and written language.

In the Mille Lacs decision, it was determined that the treaty rights of an Indian tribe to hunt, fish, and gather within state boundaries did not inherently conflict with the state's sovereignty. Instead, the rights enshrined in the treaty could harmoniously coexist with the state's management prerogatives. Notably, the Mille Lacs judgment also points out the precedent set in United States v. Dion.[24] In the case of United States v. Dion, the U.S. Supreme Court ruled that the Eagle Protection Act, which bans hunting of bald and golden eagles with limited exceptions, effectively abrogated the Yankton Sioux Tribe's treaty rights from 1858 to hunt these birds on their reservation.

This decision came after a tribal member was prosecuted for shooting several eagles. The Court held that for Congress to override treaty rights, clear intent must be displayed, and such intent was evident in the Act's provisions and its legislative history. Consequently, the respondent could not claim his treaty rights as a defense under the Endangered Species Act[25]. The United States v. Dion created a legal foundation that if Congress intends to nullify or alter treaty rights it must be explicit and unambiguous. This perspective was further illuminated by the Mille Lacs ruling, which sharply countered the arguments set forth in Race Horse and Repsis I & II. In other words, because the law admitting Wyoming into the Union said nothing about Indian treaty rights, it did not clearly or explicitly revoke them—and without such clear language, the rights should remain intact.

---

[24] *United States v. Dion*, 476 U.S. 734 (1986).
[25] *Endangered Species Act of 1973*, Pub. L. No. 93-205, 87 Stat. 884 (codified as amended at 16 U.S.C. §§ 1531–1544).

Grasping the profound implications of such judicial interpretations, the Shoshone-Bannock Tribes keenly presented an Amicus Curiae brief, bolstering Herrera's position.

While deliberating on the Herrera v. Wyoming case, the Supreme Court used insights from the Mille Lacs decision and delved into the actual treaty negotiations between the Crow Tribe and the U.S. These negotiations, dating back to 1867, saw the involvement of key federal representatives, notably Commissioner of Indian Affairs, Nathaniel G. Taylor. During these talks, Taylor recognized the incursions by white settlers onto Crow lands and the consequent depletion of game. In response, he proposed the establishment of a designated reservation for the Crow Tribe, and to buy the rest of their land. Taylor also emphasized that the Tribe would have "the right to hunt upon" the land it ceded to the Federal Government "as long as the game lasts."

During the negotiations with federal representatives, Black Foot, a prominent Crow leader, voiced his concerns, stating,

> You speak of putting us on a reservation and teaching us to farm... That talk does not please us. We want horses to run after the game, and guns and ammunition to kill it. I would like to live just as I have been raised.[26]

Another Crow leader, Wolf Bow, echoed this sentiment, noting, "You want me to go on a reservation and farm. I do not want to do that. I was not raised so".[27] By the spring of the following year, the Crow Tribe and the U.S. formalized these discussions through the 1868 Treaty with the Crow. Under this treaty, the Crow Tribe relinquished over 30 million acres of their original homeland to the U.S. While they consented to establish the reservation as their enduring home, not venturing to settle elsewhere permanently, the U.S., in return, committed to erect structures, supply farming tools and materials, and other necessities for the tribe. Article IV of the Treaty with the Crow also pledged that

> The Indians...shall have the right to hunt on the unoccupied lands of the United States so long as game may

---

[26] Institute for the Development of Indian Law. 1975. *Proceedings of the Great Peace Commission of 1867-1868*. Washington D.C.: The Institute for the Development of Indian Law, 86.
[27] Ibid., 89.

be found thereon, and as long as peace subsists among the whites and Indians on the borders of the hunting districts.[28]

In the Herrera v. Wyoming[29] ruling, which was a close 5 to 4 decision, the Supreme Court determined that there was no indication that Congress ever meant to revoke the off-reservation Indian hunting treaty rights when Wyoming joined the Union. That conclusion in itself was a major victory for not only the Crow, but the Shoshone-Bannock and Eastern Shoshone. While it was somewhat questionable that the Mille Lacs case did not explicitly overturn Race Horse, the Supreme Court ruled in Herrera v. Wyoming that it effectively did. Justice Sotomayor delivered the opinion of the court and wrote that the Race Horse decision has been "repudiated to the extent it held that treaty rights can be impliedly extinguished at statehood."[30] In other words, the Shoshone-Bannock, Crow, and Eastern Shoshone Tribes off-reservation hunting treaty rights had indeed survived statehood.

The Supreme Court also concurred with Herrera's assertion that the establishment of the Bighorn National Forest did not inherently mean the land had become "occupied". Emphasizing the importance of interpreting treaty terms in the manner Indian tribes would naturally perceive them, the Court noted, "[h]ere it is clear that the Crow Tribe would have understood the word 'unoccupied' to denote an area free of residence or settlement by non-Indians."[31] Thus, Wyoming's attempt, and the Barrett decision in Repsis II, to interpret the designation of a national forest as "occupied" did not stand. The Court, referencing the term's plain interpretation, concluded that President Grover Cleveland's proclamation designating the Bighorn National Forest did not, in fact, "occupy" it in the treaty sense. The very proclamation set aside the lands from potential settlement, aligning with the treaty's definition of "unoccupied".

However, following the Supreme Court's landmark decision in Herrera v. Wyoming, the path to full recognition and protection of off-reservation hunting rights did not bring immediate relief. While the Court held that the 1868 Treaty right survived

---

[28] *Treaty with the Crows*, 15 Stat. 649.
[29] Herrera v. Wyoming, 587 U.S. ___ (2019).
[30] Ibid.
[31] Ibid.

Wyoming's statehood and repudiated Race Horse and its reasoning, it did not definitively resolve whether Herrera's specific elk hunt was lawful. Instead, it vacated the judgment of the Wyoming District Court in Sheridan County and remanded the case for further proceedings consistent with its ruling. On remand, the state was permitted to argue whether the area where Herrera hunted was "occupied" or whether its conservation laws could still apply. Despite the Supreme Court's clarification, Wyoming has persisted in prosecuting Herrera, asserting that the prior Repsis ruling still binds the Tribe and its members under the doctrine of issue preclusion.

To put it plainly, even though the U.S. Supreme Court confirmed that the 1868 Treaty hunting right still exists, that wasn't the end of the legal battle. The Court vacated the lower court's conviction of Herrera and sent the case back to the Wyoming District Court to consider unresolved questions—like whether the area where Herrera hunted was "occupied" under the treaty, and whether state conservation laws could still apply. In short, the Supreme Court said the treaty right was valid, but left room for Wyoming to argue if Herrera still violated other state laws.

Wyoming continues to prosecute Herrera, arguing that the earlier Repsis decision should still stand under the doctrine of issue preclusion (also called collateral estoppel). This legal principle says that once a court has settled an issue between the same parties, that issue can't be argued again. Wyoming claimed that Repsis II, which had previously ruled the treaty right ended at statehood, should still prevent Herrera from asserting his treaty defense—even though Herrera v. Wyoming explicitly rejected the reasoning behind Repsis. The Supreme Court disagreed. It ruled that Mille Lacs had so thoroughly repudiated Race Horse and Repsis that the law had clearly changed. That change made an exception to issue preclusion, allowing Herrera to make his case. Therefore, the Tribe sought to reverse the previous judgment in Repsis II under Federal Rule of Civil Procedure 60(b) in Wyoming District Court.

The Federal Rule of Civil Procedure 60(b) provides a mechanism for parties to seek relief from a final judgment, order, or proceeding in certain specific circumstances. According to this rule, the Wyoming District Court has the authority to grant relief from a final judgment, based upon the higher courts ruling in Herrera v. Wyoming. In other words, the Tribe wanted to change a previous decision made against them in court (Repsis II) after a major decision was made by the Supreme Court. The Crow Tribe tried to use the Federal Rule of Civil Procedure 60(b), which lets people ask the court to change or undo a final decision in specific situations.

However, the Wyoming District Court rejected the Tribe's claims, ruling that Herrera's conviction could still stand on alternative grounds not addressed in Herrera v. Wyoming—specifically, that the land where Herrera hunted was "occupied" and that his actions violated conservation laws. In simpler terms, the court concluded that because the treaty right did not apply to "occupied" lands or override conservation concerns, the Supreme Court's ruling did not overturn his conviction. This outcome was no doubt disheartening for the Crow Tribe and others, especially considering Wyoming's long history of resisting tribal sovereignty—including the infamous 1895 killings of Bannock hunters under the governorship of William Richards. Undeterred, the Tribe and Herrera appealed the decision, and the case was taken up by the Tenth Circuit Court of Appeals, which oversees Wyoming and neighboring states, including parts of Yellowstone National Park.

The Crow Tribe contended that the District Court was wrong in claiming it could not review their Rule 60(b) motion. Additionally, the Tribe pressed the court to either independently provide Rule 60(b) relief or reconsider their prior mandate in Repsis II. In other words, the Tribe did not agree with the District Court's decision and took their case to a higher court, the Tenth Circuit. The Tribe said that the Wyoming District Court was wrong in its decision and asked this Tenth Circuit to either use the rule (60(b)) to help them or to reconsider the previous decision made against them (Repsis II).

On July 24, 2023, the Tenth Circuit Appeals Court found that the Wyoming District Court had indeed overstepped by claiming it could not re-evaluate the Tribe's request after its first judgment[32]. The Tenth Circuit also believed the Wyoming District

---

[32] *Crow Tribe of Indians v. Repsis*, No. 21-8050, 2023 WL 4717367 (10th Cir. July 24, 2023).

Court was in a better position to consider the case's details and decide on granting a type of relief known as Rule 60(b). Although the Tenth Circuit did not itself rule on the merits of the Tribe's request, it vacated the District Court's judgment and remanded the case—sending it back for reconsideration by the same court that had earlier shown strong resistance to overturning Repsis II. This action seemingly highlights legal stratagems and divergent perspectives across judiciary levels.

The protracted legal battle faced by the Crow Tribe, and by default the Shoshone-Bannock Tribes, exemplifies the complex and often arduous journey Federally Recognized Tribes undertake to assert their historical and treaty-backed rights. Forced to navigate a labyrinthine legal system, these tribes confront many challenges, from varying court interpretations to precedent-based pushbacks, all of which demand considerable time, financial resources, and unyielding perseverance. Even as landmark decisions, such as Herrera v. Wyoming, emerge as moments of hope in the struggle to recognize Indian Treaty Rights, they are often preceded and followed by layers of judicial deliberations, appeals.

Chapter 7 – Bibliography

Crow Tribe of Indians v. Repsis, 73 F.3d 982 (10th Cir. 1995).

Crow Tribe of Indians v. Repsis, 866 F. Supp. 520 (D. Wyo. 1994).

Crow Tribe of Indians v. Repsis, No. 21-8050, 2023 WL 4717367 (10th Cir. July 24, 2023).

Echo-Hawk, Walter. In the Courts of the Conqueror: The 10 Worst Indian Law Cases Ever Decided. Golden, CO: Fulcrum Publishing, 2018.

Endangered Species Act of 1973. Pub. L. No. 93-205, 87 Stat. 884 (codified as amended at 16 U.S.C. §§ 1531–1544).

Herrera v. Wyoming, 587 U.S. ___ (2019).

Idaho v. Tinno, 94 Idaho 759, 497 P.2d 1386 (1972).

Institute for the Development of Indian Law. Proceedings of the Great Peace Commission of 1867–1868. Washington, D.C.: The Institute for the Development of Indian Law, 1975.

Jones v. Meehan, 175 U.S. 1 (1899).

Minnesota v. Mille Lacs Band of Chippewa Indians, 526 U.S. 172 (1999).

Treaty with the Crow Indians, May 7, 1868, 15 Stat. 649.

Treaty with the Red Lake and Pembina Bands of Chippewa Indians, October 2, 1863, 13 Stat. 667.

Treaty with the Yakama, June 9, 1855, 12 Stat. 951.

United States v. Dion, 476 U.S. 734 (1986).

United States v. Winans, 198 U.S. 371 (1905).

Ward v. Race Horse, 163 U.S. 504 (1896).

Chapter 8 – Species Conservation

Taking a step back and looking at the full picture, one thing is clear: despite years of litigation, the issue of off-reservation treaty hunting rights in Wyoming remains unresolved. As of this writing, neither the Supreme Court, the Tenth Circuit Court of Appeals, nor the Wyoming District Court has taken firm, decisive action to fully recognize or enforce those rights. There is a growing sense that the courts—at every level—understand that what's happening isn't right or consistent with treaty law, yet they stop short of granting meaningful relief to the Tribes.

Rather than issuing a definitive ruling, the Supreme Court left the question in the hands of the Wyoming District Court. As detailed earlier, the primary issue the Wyoming District Court must address is whether the area where Herrera hunted qualifies as "unoccupied" as the Indians would have understood. Beyond this, the court is also tasked with determining if Wyoming can set hunting limits on the Crow Tribe, specifically for the purposes of species conservation. The exploration and deliberation on this latter point is now discussed.

To figure out whether Wyoming can legally place hunting restrictions on the Crow Tribe for conservation reasons, the District Court will likely take several steps. First, it will need to look closely at federal, state, and local wildlife laws, as well as any current hunting limits. Since many different species could be involved, this process could take quite a bit of time. The court will also need to review past court decisions on similar issues. On top of that, it may consider how the Crow Tribe manages its own hunting and what rules they already have in place. Both the Tribe and the State of Wyoming will be able to make their case by submitting legal arguments and supporting documents.

It's still unclear exactly how the Wyoming District Court will handle the question of whether conservation laws can limit tribal hunting rights. But chances are, the court will look at past cases to help make its decision. One of the key examples is the Puyallup cases[1], especially Puyallup Tribe v. Department of Game of

---

[1] *Puyallup Tribe v. Department of Game of Washington*, 391 U.S. 392 (1968) (*Puyallup I*); *Department of Game of Washington v. Puyallup Tribe*,

Washington (1968)², which dealt with how treaty rights and wildlife conservation laws can sometimes clash. The Puyallup cases—known as the Puyallup Trilogy—tell a story that every hunter and fisherman should care about. At the heart of it was a simple question: could the Puyallup Tribe keep fishing the way their ancestors always had, or could the state shut them down in the name of conservation?

This chapter looks at those cases and others not just to guess how the court might rule in the Herrera case, but also to give readers a better understanding of Indian hunting and fishing rights. It is important to note that the treaties did not grant rights to Indian tribes but instead affirmed the inherent rights they already held. Despite this, tribes have faced relentless challenges in securing recognition of these rights, particularly from state governments. The ongoing struggle highlights the importance of honoring treaty obligations and respecting tribal sovereignty, though views on how to balance these with state interests may differ.

The Puyallup Trilogy affirmed that while Tribes hold treaty-protected fishing rights, those rights can be limited by state conservation laws—provided the regulations are necessary, non-discriminatory, and the least restrictive means available. However, given Wyoming's long and often hostile history toward Indian hunting, there is a real concern that the state may invoke conservation as a pretext to impose regulations that unfairly burden Tribes or bring them under state control. Understanding this dynamic is critical when assessing whether state policies are truly about conservation or simply about restricting tribal rights. The cases that follow shed light on how courts have interpreted the concept of "conservation necessity" and emphasize that state regulations must stem from genuine environmental concerns—not in discrimination or political convenience.

It started in the late 1960s, when the Tribe was fighting for the right to use nets to catch steelhead in the Puyallup River—something they had done for generations. In Puyallup I, the U.S. Supreme Court said yes, tribes do have treaty rights to fish. But it also said those rights can be reasonably regulated for conservation

---

414 U.S. 44 (1973) (*Puyallup II*); *Puyallup Tribe, Inc. v. Department of Game of Washington*, 433 U.S. 165 (1977) (*Puyallup III*).
² *Puyallup I*, 391 U.S. at 392.

purposes. However, the Court wasn't convinced that the state's total ban on net fishing was truly about conservation. So, it sent the case back to the state court to take a closer look and justify the restriction.

Then came Puyallup II (1973)[3], where the Court made it clear: banning tribal net fishing altogether wasn't allowed. The state couldn't just wipe out the Tribe's fishery. Instead, it had to figure out a fair way to share the fish with the Indians. Finally, in Puyallup III (1977)[4], the Court struck a balance. It said the Tribe had a guaranteed right to fish, but that right was "in common with all citizens of the Territory"[5]. That meant the state could limit fishing to protect the steelhead run—but only if the rules were necessary, backed by science, and applied fairly. After hearing from experts on both sides, the Court approved a plan giving the Tribe 45% of the fishable steelhead run. Apparently, the decision on allocation relied on the state's calculations, leaving the final allocation feeling somewhat one-sided.

These cases mattered then—and they still matter now. Steelhead and salmon populations on the Columbia and Snake Rivers have declined drastically due to dams and habitat loss. Today, many runs are threatened. So yes, conservation is important—but so is honoring the promises made in treaties. One should also ask a fundamental question: who is truly responsible for the decline of anadromous fish? It was not the Tribes who built the dams or disrupted the ecosystems. Yet tribal harvests—alongside state-regulated harvests—are often reduced under the banner of conservation necessity.

The difference is that these reductions can directly restrict rights that were explicitly reserved in treaties. This raises serious concerns about fairness, accountability, and the U.S.' obligation to uphold its treaty commitments. It also highlights the importance of actively engaging Tribes in decisions that could impact their treaty rights. Too often, federal agencies treat government-to-government consultation as a procedural formality—checking a box rather than engaging in genuine, sovereign-to-sovereign dialogue. As a result, Tribal concerns are frequently sidelined or

---

[3] *Department of Game v. Puyallup Tribe*, 414 U.S. 44 (1973)
[4] *Puyallup II, 414 U.S.* at 44.
[5] *Treaty of Medicine Creek*, December 26, 1854, 10 Stat. 1132; *Puyallup III*, 433 U.S. at 165.

treated as merely advisory, rather than as the legally and morally significant input they are.

To provide context on the tense relationship between the Washington Department of Game and the Puyallup Tribe, testimony from three Tribal officers during Puyallup III highlighted longstanding patterns of mistreatment. According to their accounts, Tribal members faced repeated arrests, incarceration, and degrading treatment by state officials, which they believed was part of a deliberate effort to interfere with their treaty-protected fishing activities. The officers described how the State appeared to be using its authority to obstruct the Tribe's ability to earn a livelihood, creating an environment of sustained pressure and conflict. They also reaffirmed that the Tribe had a valid treaty with the U.S. and maintained that the fishery was a resource rightfully belonging to the Puyallup people.

In the end, the Puyallup decisions marked a significant moment for tribal fishing rights, establishing that a state cannot assert jurisdiction over a federally recognized Indian Tribe due to its sovereign immunity. However, the court did determine that neither the Tribe nor its members possess an exclusive right to fish in areas covered by the Treaty of Medicine Creek, emphasizing that the treaty rights are shared with all citizens and subject to state conservation regulations. This decision acknowledged the state's authority to impose reasonable limits on steelhead trout fishing to ensure apportionment between Indian and non-Indian fishers.

Federal Indian law established by the Puyallup decisions revealed the judiciary's struggle to balance tribal treaty rights with state conservation interests, often stopping short of fully affirming the strength and exclusivity of those rights. That is what makes the Boldt Decision in Washington v. Washington State Commercial Passenger Fishing Vessel Association[6] so pivotal. Building upon the legal foundations laid in the Puyallup Trilogy, the Boldt Decision marked a major turning point: it clearly upheld the binding nature of treaties and recognized that Washington tribes were entitled to harvest up to 50 percent of harvestable fish runs in their usual and accustomed waters.

---

[6] *Washington v. Washington State Commercial Passenger Fishing Vessel Association*, 443 U.S. 658 (1979).

Unlike earlier rulings that left tribal rights vulnerable to regulatory erosion, Boldt emphasized that treaties are the supreme law of the land, not vague promises subject to state interpretation. It rejected the idea that state conservation laws could be used to undermine treaty-guaranteed access to a subsistence and commercial resource. In the broader context of this chapter, Boldt stands as one of the strongest judicial affirmations of Indian treaty rights—not only for fishing, but also for the principle that treaty promises must be honored in full, even when inconvenient to state agendas. Its legacy continues to shape the legal terrain surrounding Indian hunting and fishing across the U.S., and could potentially influence the Herrera case in Wyoming, where courts have so far failed to offer similar clarity or relief.

While the Boldt Decision expanded tribal rights to off-reservation fishing in Washington, the outcome in Oregon Department of Fish and Wildlife v. Klamath Indian Tribe,[7] illustrates the limitations of treaty rights when explicit language or later agreements narrow their scope. The Klamath Tribes' 1864 Treaty[8] guaranteed them exclusive fishing rights within their reservation. However, after a boundary dispute and subsequent 1901 Cession Agreement[9], the U.S. Supreme Court held that the Tribes' rights did not extend to lands that were later ceded. Unlike the treaties at issue in Boldt, the Klamath treaty did not include language reserving rights in off-reservation areas, which ultimately limited the Court's interpretation in favor of the state's regulatory authority. The contrasting outcomes in these two cases underscore how critical treaty language—and later federal actions—are in determining the scope of Indian hunting and fishing rights.

The Puyallup Trilogy, Boldt Decision, and Oregon Department of Fish and Wildlife v. Klamath Indian Tribe highlight the evolving and varied federal court interpretations of Indian treaty rights, particularly for off-reservation fishing and hunting.

---

[7] *Oregon Department of Fish and Wildlife v. Klamath Tribe*, 473 U.S. 753 (1985).
[8] *Treaty with the Klamath, Modoc, and Yahooskin Band of Snake Indians*, October 14, 1864, 16 Stat. 707.
[9] Agreement with the Klamath and Modoc, and the Yahooskin Band of Snake, June 17, 1901.

The Puyallup Trilogy recognized treaty fishing rights but permitted state conservation regulations to limit their scope. The Boldt Decision marked a breakthrough, fully honoring the "usual and accustomed places" clause to grant Washington tribes 50% of harvestable fish. Conversely, the Klamath decision restricted rights to the post-cession reservation, as the treaty lacked off-reservation guarantees and a 1901 agreement narrowed its scope. These cases, alongside Herrera v. Wyoming[10], where treaty language remains unresolved, show that tribal rights' strength depends on precise treaty terms and the courts' fidelity to them.

Today, the state of Wyoming will likely stress to the court the need to impose a conservation necessity on game and probably fish species. As for elk, which have been at the heart of the issue since the beginning, Wyoming is grappling with an overpopulation of elk, particularly in its eastern and northeastern regions, leading to conflicts among lawmakers, ranchers, hunters, and the Wyoming Department of Game and Fish[11]. The elk population in some areas is reportedly up to four times higher than the department's target numbers, causing challenges for ranchers. While elk have thrived, mule deer and antelope populations suffered from winterkill and diseases.

To manage elk numbers, the state has considered longer hunting seasons and issuing "lethal take" permits on private land. But despite the urgent need for population control, Wyoming has shown no interest in allowing Indian hunting to be part of the solution. In fact, based on its troubling history, the state has taken extreme steps—including violence—to keep Indian hunters out.

Some may argue that states do have authority to regulate wildlife, even when Indian treaty rights are involved. That's true—but only under narrow legal limits. Several court cases have addressed this balance. As mentioned in the preceding chapter, the U.S. Supreme Court in Minnesota v. Mille Lacs Band of Chippewa Indians[12] ruled that the Mille Lacs Band retained their treaty rights to hunt, fish, and gather on ceded lands. However,

---

[10] Herrera v. Wyoming, 587 U.S. ___ (2019).
[11] Mark Heinz. "Wyoming Has Too Many Elk, And Nobody's Sure What To Do About It," *Cowboy State Daily*, August 11, 2023.
[12] *Minnesota v. Mille Lacs Band of Chippewa Indians*, 526 U.S. 172 (1999).

the Court also clarified that these rights are not absolute. States may impose non-discriminatory regulations for genuine conservation purposes—but only if they meet a high standard and do not violate treaty protections.

This standard has been shaped by earlier cases like Puyallup Tribe v. Department of Game of Washington (1968), which held that states can regulate treaty hunting and fishing only if the regulations are necessary for conservation, applied equally, and are the least restrictive means available. In other words, states can't use conservation as a cover to block Indian hunting rights. The Supremacy Clause of the Constitution makes it clear: treaties are the supreme law of the land and override conflicting state laws.[13]

So yes, conservation regulations can legally affect tribal rights—but only under strict conditions. The state must show that its actions are essential for protecting a species and that no less burdensome option exists. Regulations cannot be designed to exclude or punish tribes specifically. If they are, such regulations may violate treaty rights and could also raise constitutional concerns, including potential violations of the Equal Protection Clause[14]—especially if they are applied in a discriminatory or unequal manner without legitimate justification.

Some tribal members may wonder: would the courts recognize the Tribe's traditional cultural knowledge regarding species conservation? After all, our people managed these lands for generations before the arrival of settlers. Elk, deer, buffalo, fish, and clean water were abundant—not by accident, but through our traditional systems of stewardship. We had rules—*Deniwape* and *Tenichui*—that shaped our behavior and kept ecosystems healthy.

Yet in today's courtrooms, it is highly likely this knowledge would be dismissed. Even when tribal elders speak with clarity and truth, their words are weighed less than a state biologist with a model. Western legal systems favor state authority and data that fits within their framework. If traditional knowledge is admitted at all, it's often ignored—and rarely carries weight in decisions. To put it plainly, the system wasn't built for us and that is why the

---

[13] U.S. Const., art. VI, cl. 2.
[14] U.S. Const. amend. XIV, § 1.

U.S. court system is referred to by some Indians as the Courts of the Conquer.

Chapter 8 – Bibliography

Agreement with the Klamath and Modoc, and the Yahooskin Band of Snake, June 17, 1901.

Department of Game of Washington v. Puyallup Tribe, 414 U.S. 44 (1973).

Heinz, Mark. "Wyoming Has Too Many Elk, And Nobody's Sure What To Do About It." *Cowboy State Daily*, August 11, 2023.

Herrera v. Wyoming, 587 U.S. ___ (2019).

Minnesota v. Mille Lacs Band of Chippewa Indians, 526 U.S. 172 (1999).

Oregon Department of Fish and Wildlife v. Klamath Tribe, 473 U.S. 753 (1985).

Puyallup Tribe v. Department of Game of Washington, 391 U.S. 392 (1968).

Puyallup Tribe, Inc. v. Department of Game of Washington, 433 U.S. 165 (1977).

Treaty of Medicine Creek, December 26, 1854, 10 Stat. 1132.

Treaty with the Klamath, Modoc, and Yahooskin Band of Snake Indians, October 14, 1864, 16 Stat. 707.

U.S. Constitution, amend. XIV, § 1.

U.S. Constitution, art. VI, cl. 2.

Washington v. Washington State Commercial Passenger Fishing Vessel Association, 443 U.S. 658 (1979).

Chapter 9 - Defining "Unoccupied"

For more than a century, the meaning of the phrase "the right to hunt on the unoccupied lands of the United States so long as game may be found thereon" [1] has remained unsettled in the eyes of the law. At the time of this writing, the U.S. District Court in Wyoming is once again confronted with critical questions—questions that go to the heart of what was promised in the Fort Bridger Treaties of 1868.

The previous chapter examined how states and courts have used the concept of wildlife conservation to limit treaty rights. This chapter shifts focus to another unresolved issue: how to interpret the word "unoccupied." Specifically, it asks whether places like the Bighorn National Forest—where Clayvin Herrera exercised his treaty right to hunt—can truly be considered "occupied," and if so, by what standard? The goal here is to explore how tribal leaders at the time of the treaty would have understood that term, and what it meant to them when they agreed to those conditions. This is not just a legal debate—it's a cultural and historical one that continues to shape the boundaries of tribal sovereignty.

At present, neither Congress nor the courts have provided a definitive interpretation of the term "unoccupied" as used in the Fort Bridger and Fort Laramie Treaties of 1868. In the likely absence of legislative clarity, the courts have tended to focus on the physical and legal character of the landscape where the alleged treaty violation occurred. In the case of Herrera, this inquiry centers on the Bighorn National Forest, where he harvested an elk pursuant to what he believed were his protected treaty rights.

While not controlling in Wyoming, the Idaho case State v. Cutler[2], offers important insight into how state courts may interpret the concept of "unoccupied" in the context of off-reservation hunting rights. In that case, commonly referred to as Cutler, members of the Shoshone-Bannock Tribes were charged with misdemeanor violations for possessing unlawfully taken wildlife on Sand Creek Ranch—a state-managed wildlife area. The

---

[1] Treaty with the Eastern Band Shoshoni and Bannock, July 3, 1868, 15 Stat. 673.
[2] *State v. Cutler*, 109 Idaho 448, 708 P.2d 853 (1985).

defendants argued that their conduct was protected under the 1868 Fort Bridger Treaty, which guaranteed the right to hunt on the "unoccupied lands of the United States."[3]

The magistrate court rejected this argument, holding that Sand Creek Ranch did not constitute "unoccupied" land within the meaning of the 1868 Fort Bridger Treaty. That decision was affirmed by the District Court of Fremont County and ultimately upheld by the Idaho Supreme Court in State v. Cutler[4]. What follows is a closer examination of the facts and legal reasoning behind the Idaho Supreme Court's final ruling, and how it may inform contemporary interpretations of treaty hunting rights in both state and federal jurisdictions.

On November 10, 1978, officers from the Idaho Department of Fish and Game encountered four individuals parked in a pickup truck just off the main road within Sand Creek Ranch. In the bed of the truck were two elk, and a third elk lay nearby. The individuals admitted to harvesting the elk and presented their Shoshone-Bannock Tribal enrollment cards, asserting their treaty-protected right to hunt on the land. The officers later identified the kill sites within the boundaries of Sand Creek Ranch.

The Shoshone-Bannock defendants were charged with misdemeanor game violations in the Magistrate Division of Fremont County. As part of their defense, they moved to dismiss the charges, invoking the 1868 Fort Bridger Treaty and asserting their right to hunt on "unoccupied lands of the United States." In support of their motion, they submitted affidavits, historical documents, and legal memoranda. After reviewing the full evidentiary record and legal arguments from both parties, the magistrate issued a written opinion. The court concluded that the location where the game was taken—within the boundaries of Sand Creek Ranch—did not qualify as "unoccupied" land under the treaty. Accordingly, the motion to dismiss was denied.

At the trial set for December 16, 1980, the defendants waived their right to a jury and submitted a signed stipulation of facts. In the stipulation, they admitted that they had hunted on state-owned lands within the Sand Creek Ranch section of the Sand Creek Wildlife Management Area at the dates and times

---

[3] *Treaty with the Shoshoni and Bannock*, 15 Stat. 673.
[4] *State v. Cutler*, 109 Idaho 448, 708 P.2d 853 (1985).

alleged, and that they had possessed elk and deer taken during Idaho's closed hunting season. In the same filing, the defendants renewed their motion to dismiss the charges based on the 1868 Fort Bridger Treaty, incorporating the affidavits, exhibits, and legal arguments previously submitted. While the State did not object to the stipulated facts—according to the judgment of conviction—no formal written agreement from the prosecution appears in the appellate record. Upon accepting the defendants' admissions, the magistrate court found the allegations in the complaints to be true and entered guilty verdicts. In doing so, the court also relied on its prior written order from November 7, 1980, which rejected the treaty-based motion to dismiss.

At the time of Cutler, there was limited judicial precedent addressing whether state-owned lands qualified as "unoccupied lands of the United States" in the context of off-reservation Indian hunting rights. Earlier decisions, such as Idaho v. Tinno[5], had concluded that federal lands—specifically the Challis National Forest—could be considered "unoccupied," thus falling within the scope of treaty-protected hunting rights. However, the legal status of privately held or state-managed lands remained unresolved. The applicability of the 1868 Fort Bridger Treaty to such lands had not been squarely addressed by Idaho courts. In related contexts, courts had begun to draw distinctions. For example, in Idaho v. Coffee[6], the Idaho Supreme Court held that privately owned land outside the boundaries of an Indian reservation did not qualify as "open and unclaimed" under the hunting clause of the 1855 Treaty of Hellgate[7]. This emerging distinction between federal, state, and private lands set the stage for Cutler to become a key test case in clarifying how treaty hunting rights apply to state-owned wildlife management areas.

Although the phrase "open and unclaimed" differs from "unoccupied lands of the United States," both formulations appear in nineteenth-century Indian treaties and reflect similar concerns about off-reservation hunting rights. The recurrence of such language is not coincidental. Treaties negotiated during the same era often employed overlapping terms, particularly when a single federal official directed the negotiations. One such figure was Isaac

---

[5] Idaho v. Tinno, 94 Idaho 759, 497 P.2d 1386 (1972).
[6] *Idaho v. Coffee*, 97 Idaho 905, 556 P.2d 1185 (1976).
[7] *Treaty of Hellgate*, July 16, 1855, 12 Stat. 975.

Stevens, then Governor of Washington Territory and Superintendent of Indian Affairs, who played a central role in drafting multiple agreements in the Pacific Northwest. Treaties negotiated under his leadership—such as the 1854 Treaty of Medicine Creek[8] and the 1855 Treaty of Hellgate—share consistent language concerning hunting, fishing, and gathering rights, and are collectively referred to as the Stevens Treaties. While the language in Article 4 of the 1868 Treaty with the Crows and the 1868 Treaty with the Eastern Band of the Shoshoni and Bannock is similarly worded, these agreements were not negotiated by Stevens and are therefore not categorized as Stevens Treaties.

When the interpretation of a treaty term has been firmly established in case law, courts often look to that precedent when construing similar or identical language in other treaties. In Idaho v. Cutler, the Idaho Supreme Court considered prior rulings addressing the phrase "open and unclaimed," even though the Fort Bridger Treaty uses the distinct term "unoccupied lands of the United States." The court ultimately concluded that privately owned lands outside a reservation did not fall within the scope of off-reservation hunting rights—echoing the reasoning in earlier cases such as Idaho v. Coffee. The reliance on precedents using slightly different language illustrates the fluidity and unpredictability of judicial treaty interpretation. This interpretive variability is further demonstrated by United States v. Hicks[9] in which a federal district court held that the establishment of Olympic National Park effectively terminated the Quinault Tribe's hunting rights under the Treaty of Olympia[10]. The lack of clear, controlling precedent on how to apply the Fort Bridger Treaty's language to state-managed lands made Cutler a particularly complex and consequential case for the Idaho Supreme Court.

In assessing the implications of the 1868 Fort Bridger Treaty, it was acknowledged that the interpretation of such treaties presents a federal question, with the U.S. Supreme Court serving as the final arbiter. In U.S. v. Shoshone Tribe of Indians[11] the Court emphasized that Indian treaties must not be interpreted

---

[8] *Treaty with the Nisqualli, Puyallup, and Other Tribes*, December 26, 1854, 10 Stat. 1132
[9] *United States v. Hicks*, 587 F. Supp. 1162 (W.D. Wash. 1984).
[10] *Treaty with the Quinaielt, etc.*, July 1, 1855, 12 Stat. 971.
[11] *United States v. Shoshone Tribe of Indians*, 304 U.S. 111 (1938).

narrowly or through the lens of legal formalism, but rather in a manner consistent with the likely understanding of the tribal signatories. This interpretive approach was reaffirmed in Idaho v. Tinno[12] where the Idaho Supreme Court stressed that treaty language should be construed in light of how the signatory tribes would have reasonably understood its terms. The central issue in Cutler revolved around the meaning of the phrase "unoccupied lands of the United States" and whether that language extended treaty hunting rights to lands owned or managed by state or private entities.

The Idaho Supreme Court acknowledged that the distinction between federal and state land ownership would not have been apparent to the Shoshone and Bannock leaders at the time of the 1868 Fort Bridger Treaty. The Court relied on historical accounts from figures such as Chief Washakie and Chief Taghee to support its view that the tribal leadership anticipated the advance of white settlement and understood that treaty hunting rights would diminish over time as lands became occupied and game became scarce. With that context, the Court turned to the specific facts surrounding Sand Creek Ranch. To support its conclusion that the area did not qualify as "unoccupied lands of the United States" under the treaty, the Court examined the property's chain of title and historical use, tracing its transition from private ownership to state management for wildlife conservation.

Between 1904 and 1934, the lands comprising Sand Creek Ranch were conveyed through federal patents to various private individuals. By 1944, Edgar Chapman had consolidated ownership and operated the property as a working cattle ranch, cultivating grain and hay to support his livestock. However, migrating elk herds increasingly disrupted his operations, consuming feed and damaging pastures. After unsuccessful attempts to mitigate the conflict, it became clear to the Idaho Fish and Game that protecting the elk population would require acquiring the land. Following the state's purchase, the property was repurposed and managed as a wildlife refuge, with a particular focus on elk conservation. The state implemented land management practices including fencing, seasonal grain

---

[12] Idaho v. Tinno, 94 Idaho 759, 497 P.2d 1386 (1972).

cultivation, water development projects, and the construction of facilities to support its wildlife objectives.

The Court's ruling placed significant weight on the land's historical ownership in determining whether it qualified as "unoccupied" under the Fort Bridger Treaty. Notably, the phrase "so long as game may be found thereon," a central element of the treaty's language, was absent from the Court's reasoning. This omission reflects a judicial tendency to prioritize property ownership and physical indicators of land use over the ecological conditions necessary for sustaining game. By overlooking the presence of wildlife as a meaningful factor, the decision diminished the role that habitat plays in the exercise of treaty-protected hunting rights. One could reasonably argue that this interpretation reveals a bias toward settled land tenure systems, rather than a holistic understanding of the treaty's original intent.

Building on its prior analysis, the Idaho Supreme Court grounded its interpretation of "unoccupied" in the continued use and function of the land, rather than in a mere change of ownership. The Court emphasized that the land's essential character remained consistent even after its transfer from private to state ownership. Indicators of sustained occupation—such as fencing, signage, buildings, and equipment—remained intact. The state's active management of the property for wildlife conservation, including regulated hunting seasons, further reinforced the conclusion that the land had never reverted to an "unoccupied" state. In the Court's view, the critical issue was not the identity of the landholder, but whether the land's use aligned with the meaning of "unoccupied" as understood in the treaty context. On that basis, the Court upheld the trial court's determination that the hunting in question did not occur on "unoccupied lands of the United States" within the meaning of the 1868 Fort Bridger Treaty.

The Idaho Supreme Court's reasoning in concluding that Sand Creek Ranch was "occupied" becomes difficult to justify when viewed in light of the similarities between its management and that of federal public lands. Sand Creek Ranch formed part of the larger 27,000-acre Sand Creek Wildlife Management Area in Fremont County. Of this, approximately 1,000 acres were federally owned, interspersed among 4,760 acres held by the State of Idaho. The entire management area functioned as a coordinated wildlife restoration initiative, administered by the Idaho Fish and Game under the authority of two key federal statutes: the Federal Aid in Wildlife Restoration Act and the Fish and Wildlife Coordination Act of 1934. Importantly, about 75 percent of the funding used to acquire the state-owned portions, including Sand Creek Ranch, came from federal sources. While the Idaho Fish and Game conducted day-to-day management, the federal government retained supervisory authority. Given these facts, the distinction drawn by the Court between Sand Creek Ranch and federally managed lands such as national forests—lands often deemed "unoccupied" for treaty purposes—appears strained and inconsistent.

Historically, the entirety of the Sand Creek Wildlife Management Area lay within the homeland territory of the Shoshone-Bannock Tribes. Following the 1868 Fort Bridger Treaty, the United States retained continuous ownership of all federally managed tracts in the region. In contrast, lands now under state ownership were originally federal public domain lands that were transferred to the State of Idaho or to private individuals upon Idaho's admission to the Union in 1890. These lands later returned to state control through private sale. The central legal question in Cutler was whether the 1868 Treaty conferred upon the Shoshone-Bannock Tribes a continuing right to hunt on such lands. The magistrate court concluded that the Sand Creek Ranch did not constitute "unoccupied lands of the United States." Rather than addressing whether state-owned land met the "lands of the United States" standard under the treaty, the magistrate based its decision on two key factors. First, the court reasoned that a state agency possesses the authority to hold and manage land in a manner functionally equivalent to private ownership. Second, the court pointed to visible indicators of land occupation—such as fencing, signage, and structural improvements—as evidence that the area was not unoccupied in the treaty's intended sense.

The Cutler decision rested on several key findings. First, the Idaho Supreme Court concluded that the Shoshone signatories to the 1868 Fort Bridger Treaty understood that land could be considered "occupied" even in the absence of direct physical settlement, particularly when managed by a governmental entity. Second, the Court reasoned that the tribes recognized their off-reservation hunting rights would diminish over time, as non-Indian settlement expanded and game populations declined. Based on this logic, the Court determined that Sand Creek

Ranch—originally a privately owned cattle operation—was clearly excluded from the scope of the treaty's hunting protections. In the Court's view, the transfer of the ranch to state ownership did not alter its essential character; the only meaningful change was the substitution of elk for cattle. However, a critical review of the Court's reasoning reveals substantial weaknesses. The conclusion that Sand Creek Ranch remained "occupied" under the treaty is based on a narrow interpretation of land use and fails to account for broader historical, cultural, and ecological considerations that should inform the application of treaty rights.

The Idaho Supreme Court's conclusion that the Shoshone signatories to the 1868 Fort Bridger Treaty understood land could be "occupied" without direct physical presence was based largely on a single assumption: that tribal leaders, by having visited white settlements such as Fort Bridger, Fort Laramie, and Salt Lake City, had thereby acquired an understanding of Euro-American legal concepts of land tenure and government occupation. From this, the Court inferred that the tribes fully comprehended the Western legal meaning of "occupancy" as used in the treaty. Yet this assumption lacks supporting evidence and reflects a problematic judicial posture. It overlooks the vast cultural differences in how land, presence, and use were conceptualized by Indian peoples. The idea that brief exposure to settler institutions conferred a sophisticated grasp of Anglo-American property law is not only unfounded but also rooted in a form of judicial ethnocentrism. In the absence of direct testimony or contemporaneous documentation from the signatory tribes themselves, the Court's reasoning appears to rest more on projection than historical fact. This raises a critical question: on what basis did the Court feel justified in asserting such a conclusion—and was that basis consistent with the interpretive canons meant to govern Indian treaties?

To fully understand the intentions and mutual understandings between the Shoshone leaders and federal negotiators at the time of the 1868 Fort Bridger Treaty, it is essential to closely examine the language and implications of Article II, which defines the territorial boundaries and conditions of land use established for the Shoshone people. Central to the present analysis is whether the Shoshone signatories in 1868 would have interpreted the term "occupy" in the same manner as the federal drafters—an issue that cannot be resolved through textual analysis alone, but must be approached with attention to the historical, cultural, and diplomatic context in which the treaty was negotiated. The meaning of "occupation" as it appears in Article II must be interpreted not solely through modern legal frameworks, but in light of the likely understanding of the tribal leadership, shaped by their lived experiences, interactions with federal agents and immigrants, and the socio-political conditions of the time. The relevant portion of Article II reads as follows:

> ...The United States further agrees that the following district of country, to wit: Commencing at the mouth of Owl Creek and running due south to the crest of the divide between the Sweet-water and Papo Agie Rivers; thence along the crest of said divide and the summit of Wind River Mountains to the longitude of North Fork of Wind River; thence due north to mouth of said North Fork and up its channel to a point twenty miles above its mouth; thence in a straight line to head-waters of Owl Creek and along middle of channel of Owl Creek to place of beginning, shall be and the same is set apart for the absolute and undisturbed use and occupation of the Shoshonee Indians herein named, and for such other friendly tribes or individual Indians as from time to time they may be willing, with the consent of the United States, to admit amongst them; and the United States now solemnly agrees that no persons except those herein designated and authorized so to do, and except such officers, agents, and employés of the Government as may be authorized to enter upon Indian reservations in discharge of duties enjoined by law, shall ever be permitted to pass over, settle upon, or reside in the territory described in this article for the use of said Indians, and henceforth they will and do hereby relinquish all title, claims, or rights in and to any portion of the territory of the United States, except such as is embraced within the limits aforesaid.[13]

Like many treaties negotiated during the era of westward expansion, the 1868 Fort Bridger Treaty was drafted within a framework shaped by Euro-American legal norms and territorial ambitions. The treaty emerged at a time when federal policy and settler migration were rapidly encroaching on Tribal homelands.

---

[13] Fort Bridger Treaty, art. 2, 15 Stat. 673.

As such, its language reflects a distinctly Western conception of land, law, and control. In Euro-American legal tradition, the term "occupy" typically connotes physical residence, legal possession, or administrative control over a defined area. Article II of the treaty, with its detailed survey-style description of reservation boundaries, illustrates this worldview—a mapped, surveyed, and fixed understanding of land tenure that contrasts with more fluid and relational Indian conceptions of territory and use. This disparity in meaning raises important questions about how "occupation" would have been interpreted by the Shoshone signatories at the time the treaty was signed.

Conversely, many—if not all—American Indian nations, including the Shoshone and Bannock, held fundamentally different understandings of land, its use, and what it meant to occupy a place. While we cannot speak with absolute certainty about their precise interpretations in 1868, it is reasonable to infer that leaders such as Chief Washakie and Chief Taghee viewed land in terms of its use for hunting, gathering, seasonal movement, and spiritual purposes, rather than through the lens of fixed boundaries or exclusive ownership as understood in Euro-American law. For these Tribes, the concept of "occupation" was likely more fluid, grounded in patterns of subsistence, kinship, and ceremonial significance. As the anthropologist Sven Liljeblad observed,

> In 1868, when his spokesmen signed the treaty with the United States Government, a Bannock Indian's native land was anywhere between the Weiser River and Yellowstone where he could find something to eat. He also considered open to his exploitation the areas beyond, as far as he dared to go and could safely pitch his tipi.[14]

To be fair, the Shoshone and Bannock leaders who participated in the 1868 treaty negotiations were not entirely unfamiliar with the federal government's intentions or territorial frameworks. Through repeated dealings with U.S. officials, they were likely exposed to the government's concepts of land ownership, settlement, and control. However, exposure alone does not equate to full comprehension—especially when such complex

---

[14] Sven Liljeblad, *Indian Peoples in Idaho* (Pocatello: Idaho State College, 1957), 52.

legal and cultural ideas were conveyed over a short period, often through translators whose interpretations may have lacked precision or failed to capture the deeper meanings of either side. There remains a meaningful distinction between being introduced to a foreign legal framework and truly understanding its long-term implications—particularly when treaty language carried consequences that would unfold generations later.

Furthermore, historical accounts reveal that treaty negotiations were frequently marked by profound misunderstandings. Language barriers, differing worldviews regarding land and legal authority, and stark power imbalances almost certainly led Indian Tribes and U.S. negotiators to interpret treaty provisions in fundamentally different ways. Compounding these differences is the well-documented reality that the U.S. has repeatedly violated the terms of its treaties with Indian Nations. One example lies in the clause of the 1868 Fort Bridger Treaty stating that the land "shall be and the same is set apart for the absolute and undisturbed use and occupation of the Shoshonee Indians".[15] This language conveys an assertion of exclusive territorial rights, but it could also be read as an attempt to limit the Shoshone's traditional nomadic practices, confining them to a fixed geographic area. While Shoshone leaders may have understood "occupy" in a general sense—to live on or use the land—it is far less certain they grasped the term in the rigid, exclusive, and legalistic way the federal government intended.

Given the wide cultural, linguistic, and philosophical gaps between the parties, it is highly unlikely that their understandings of "occupation" were fully aligned. One might even argue that it is the Euro-American legal tradition that has failed to define the term consistently, reshaping its meaning to fit shifting political or economic objectives. Historically, millions of acres of Indian reservation land—clearly within established treaty boundaries—have been deemed "unoccupied" and opened to non-Indian settlement simply because the Tribes were not using the land in a way recognized by federal authorities. This raises a critical point: the definition of "occupied" and "unoccupied" has never been stable. Instead, it has evolved—often to the detriment of Indian land rights—and its meaning in U.S. courts remains

---

[15] *Fort Bridger Treaty*, art. 2, 15 Stat. 673.

unpredictable. In this sense, the legal terrain surrounding these terms is not just uncertain—it is a dangerously slippery slope.

Nonetheless, the Idaho Supreme Court's decision in Idaho v. Tinno offers a substantive critique of the narrow interpretation later applied in Cutler. In Tinno, the Court interpreted Article IV of the 1868 Fort Bridger Treaty to affirm that the Shoshone and Bannock retained the right to hunt on lands not settled or claimed by non-Indians. The Court wrote,

> In agreeing to settle on a permanent basis [on reservations] they [the Indians] still were expecting rights to harvest food on the unsettled lands as a means of subsistence and as an integral part of their way of life.[16]

This interpretation recognizes that the treaty's hunting clause was not a temporary accommodation but a fundamental element of the Tribes' continued survival and cultural identity. The records of the 1868 treaty negotiations, along with broader historical evidence, support the reasoning advanced in Tinno— namely, that the treaty preserved hunting rights on lands beyond the reservation so long as those lands remained unsettled and game was present.

On July 3, 1868, General C.C. Augur, a member of the Indian Peace Commission, met with the Eastern Band of the Shoshone and the Bannock to explain the U.S.' objectives in negotiating a treaty. Speaking on behalf of the federal government, he outlined the broader goals of peace, land cession, and relocation, while assuring the Tribes that certain rights—such as the ability to hunt—would be preserved. He stated:

> About a year ago, the great council and your great Father in Washington sent out a Commission to have a talk with the Indian tribes in the west, to make peace with such as were hostile, and to arrange with all of them that hereafter, there should be no more war between the white men and the Indians... The Shoshone and Bannocks are at peace with the whites, and have been for years. All we have to do therefore is to arrange matters, that there may never hereafter be a cause of war between them. There are a great many white men in your country now, and as soon as the

---

[16] Idaho v. Tinno, 94 Idaho 759 (1972).

Railroad is completed there will be many more. They will wish to remain and make homes here, and your great Father desires that they should do so...

He [U.S. President] wishes, however, to set apart a portion of it [homelands] for your permanent homes, and into which no white men will be permitted to come or settle. Upon this reservation he wishes you to go with all your people as soon as possible and to make it your permanent home, but with permission to hunt wherever you can find game.[17]

Although questions remain about how clearly the Shoshone and Bannock understood the geographic scope of their post-treaty hunting rights, it is evident that U.S. representatives conveyed an intention to preserve those rights, at least in principle. During negotiations, General Augur explicitly stated that the Tribes would retain the right to hunt wherever they can find game, a sentiment later codified in Article IV of the 1868 Fort Bridger Treaty through the phrase "so long as game may be found thereon." Additional evidence of this understanding appears in the reports of Indian Agent James Patten, who wrote that "Shoshone also understand that with the treaty of 1868 permission was given to them to hunt as long as game may be found thereon and that the same does not interfere with white settlers".[18] A similar interpretation was voiced during the ratification of the 1868 Fort Laramie Treaty with the Crow. When discussing Article IV, Senator James Harlan of Iowa remarked:

a provision permitting these Indians to hunt, so long as they can do so without interfering with the settlements. So long as outside lands, outside of the reservation, may not be occupied by settlements, and may be occupied by game, they may hunt to the game.[19]

---

[17] C. C. Augur, transcript of Fort Bridger Treaty Negotiations, October 4, 1868, reproduced at the National Archives, 4-5.
[18] State of Idaho v. Curtis Cutler, et al., 708 P.2d 853 (Idaho 1985).
[19] Crow Tribe of Indians. *Brief of the Crow Tribe of Indians as Amicus Curiae in Support of Petitioner,* No. 17-532, Supreme Court of the United States, on writ of certiorari to the District Court of Wyoming, Sheridan County. Counsel: Heather Daphne Whiteman Runs Him et al., Native American Rights Fund; Dennis M. Bear Don't Walk, Crow Agency, MT.

Although attorneys often build careers around parsing language to serve particular legal arguments, the weight of historical evidence strongly supports the conclusion that both U.S. negotiators and the Indian headmen involved in the 1868 treaty discussions understood Article IV as guaranteeing the right to hunt beyond reservation boundaries—provided such hunting did not interfere with white settlements and game, fish, or native plants remained available. Article IV of the Fort Bridger Treaty was crafted, in part, to reconcile two fundamentally different lifeways: the settler model of fixed, agricultural land use, and the more mobile, seasonal hunting and gathering traditions of the Indian Tribes. While Indian subsistence practices did not easily fit within the rigid frameworks of white settlement, they remained compatible with vast areas of land that were undeveloped, uncultivated, and free from permanent non-Indian occupation. In this sense, Article IV functioned as a compromise—an attempt to protect traditional Indian use of land in a rapidly changing territorial landscape.

The Cutler Court, along with other decisions, has acknowledged that national forests and other federally managed public lands may be classified as "unoccupied lands of the United States" within the meaning of the 1868 Fort Bridger Treaty and similar agreements. This position is supported by precedent in cases such as Idaho v. Tinno, Idaho v. Arthur[20], and Swim v. Bergland[21]. In each of these cases, courts upheld the view that Indian treaty hunting rights extended to federal lands not actively settled or claimed. The supposed distinctions drawn between state and federal lands—based on features like fences, signs, campgrounds, temporary occupancy by personnel, or minor infrastructure improvements such as earthen dams—appear superficial and unconvincing, especially given the largely parallel approaches to land management seen across the West.

For example, the Bureau of Land Management (BLM) operates under the statutory framework of the Federal Land Policy and Management Act of 1976 (FLPMA). This legislation directs the BLM to manage public lands for multiple uses, including energy development, livestock grazing, outdoor recreation, and wildlife habitat conservation. Like the U.S. Forest Service, the BLM is also

---

[20] *Idaho v. Arthur*, 74 Idaho 251, 261 P.2d 135 (1953).
[21] *Swim v. Bergland*, 696 F.2d 712 (9th Cir. 1983).

bound by the requirements of the Endangered Species Act, which obligates the agency to protect and restore habitats for listed species. At the core of the BLM's land management philosophy is the principle of multiple use and sustained yield—a mandate to balance present-day resource use with long-term ecological health. Both the BLM and Forest Service are required to develop land use plans through public participation and interagency coordination. This collaborative planning process is intended to ensure that the diverse interests associated with public lands are considered equitably, with particular attention to the conservation of fish and wildlife habitat, including for threatened and endangered species.

Anyone who has spent time on BLM or Forest Service lands knows they often feature fences, posted signs, campgrounds, water projects, and other modest infrastructure. These same features are also present on state-managed lands, including places like Sand Creek Ranch. In practice, there is little functional difference in how state and federal lands across the West are managed—both emphasize wildlife conservation, multiple-use access, and are often open to hunting by both Indian and non-Indian users. This raises a critical flaw in the Cutler decision: the Court's determination that Sand Creek Ranch was "occupied" fails to recognize that, from the perspective of a Shoshone or Bannock treaty signatory, there would have been no discernible distinction between the state-managed landscape of Sand Creek and the federal lands that courts have repeatedly deemed "unoccupied." The built features and use patterns are materially the same. If national forests can be considered "unoccupied" under the treaty, it is difficult to justify why similarly managed state lands would not be—unless one adopts a legal double standard untethered from the treaty's original understanding.

Although no definitive legal standard has been established for what constitutes "occupied" land under the 1868 Fort Bridger Treaty, the Cutler decision offers a set of criteria—referred to as the indicia of occupancy—that the Idaho Supreme Court found persuasive. These included the presence of cattle, fencing, cultivated fields, buildings, and other physical modifications to the land. The Court concluded that such features would have signaled to the signatory Indians that these lands were actively occupied by settlers and thus excluded from the scope of their treaty-based hunting rights. Importantly, the Court also asserted that the subsequent transfer of title from private ownership to the State of

Idaho did not alter the land's classification under the treaty. Although livestock were removed following the transfer, other indicators of occupation were added or maintained—such as continuous fencing, signage, structures, machinery, water infrastructure, cattle guards, roads, and recreational campgrounds. While the Court noted that its decision did not rest solely on the presence of these features, it emphasized that the indicia of occupancy were particularly strong in this case. Ultimately, the Court affirmed that determinations under the Fort Bridger Treaty must be made on a case-by-case basis, with close attention to the specific facts and characteristics of the land in question.

The presence of native wildlife and flora—such as elk, deer, buffalo, bighorn sheep, pinenuts, salmon, trout, and other culturally significant plant species—should serve as a meaningful indicator in determining whether land is "occupied" or "unoccupied" under treaty language. These species not only reflect the ecological health of a landscape but also carry deep historical and subsistence value for Indian communities. Their continued existence on a tract of land strongly suggests that the area remains in a relatively undisturbed, natural state—a condition consistent with how "unoccupied lands" would likely have been understood by the treaty signatories. Yet courts have largely failed to consider the presence of native species as a legal indicium of unoccupancy. Recognizing this connection would allow for a more culturally and ecologically grounded interpretation of treaty rights, aligning legal definitions with the lived relationships Indian Nations have long maintained with the land.

The continued vitality of these species should therefore be treated not as incidental, but as central to any analysis of whether a given landscape falls within the treaty-protected right to hunt on "unoccupied lands of the United States." This principle—anchoring legal meaning in the presence of game and the enduring relationships between Indian people and their traditional food sources—is the primary reason why this book bears the title *So Long As Game May Be Found Thereon...* It reflects not only the literal wording of the treaty but also the enduring vision of a world in which Indian rights are inseparable from the health of the land and the lives that depend on it.

Chapter 9 - Bibliography

Augur, C. C. *Transcript of Fort Bridger Treaty Negotiations*, October 4, 1868. Reproduced at the National Archives.

Crow Tribe of Indians. *Brief of the Crow Tribe of Indians as Amicus Curiae in Support of Petitioner*, No. 17-532. Supreme Court of the United States, on writ of certiorari to the District Court of Wyoming, Sheridan County. Counsel: Heather Daphne Whiteman Runs Him et al., Native American Rights Fund; Dennis M. Bear Don't Walk, Crow Agency, MT.

Idaho v. Arthur, 74 Idaho 251, 261 P.2d 135 (1953).

Idaho v. Coffee, 97 Idaho 905, 556 P.2d 1185 (1976).

Idaho v. Cutler, 109 Idaho 448, 708 P.2d 853 (1985).

Idaho v. Tinno, 94 Idaho 759, 497 P.2d 1386 (1972).

Liljeblad, Sven. *Indian Peoples in Idaho*. Pocatello: Idaho State College, 1957.

Swim v. Bergland, 696 F.2d 712 (9th Cir. 1983).

Treaty with the Eastern Band of Shoshoni and Bannock, July 3, 1868, 15 Stat. 673.

Treaty with the Nisqualli, Puyallup, and Other Tribes (Treaty of Medicine Creek), December 26, 1854, 10 Stat. 1132.

Treaty with the Quinaielt, et al. (Treaty of Olympia), July 1, 1855, 12 Stat. 971.

Treaty with the Shoshoni and Bannock, July 3, 1868, 15 Stat. 673.

Treaty of Hellgate, July 16, 1855, 12 Stat. 975.

United States v. Hicks, 587 F. Supp. 1162 (W.D. Wash. 1984).

United States v. Shoshone Tribe of Indians, 304 U.S. 111 (1938).

Chapter 10 - Make Said Reservations their Permanent Home

On October 17, 2023, the U.S. Court of Appeals for the Ninth Circuit issued an important ruling in Northwestern Band of the Shoshone Nation v. Wooten, a case that centered on the meaning of hunting rights in the 1868 Treaty of Fort Bridger.[1] The treaty promises that the Tribe would make its reservation a permanent home, but it also says "they will make no permanent settlement elsewhere; but they shall have the right to hunt on the unoccupied lands of the United States so long as game may be found thereon…" At the heart of the Wooten case was a disagreement over what that language really means. The Northwestern Band argued that their treaty rights allow them to hunt outside of Idaho's regular state hunting seasons—just as their ancestors did. But the Idaho Fish and Game disagreed. The Tribe took the issue to court, challenging Idaho's enforcement officer, Greg Wooten, and asking for their treaty rights to be upheld.

The dispute began when Idaho Fish and Game officers cited members of the Northwestern Band of the Shoshone Nation for hunting big game outside the regular state hunting season. The hunters defended their actions, arguing that the 1868 Fort Bridger Treaty protected their right to hunt on unoccupied lands, regardless of state-imposed seasons. Idaho officials disagreed, asserting that the treaty's hunting rights only applied to Tribes who live full-time on federally recognized Indian reservations. Because the cited hunters didn't reside on a reservation, the state claimed the treaty didn't cover them. This raised important legal questions about Tribal sovereignty and how the treaty's language should be interpreted—particularly whether living on a reservation is a condition for exercising treaty rights. While the individuals cited may not live on a reservation, many members of the Northwestern Band do, including those who reside at Fort Hall, especially in the Bannock Creek District.

The Northwestern Band of the Shoshone gained federal recognition in 1987, but their connection to the 1868 Fort Bridger

---

[1] *Northwestern Band of the Shoshone Nation v. Wooten,* No. 22-35140, 2023 WL 6822995 (9th Cir. Oct. 17, 2023).

Treaty goes back much further. In 1962, the Indian Claims Commission ruled that the Northwestern Band was legally bound by that treaty—even though their own leader, Chief Pocatello, hadn't signed it. Instead, the U.S. had treated Chief Washakie[2], a leader of a different Shoshone group, as representing all the Shoshone people at the time. Chief Pocatello had signed a different treaty in 1863—the Treaty of Box Elder[3]—which covered Northwestern Shoshone territory stretching from Raft River on the west to the Portneuf Mountains on the east. That treaty didn't clearly define the northern or southern borders of the land, but the area included key hunting grounds in what's now southern Idaho and northern Utah. The Indian Claims Commission acknowledged that this land was especially important to the Northwestern Band. It's also important to understand that Pocatello led a distinct band of Shoshone, separate from other Shoshone and Bannock leaders. He only rose to broader leadership status after the Bear River Massacre devastated several major Shoshone bands, forcing a reshuffling of tribal leadership.

Figuring out where Indian treaty hunting rights apply isn't simple. It often falls to U.S. courts to draw lines on a map—something that requires digging deep into ethnographic, linguistic, archaeological, and historical evidence to understand how Tribes traditionally used the land. But of all these sources, historical records often prove to be the most problematic. Treaties, government maps, and official documents are usually incomplete, one-sided, or just plain wrong. They were often written by non-Indians who had little understanding of Indian land use or values. Meanwhile, tribal oral histories—stories passed down through generations—carry deep knowledge about hunting grounds, seasonal patterns, and spiritual relationships with the land. Yet too often, courts and agencies have ignored or downplayed these accounts, treating written documents as the only "real" evidence. That's a serious problem. As linguistic anthropologist Dr. Sven Liljeblad once wrote, "The oral traditions of the Indians themselves proved to be more reliable, accurate, and exhaustive sources than

---

[2] *Shoshone Tribe of Indians of Wind River Reservation, Wyoming v. United States*, 11 Ind. Cl. Comm. 387 (1962), 402-404.
[3] Treaty with the Shoshoni—Northwestern Bands, July 30, 1863, 13 Stat. 663.

the written accounts of early travelers."⁴ Correcting these biases while building a credible case rooted in legally acceptable evidence remains a critical challenge.

Trying to define where tribes can legally hunt under their treaty rights isn't just a matter of drawing lines on a map—it's a lot more complicated. Tribal territories often overlap with state lands, private property, or other tribal claims, and sorting that out means dealing with layers of legal and political red tape. On top of that, traditional tribal lands weren't fenced off or fixed in place—they shifted with the seasons, as people moved to follow game, fish runs, and harvest cycles. That makes it hard to apply today's rigid legal boundaries to lands that were once used in a much more flexible, natural way.

There's also the issue of cultural sensitivity. Some places, stories, or practices tied to hunting are considered sacred and aren't meant to be shared with the public—or even with outsiders doing research. Respecting those boundaries while still gathering enough evidence to make a strong legal case is a real challenge. It takes work across multiple fields—history, law, anthropology, and ecology—to build a complete picture that both courts and tribal communities can stand behind. And just when a clear understanding starts to form, legal standards can shift. Courts and agencies often reinterpret what treaty rights mean or how they apply to things like land and wildlife, so what's considered legal today might be ruled differently tomorrow.

Optimally, doing this kind of work takes time, funding, and access to experts and historical records, and—critically—knowledgeable tribal members who hold the lived experience and oral history necessary to understand the land and its traditions. This type of knowledge and resources are often limited or difficult to secure. Ideally, it should be a collaborative effort involving tribal members, researchers, legal experts, and even regulatory agencies, all working together with a shared respect for tribal sovereignty and cultural values. That's the only way to build an outcome that's not only legally sound, but also honest and fair to the people whose rights are on the line. But when the process becomes adversarial and constrained by rigid court timelines, it

---

⁴ Liljeblad, *Indian Peoples in Idaho* (Pocatello: Idaho State College, 1957), 7.

leaves little room for mutual understanding—often leading to outcomes that fail to account for the rights, history, and perspectives of the Indian people who are most affected.

Thus, the historical record is far from complete, but that has not stopped historians and anthropologists with providing descriptions of the traditional homelands of the Northwestern Band of the Shoshone Nation. These interpretations are based on available sources and research, but they should be understood as approximations, limited by gaps and biases in historical documentation. According to historian Brigham D. Madsen, the Northwestern Band's territory at the time of early white settlement included the major river systems that flow into the Great Salt Lake in what is now northwestern Utah. Their range extended north to the Portneuf River, west to the Raft River watershed in southern Idaho, and into northeastern Nevada[5]. An 1859 estimated the population to be about one thousand[6]. It is also important to mention there was more than one leader.

Among these leaders, none became more well-known—or more closely associated with the defense of Shoshone lands—than Chief Pocatello. After the Bear River Massacre, he emerged as the primary chief and was known for taking action to protect a homeland that stretched from the Raft River and the northern shores of the Great Salt Lake to the Portneuf River in what is now southern Idaho.[7] This territory encompassed critical emigrant routes, including the California Trail and the Salt Lake Road, through which thousands of settlers traveled during the westward expansion. These settlers often disregarded Shoshone sovereignty, depleting resources and disrupting traditional lifeways. For years, Pocatello's people and other Northwestern Band Shoshone faced harassment, resource theft, and unprovoked violence from settlers and U.S. military forces, who at times indiscriminately killed Shoshone men, women, and children along these trails[8]. The Cache Valley, located between the Wasatch and Bear River Mountains in northern Utah, was at the heart of the Northwestern

---

[5] Brigham D. Madsen, *Chief Pocatello: The "White Plume"* (Salt Lake City: University of Utah Press, 1985),14-15.
[6] Ibid., 39.
[7] Ibid., 18.
[8] Brigham D. Madsen, *The Shoshoni Frontier and the Bear River Massacre* (Salt Lake City, UT: University of Utah Press, 1985), 57-73.

Shoshone homeland. It was in this valley that Chief Bear Hunter's people lived—and where they suffered the horrific Bear River Massacre in 1863 at the hands of the U.S. military[9].

Like many tribes in the region, the Northwestern Band of the Shoshone followed seasonal rounds, traveling to harvest food and materials and returning to favored wintering areas that offered shelter and resources. Their proximity to the Ute suggests they may have been among the first Shoshone bands to adopt the horse, which transformed their mobility and hunting practices. They were also known to travel eastward to the Great Plains for annual buffalo hunts, often joining with the Fort Hall Shoshone, Bannock, and Chief Washakie's people[10]. These hunts were vital not only for food and supplies, but also no doubt contributed to maintaining alliances and cultural ties among the tribes of the Intermountain West.

The connection to the land and seasonal movement across a wide territory is central to the legal recognition they later sought. In Northwestern Band of the Shoshone Nation v. Wooten, the court acknowledged that the Shoshone people, from time immemorial, lived on, traveled through, and relied upon a vast expanse of land for hunting, fishing, and gathering. The case emphasized the Shoshone's enduring relationship with the landscape and affirmed that their survival was rooted in these traditional practices.[11] It also recognized the longstanding ties between the Shoshone and the Bannock, and described how increasing pressures from white settlers, including depletion of game and acts of violence, led to rising tensions. These tensions ultimately exploded into the Bear River Massacre, a tragic event that marked a turning point and ushered in the treaty-making era between the U.S. government and the Shoshone and Bannock peoples.

In the years that followed, as documented in the Indian Claims Commission proceedings, the U.S. government began efforts to concentrate scattered tribal groups onto federally managed reservations. In 1873, it established a commission tasked with surveying the tribes in the region, estimating their

---

[9] Ibid., 15
[10] Ibid.,
[11] *Northwestern Bands of Shoshone Indians v. United States*, 95 Ct. Cl. 677 (1942), aff'd, 324 U.S. 335 (1945) (*Northwestern Bands I*).

populations, and evaluating the feasibility of relocating them to one or more reservations where they could be brought under closer federal supervision.[12] By then, the Northwestern Band of the Shoshone had become widely dispersed. Some had moved to the Wind River Reservation in Wyoming, while around 400 were living on the Fort Hall Reservation in Idaho, and another 400 were reported living in southern Idaho[13], apparently outside of any formal reservation boundaries. Even Chief Pocatello—the prominent Shoshone leader who signed the 1863 Treaty of Box Elder—ultimately relocated to Fort Hall and began living the reservation life in the Bannock Creek area[14]. A separate group had settled in northeastern Nevada on land set aside by an Indian agent, which was later formalized as a reservation through an apparent 1877 Executive Order—but that reservation was short-lived. It was dissolved in 1879, and its Shoshone residents were moved to Duck Valley, a reservation established for the Western Shoshone. Still, not all Northwestern Shoshones relocated. A portion of the group remained in northern Utah and would later organize other Northwestern Band Shoshone Indians to become federally recognized as the Northwestern Band of the Shoshone Nation. Today, the U.S. government maintains a distinct government-to-government relationship with this Band, along with the Eastern Shoshone Tribe at Wind River and the Shoshone-Bannock Tribes at Fort Hall.

In 1985, the Northwestern Band solicited the Bureau of Indian Affairs, also known as the BIA, for an affirmation of their hunting and fishing rights as stipulated by the 1868 Fort Bridger Treaty. Lawrence E. Cox, the Acting Regional Solicitor of the Pacific Northwest Region, acknowledged that "the Northwestern Band does possess treaty protected hunting and fishing rights which may be exercised on the unoccupied lands within the area acquired by the United States pursuant to the 1868 Treaty of Fort Bridger".[15] The conclusion was drawn upon the acceptance of the Indian Claims Commission's determinations, one of which included "that Chief Washakie represented the interests of all

---

[12] *Northwestern Bands I*, 95 Ct. Cl. at 677.
[13] Ibid., 677–78.
[14] Madsen, *Chief Pocatello*, 105.
[15] Lawrence E. Cox, Memorandum, Acting Regional Solicitor of the Pacific Northwest Region, March 20, 1985.

Shoshone Indians, including the absent Northwestern Band led by Pocatello,"[16] during treaty negotiations.

In 1997, two members of the Northwestern Band, Shane and Wayde Warner, were charged by the state of Idaho for hunting big game outside the designated hunting season, an act considered a misdemeanor. In their defense, the Warners invoked the right to hunt under the 1868 Fort Bridger Treaty. However, their defense was dismissed by the state court which construed the Treaty as limiting the hunting privilege to Indians permanently residing on a reservation. This interpretation was formalized in State of Idaho v. Warner, where the court concluded that the treaty's hunting rights were limited to members of the Eastern Shoshone Tribe at the Wind River Reservation and the Shoshone-Bannock Tribes at the Fort Hall Reservation.[17]

That court determined the Northwestern Band could not lay claim to the Treaty-guaranteed hunting rights without demonstrating political unity with either of those tribes. The decision relied in part on precedent from a Ninth Circuit case, which established that treaty rights require sufficient political continuity to ensure that such rights are exercised in a manner consistent with the original treaty agreements.[18]

In 2019, the issue resurfaced when two other Northwestern Band members, Wyatt Athay and Shanelle Long, were cited by Idaho officials for hunting without state-issued tags. Like the Warners, they asserted that their actions were protected under the 1868 Fort Bridger Treaty. Rather than proceeding immediately to trial, the parties agreed to delay the case, pending resolution of a broader legal challenge in which the Northwestern Band is actively seeking a formal judicial declaration affirming their right to hunt under the Treaty. This ongoing litigation could have significant implications for tribal hunting rights in Idaho and beyond.

Returning to the Wooten case—the primary focus of this chapter—the Northwestern Band of the Shoshone Nation brought a federal lawsuit seeking formal recognition of their hunting rights

---

[16] Ibid.
[17] *State of Idaho v. Warner*, Idaho Case Nos. CR-98-00014 and CR-98-00015 (Idaho Dist. Ct., November 1, 2000).
[18] *United States v. Oregon*, 29 F.3d 481, 484, 486 (9th Cir. 1994), amended by 43 F.3d 1284 (9th Cir. 1994).

under the 1868 Fort Bridger Treaty[19]. As is common in Indian law, the case became procedurally complex. Idaho responded by filing motions to dismiss, arguing that the court lacked jurisdiction, that the complaint failed to state a claim, and that the absence of necessary parties—most notably the Shoshone-Bannock Tribes—meant the case could not proceed fairly. While these arguments are grounded in procedural law, they also reflect broader tensions about how treaty rights are interpreted and shared among related tribes.

On one hand, it is reasonable to argue that other treaty signatories should be included in litigation that might impact their rights. On the other hand, it puts the Shoshone-Bannock Tribes in a difficult position—potentially being pulled into a federal case that stems from actions taken by members of another tribe, not their own. That kind of legal entanglement can create unwanted political and legal consequences for a tribe that didn't initiate the conflict, yet now must defend its interests in court. This situation highlights how fragmented federal Indian policy and overlapping treaty interpretations can place tribes at odds with one another, even when their long-term interests might otherwise align.

One part of the case that's worth understanding is why the State of Idaho itself wasn't ultimately held responsible in the lawsuit. Early on, the district court ruled that the Eleventh Amendment to the U.S. Constitution protected Idaho from being sued directly. That amendment basically says states can't be dragged into federal court without their consent—a legal shield known as "sovereign immunity." Because of that, the judge approved Idaho's motion to dismiss, but only for the State itself—not for its officers, like Greg Wooten. The Northwestern Band didn't challenge this part of the ruling, choosing instead to focus on the broader question of their hunting rights under the Treaty. While it might seem like a technical detail, it shows how hard it can be to hold state governments accountable in federal court—even when the issues at stake involve treaty rights that predate the states themselves.

The court also upheld the defendants' motion to dismiss under Rule 12(b)(6)[20], which is used when a lawsuit doesn't clearly

---

[19] *Northwestern Band v. Wooten*, No. 22-35140, 2023 WL 6822995
[20] *Fed. R. Civ. P.* 12(b)(6).

present a legal claim the court can act on. In this case, the argument was that the 1868 Fort Bridger Treaty only protects hunting rights for those living full-time on reservations like Fort Hall or Wind River—something the Northwestern Band members cited in the case did not do. The state also argued that even if the Northwestern Band had ties to the Treaty, they couldn't use those rights on their own because they weren't politically unified with either of the tribes that originally negotiated it—the Eastern Shoshone or the Shoshone-Bannock. Whether that's true or not is still up for debate. Future decisions will need to examine whether the Northwestern Band has maintained strong enough political ties to those tribes—looking at their shared history, leadership structures, and how they've worked together in recent years.

The district court ultimately sided with the state's interpretation of the treaty, agreeing that the Northwestern Band's hunting rights might depend on more than just their ancestry. But the court stopped short of deciding whether the Band had actually maintained strong political ties with the Shoshone-Bannock or Eastern Shoshone Tribes—leaving that question for another day. The court also didn't rule on another argument raised by the state: that the case should be thrown out because a key party, the Shoshone-Bannock Tribes, weren't included in the lawsuit. That question, too, remains unresolved for now.

Interestingly, the Shoshone-Bannock Tribes themselves stepped in to support the State of Idaho, filing an amicus brief urging the court to uphold the dismissal. Idaho also included a declaration from Devon Boyer, Chairman of the Fort Hall Business Council, to back its argument that the case couldn't fairly move forward without the Tribes being involved. In his statement, Chairman Boyer pointed to the Shoshone-Bannock Tribal Code, which clearly states: "Only enrolled members of the Shoshone-Bannock Tribes who make the Fort Hall Reservation their permanent home shall enjoy the off-Reservation Tribal hunting and fishing rights as set forth pursuant to the Fort Bridger Treaty of July 3, 1868, and subsequent agreements between the Shoshone-Bannock Tribes and the United States government."[21] That position highlights just how sensitive this issue is—not just for the Northwestern Band, but also for the Shoshone-Bannock

---

[21] *Northwestern Band v. Wooten*, No. 22-35140, 2023 WL 6822995

Tribes who see these rights as tied to place, membership, and long-standing agreements with the federal government.

The Shoshone-Bannock Tribes filed a legal brief supporting the State of Idaho and agreeing with the district court's decision to dismiss the Northwestern Band's lawsuit. In doing so, they pointed to their own Tribal Code, which says that off-reservation hunting and fishing rights under the 1868 Fort Bridger Treaty only apply to enrolled members who live permanently on the Fort Hall Reservation. By highlighting this rule, the Shoshone-Bannock Tribes reinforced the argument that the Northwestern Band's claim lacked legal standing—and that the case couldn't move forward fairly without their involvement.

The key issue before the Ninth Circuit was whether the 1868 Fort Bridger Treaty limits hunting rights only to those Shoshone who live permanently on the Fort Hall or Wind River Reservations. The appeals court reviewed this question *de novo*, meaning it took a fresh look at the treaty's language without being bound by the lower court's interpretation. This approach followed established precedent allowing appellate courts to independently evaluate treaty terms and their meaning in modern legal contexts.[22]

The Ninth Circuit's decision in Northwestern Band of the Shoshone Nation v. Wooten began by reaffirming a basic principle: a treaty is a binding agreement between two sovereign nations. Drawing from prior rulings, the court emphasized that Indian treaties must be interpreted the way the tribal signers would have naturally understood them at the time.[23] This perspective, explored in earlier chapters, shaped how the court approached Article IV of the 1868 Fort Bridger Treaty—the section at the heart of the dispute. Idaho officials argued that this article grants hunting rights only to those who live permanently on reservations like Fort Hall or Wind River. But the Northwestern Band disagreed, asserting that the treaty protects their right to hunt on unoccupied lands in their traditional territory, without requiring

---

[22] *United States v. State of Washington*, 969 F.2d 752, 754 (9th Cir. 1992).

[23] *Herrera v. Wyoming*, 139 S. Ct. 1686, 1699 (2019); *Washington v. Washington State Commercial Passenger Fishing Vessel Association*, 443 U.S. 658, 675 (1979), modified sub nom. *Washington v. United States*, 444 U.S. 816 (1979).

them to move to a reservation. After weighing both sides, the Ninth Circuit found the Tribe's reading of the treaty more convincing.

To understand what the 1868 Treaty of Fort Bridger really meant to the Shoshone signers, the court didn't just look at the plain wording. It looked at the bigger picture—how the treaty came about, what was discussed during negotiations, and how both sides understood and acted on its terms afterward. This method is supported by the U.S. Supreme Court in the Mille Lacs decision, where the Court stressed the need to consider "the history of the treaty, the negotiations, and the practical construction adopted by the parties."[24] And when any part of a treaty is unclear, the law says those ambiguities must be interpreted in favor of the Indian signatories.

Turning to the treaty text, the Ninth Circuit began its analysis with Article I, which committed both parties to peaceful relations. Article II marked a major shift for the Tribes: they agreed to give up claims to their traditional homelands, signaling the end of a nomadic lifestyle that once spanned large regions of the Western U.S. In return, the U.S. promised land for the Shoshone's exclusive use—what would become the Wind River Reservation. The treaty also addressed the Bannock Tribe, stating that when they either requested or were directed by the President to move to a reservation, a suitable area would be set aside for them within their homeland territory. This reservation was to include parts of the Portneuf and Kamas Prairie regions and provide the Bannock with the same benefits promised to the Shoshone, adjusted proportionally to their population—excluding the agency house and agent's residence. Article III outlined the U.S. government's obligation to provide schools, agency buildings, and other facilities on the Shoshone reservation. But it was Article IV that would later become a focal point of legal debate. It stated that the Tribes would make the reservation their permanent home and not settle permanently elsewhere. At the same time, it preserved their right to hunt on "right to hunt on the unoccupied lands of the United States".[25]

---

[24] *Minnesota v. Mille Lacs Band of Chippewa Indians*, 526 U.S. 172 (1999).
[25] Treaty with the Eastern Band Shoshoni and Bannock, 1868, 15 Stat. 673.

After reviewing Article IV within its full historical and legal context, the Ninth Circuit concluded that the Tribes likely understood the Treaty as requiring them to give up their land and settle on reservations—but not to surrender their hunting rights across those same lands. In other words, the right to hunt wasn't a new privilege granted by the U.S. government—it was something the Tribes believed they were keeping. The court also clarified that the phrase "the right to hunt on the unoccupied lands of the United States"[26] referred specifically to those unoccupied lands within their original homelands—not the broad application to all unoccupied lands of the U.S. as the phrase might literally suggest.

Another way to put it is this: even though other tribes weren't part of the Wooten case, the court's ruling ended up limiting hunting rights to some undefined version of original homelands which will no doubt be challenged in the future. In doing so, the court rejected the idea that treaty hunting could apply to all unoccupied lands of the U.S., as the treaty wording might literally suggest. That shift could be viewed as a major loss—not just for the Northwestern Band, but also for other tribes like the Shoshone-Bannock, the Eastern Shoshone, and possibly even the Crow. Thus, the Northwestern Band's lawsuit, which aimed at securing their own hunting rights, led to a legal interpretation that narrowed those rights for all tribes covered by the Fort Bridger Treaty.

The court also identified four conditions that limited the scope of this retained hunting right. First, the land had to be owned by the federal government. Second, it had to be unoccupied. Third, game had to still be present. And finally, the Tribes' hunting rights only continued as long as there was peace between Indians and settlers in the area.

Astonishingly, despite what seems like clear and straightforward treaty language, the Ninth Circuit concluded that the right to hunt under the 1868 Fort Bridger Treaty was not dependent on permanently living on a reservation. This was the very issue the Northwestern Band had brought to the court for clarification. Looking back at Article II, the court found no evidence that the Tribes had agreed to give up their hunting rights if they chose not to relocate. While the Fort Hall Reservation had

---

[26] Ibid.

been established the year before the treaty was signed, that applied only to the Boise and Bruneau bands of Shoshone and Bannock. There was no indication at the time that the Bannock as a whole had a reservation promised to them. In fact, Idaho's attorneys couldn't show that a second reservation had been defined or guaranteed, and the court pointed out the lack of any concrete details—no clear boundaries, no selected location, and no formal timeline.

Because of this uncertainty, the court reasoned that the Tribes would not have understood the treaty to mean they had to give up their hunting rights if they didn't move to a reservation. Another way to put it: the court concluded the Tribes would have understood the language to mean, "We're agreeing to settle down on the reservation, but we're still keeping our hunting rights on unoccupied land as long as game exists and there's peace." In effect, the court read the clause not as a contract lawyer would, but in the way it believed Indian signatories would have naturally interpreted it during treaty negotiations.

The Ninth Circuit reaffirmed that living on a reservation is not a requirement for exercising hunting rights under the Fort Bridger Treaty. The court explained that the right to hunt depended on the presence of game and the maintenance of peace, not on where a tribal member lives. This rejected Idaho's claim that only reservation residents could exercise those rights. However, the ruling was not a complete win. By interpreting "unoccupied lands of the United States" to mean only within a tribe's original homeland, the court narrowed the scope of those rights. That limitation could affect all tribes covered by the Fort Bridger Treaty. In trying to protect its own rights, the Northwestern Band's case has inadvertently defined new limits that will apply to other tribes.

Although the district court had agreed with Idaho's argument that the Tribes' promise to settle on a reservation was a key part of the treaty's bargain, the Ninth Circuit pushed back. It rejected the idea that hunting rights were granted in exchange for that promise. Instead, the court clarified that the Treaty simply recognized a right the Tribes already had—the right to hunt on their former lands. In return, the U.S. gained what it truly sought: land cessions and a commitment to peace. The lower court's reading, the Ninth Circuit concluded, misunderstood both the nature of treaty rights and what the Tribes actually gave up.

Although not part of the original district court record, a historical report from General C.C. Augur—who participated in negotiating the 1868 Fort Bridger Treaty—was appended to Idaho's appellate brief. In the report, Augur described reservation life as something that would benefit the Tribes, not as a condition for retaining hunting rights. He explained that the U.S. wanted Indians to settle on reservations so the government could more easily provide food and assistance, especially as game populations declined. At no point did Augur suggest that failure to move to a reservation would mean forfeiting the right to hunt. His words, if considered, supported the Northwestern Band's argument: that they did not need to live on a reservation to retain their rights.

Ultimately, the Ninth Circuit sided with the Northwestern Band on this core question. The court held that the 1868 Treaty of Fort Bridger does not condition the Tribes' reserved hunting rights on permanent residence on a reservation. However, the court did not resolve the entire case. Because the lower court had previously dismissed the complaint without examining Idaho's other arguments—namely, whether the Northwestern Band has maintained sufficient political cohesion with the signatory tribes, and whether the Shoshone-Bannock Tribes should have been joined as a necessary party—the Ninth Circuit sent the case back to the district court for further proceedings on those unresolved issues.

When I first heard about the Wooten case, I was concerned that the Northwestern Band of the Shoshone Nation might unintentionally jeopardize the off-reservation hunting rights of the Shoshone-Bannock Tribes. Even though I'm fluent in English and familiar with legal documents, I had always understood Article IV of the 1868 Fort Bridger Treaty to mean that hunting rights off the reservation applied only to those who lived on the reservation. The Treaty states:

> The Indians herein named agree, when the agency house and other buildings shall be constructed on their reservations named, they will make said reservations their permanent home, and they will make no permanent

settlement elsewhere; but they shall have the right to hunt on the unoccupied lands of the United States...[27]

To me, that meant if I lived off the reservation, I couldn't hunt off the reservation. And for many years, when I did live away from Fort Hall, I followed that interpretation—only hunting within reservation boundaries. I wasn't alone. At various tribal hunter meetings, I heard similar frustrations from other off-reservation tribal members who felt excluded from hunting and fishing, especially for salmon. Some argued that because they lived within the boundaries of the original Fort Hall Ceded Area, they should still have that right.

Before the Wooten case, the Shoshone-Bannock Tribes actually commissioned a legal opinion from a law firm who concluded that as long as the Shoshone-Bannock Tribes as a political organization remained on the Fort Hall Reservation, both resident and non-resident tribal members could exercise off-reservation hunting rights. But for those of us living on the reservation, the risk of a legal challenge loomed. We were worried that opening up off-reservation hunting too broadly could invite a federal case that might end with all of us losing those rights. Because of that concern, the Council had always taken a cautious approach—holding to the view that requiring residency on the reservation would help protect our hunting rights if they were ever challenged in court.

In the fall of 2022, I attended a Tribal district meeting where one of the Tribal Councilmen mentioned the idea of opening off-reservation hunting to non-resident tribal members. He also stated that the Northwestern Band was suing the state of Idaho over the residency interpretation of the Fort Bridger Treaty. He said, "We are thinking of opening it up to everyone." I offered a suggestion to the discussion by saying, "perhaps you guys (Council) should wait until the outcome of the Northwestern Band court case before making a decision." I also added, "the Tribes better start setting aside some attorney money to defend tribal members who get cited for hunting off the reservation in other states since we have tribal members spread all over the country."

I don't know whether my input played any role in the decision, but on February 6, 2024, the Fort Hall Business Council

---

[27] Fort Bridger Treaty, art. 4, 15 Stat. 673.

officially passed an amended Fish and Game Ordinance. That same day, it was approved by the BIA Superintendent Randy Thompson. The revised ordinance removed the previous distinction between resident and non-resident tribal members, effectively granting off-reservation hunting rights to all enrolled Shoshone-Bannock tribal members, regardless of where they live.

On January 26, 2023, about a week prior to the Wooten decision, I attended a talk at Idaho State University in Pocatello, Idaho, given by Darren Parry. The talk was entitled "Remembering Bear River: Hard History with Darren Parry." Mr. Parry is the former Chairman of the Northwestern Band of the Shoshone Nation and a direct descendant of Mae Timbimboo Parry, the granddaughter of a Bear River Massacre survivor who served as the Tribe's historian and record keeper. Mrs. Parry was instrumental in changing the National Monument's former name from the Bear River Battle to the Bear River Massacre.

During the questions and answer section of the talk, a participant asked, "After this atrocity [Bear River Massacre], was there ever any attempt to seek property or compensate the Shoshone in any way?"

Parry answered by saying,

> There was an act in Congress a few years later, and they tried to find us a piece of land out in Nevada and they looked at it and deemed it not very good. So, it was never done. That act of Congress is still active today, but we were never given a reservation land. So, we were one of the few tribes that did not go to a reservation. We, for, good or bad assimilated into the local culture and a . . . good in respect that were not on a reservation that has all the problems of a reservation, bad in respect that we are not on reservation we lose our language and culture quicker.

At the closing of his talk he also stated, that,

> even though the massacre was in Idaho, the federal government says we are a Utah Tribe but man there were no borders back then and we spent most our time in southern Idaho. I'd say were an Idaho Tribe as much as anything. Idaho Tribes don't want us here and that we just try to be nice.

Being aware of the ongoing Wooten case, I couldn't help but feel that his closing statement was a subtle reference to the Shoshone-Bannock Tribes' filing of an amicus brief supporting the State of Idaho's position.

Chapter 10 - Bibliography

Cox, Lawrence E. Memorandum, Acting Regional Solicitor of the Pacific Northwest Region, March 20, 1985.

Federal Rules of Civil Procedure, Rule 12(b)(6).

Herrera v. Wyoming, 139 S. Ct. 1686 (2019).

Liljeblad, Sven. Indian Peoples in Idaho. Pocatello: Idaho State College, 1957.

Madsen, Brigham D. Chief Pocatello: The "White Plume". Salt Lake City: University of Utah Press, 1985.

Madsen, Brigham D. The Shoshoni Frontier and the Bear River Massacre. Salt Lake City, UT: University of Utah Press, 1985.

Minnesota v. Mille Lacs Band of Chippewa Indians, 526 U.S. 172 (1999).

Northwestern Band of the Shoshone Nation v. Wooten, No. 22-35140, 2023 WL 6822995 (9th Cir. Oct. 17, 2023).

Northwestern Bands of Shoshone Indians v. United States, 95 Ct. Cl. 677 (1942), aff'd, 324 U.S. 335 (1945).

Shoshone Tribe of Indians of Wind River Reservation, Wyoming v. United States, 11 Ind. Cl. Comm. 387 (1962).

State of Idaho v. Warner, Idaho Case Nos. CR-98-00014 and CR-98-00015 (Idaho Dist. Ct., November 1, 2000).

Treaty with the Eastern Band Shoshoni and Bannock, July 3, 1868, 15 Stat. 673.

Treaty with the Shoshoni—Northwestern Bands, July 30, 1863, 13 Stat. 663.

United States v. Oregon, 29 F.3d 481 (9th Cir. 1994), amended by 43 F.3d 1284 (9th Cir. 1994).

United States v. State of Washington, 969 F.2d 752 (9th Cir. 1992).

Washington v. Washington State Commercial Passenger Fishing Vessel Association, 443 U.S. 658 (1979), modified sub nom. Washington v. United States, 444 U.S. 816 (1979).

Chapter 11 - Concluding Remarks

In 1868, the U.S. government entered into treaties with the Shoshone, Bannock, and Crow leaders. These agreements preserved the Tribes' right to hunt on the unoccupied lands of the U.S., so long as game could be found and peace was maintained. These rights were not granted by the government but were reserved by the Tribes as part of the treaty agreements, in exchange for their land cessions and commitment to peace.

But those rights were later dismantled in Wyoming. In Ward v. Race Horse (1896), the U.S. Supreme Court sided with the State of Wyoming and held that treaty hunting rights were no longer valid once Wyoming became a state. The effect was devastating: Indian hunting rights in Wyoming were erased for more than a century. Although the State of Wyoming and federal court system would likely never admit that the Race Horse case resulted from a conspiracy—but based on my research, and the historical evidence presented in this Chapter 6, I leave it to the reader to decide whether this was in fact a coordinated conspiracy to permanently suppress treaty-guaranteed Indian hunting rights.

Among those most familiar with hunting and fishing disputes, Tribal attorneys—and even, I suspect, some state attorneys who oppose us—recognize that Ward v. Race Horse has left a deep and lasting bias in federal Indian law. The case didn't emerge from a fair or neutral process; it was rooted in violence, sparked by the killing of Bannock Indians, and yet the courts never addressed that history. That kind of origin calls the integrity of the ruling into question. As one of our own attorneys put it plainly: Race Horse is just "bad law". When cases like Race Horse become law they represent examples of flawed jurisprudence and they undermine trust in the U.S. legal system.

Some readers might shrug and say, "So what if you can't treaty hunt? Just buy a tag like everyone else." Or, "It's the 21st century—you can get your food at the store." But these kinds of comments reflect a deep ignorance about Indian culture and a broader disregard for the long history of broken promises. What critics miss is that hunting wasn't just about getting food—it was about independence, self-reliance, and the ability of Indian people, especially men, to provide for their families, teach the next generation, and live according to their own culture and traditions.

The loss of treaty hunting rights—combined with decades of forced assimilation—has stripped many Tribes of that independence. For sovereign Nations that never surrendered those rights, it should come as no surprise that they continue to resist Wyoming's regulations and the larger system of U.S. colonial control. After all, hunting was never just a right—it was a way of life. You have to ask yourself: if the government sought to take away your right to hunt—something tied to your livelihood, culture, and identity—wouldn't you resist?

Hunting was once carried out wherever game could be found, and the very act of harvesting food from the land was a foundation of Indian independence. That independence has always stood in direct conflict with colonialism. In the past, the U.S. relied on open warfare to subjugate Indian people and force dependence. Today, the tools have changed, but the goals remain strikingly similar: the federal legal system, often backed by state governments, continues to erode tribal autonomy through litigation and regulatory control. Make no mistake—violations of treaty promises are not mere technicalities. They are acts of injustice that continue to inflict harm on Indian communities. Confronting this legacy requires more than symbolic gestures. It demands a sustained, collective effort to expose, navigate, and correct the legal and structural injustices that American Indian Tribes still face today.

Addressing these injustices ultimately depends on the actions of the Tribes themselves. Sovereignty is not a gift bestowed by the federal government—it is a reflection of power. It is earned and upheld through strength, wealth, innovation, and the collective will to assert it. Sovereignty must be exercised, not requested. It grows through discipline, economic development, legal infrastructure, and cultural unity. It is defended not just in courtrooms, but in classrooms, boardrooms, and every place where Indian people take control of their future.

This begins with disciplined leadership and a relentless commitment to strategic thinking. Tribes must invest in productive capacity, institutional development, and innovation rooted in cultural identity—what might be called *Indigenuity*. Educating youth in tribal history and governance is essential, as is confronting internal fragmentation. Unity is not a luxury; it is a necessity. Without it, the leverage needed to shape policy and secure the future erodes. With it, Indian Nations can shift from reactive to proactive—from surviving to designing their own destinies.

Sovereignty is not only built in council chambers or courtrooms. It is forged in the bodies and minds of the people—especially the men charged with leading, defending, and providing. Addiction, chronic illness, and passivity are corrosive. A sovereign Nation cannot rise if its warriors are sick, weak, numb, or broken. Discipline, physical strength, and mental clarity are prerequisites to leadership. We must return to the old ways—endurance, self-reliance, courage, and duty. A healthy, focused, and resilient people can defend their land, raise strong families, and carry the weight of sovereignty. It isn't given. It is built, protected, and earned—through strength, sacrifice, and the will to endure.

That said, non-Indian institutions, educators, and policymakers can still play a role in fostering justice and understanding. One of the most powerful tools is public education. Integrating accurate American Indian history and contemporary issues into school curricula—and ensuring Native voices are included in developing those materials—can help shift public perceptions and promote cultural respect. States like Wyoming, Idaho, and others could also support deeper historical research into events that affected the Shoshone, Bannock, Crow, and other Tribes. Funding grants or scholarships for such research could help bring long-silenced truths to light.

However, legislative actions in states like Wyoming and Idaho are moving in the opposite direction. Laws such as Wyoming's Senate File No. SF0103[1] and Idaho's House Bill No. 377[2] restrict teaching so-called "critical race theory" or "divisive concepts," placing chilling limitations on educators who seek to teach the truth about colonization, treaty violations, and the struggles of Indian people. While these laws claim to prevent guilt

---

[1] Senate File No. SF0103, 66th Wyoming Legislature, 2022 Budget Session (introduced Feb. 15, 2022), "Education–Limitations on Teaching Critical Race History–2," accessed May 18, 2025, https://wyoleg.gov/Legislation/2022/SF0103.
[2] House Bill No. 377, 66th Idaho Legislature, 1st Regular Session (2021), "Education—Dignity and Nondiscrimination in Public Education," accessed May 18, 2025,
https://legislature.idaho.gov/sessioninfo/2021/legislation/H0377/.

or bias based on race, they risk suppressing honest conversations about historical injustice. In practice, teachers will avoid these topics altogether out of fear of professional and personal repercussions—further deepening public ignorance and cutting students off from the full story of their nation's past.

A collaborative approach—especially in natural and cultural resource management—could serve as a meaningful step toward improving relations between Indian tribes and state or federal agencies. While such efforts may not stem from moral reckoning alone, they offer clear strategic value. For states like Idaho and Wyoming, joint stewardship of culturally significant landscapes could reduce legal conflict, attract tourism, and demonstrate a willingness to work with sovereign tribal nations. Sites like the Great Bannock Trail—where the Bannock were pursued dwindling populations of buffalo—deserve national recognition as historic trails or memorials. And at these places, the full story must be told. That includes the destruction of the buffalo, the long legacy of broken treaty promises, and the true cost of westward expansion.

Some may still prefer a romanticized tale of how the West was won, but the reality is far more powerful. Our history is gritty, painful, and at times evil—but it's also rich with resilience and meaning. You cannot understand the good without facing the bad. Let's hear it all, analyze it, and learn from it. That is the first real step toward reconciliation. As the next generation of tribal youth prepares to lead, their voices must be included in these decisions. True collaboration is not just symbolic—it's practical, and long overdue.

The legacy of cases like Ward v. Race Horse underscores the need to strengthen and support tribal justice systems today. Expanding tribal jurisdiction to enforce conservation laws on their own terms not only affirms sovereignty but also begins to repair the longstanding dismissal of treaty rights. Despite the damage caused by Race Horse, the Shoshone-Bannock Tribes have continued to assert their off-reservation hunting rights. In response to repeated legal challenges, the Tribes established a Fish and Game Code, created a Fish and Game Commission, and enacted hunting and fishing regulations for their members. They also formed a Fish and Wildlife Department to restore habitat and monitor game populations on and off the reservation. These efforts go hand in hand with treaty rights education—both for Tribal members and for federal land managers. Still, these initiatives come with a cost. They reflect not just sovereignty in action, but also the burden of constantly defending that sovereignty in the face of state resistance and legal uncertainty.

In sum, addressing the deep injustices faced by American Indian Tribes demands a sustained, multifaceted approach—one that recognizes their inherent rights, cultural heritage, and enduring contributions. The legacy of Ward v. Race Horse inflicted more than a legal wound; it severed generations from their ancient homelands, knowledge, and traditions. We may never fully recover the original *Newe* names of rivers, mountains, and canyons that faded from memory, nor the songs, stories, and ceremonies once tied to those sacred places. The damage extended to families like the Racehorses themselves, whose history became a legal footnote instead of a legacy. If treaty hunting is ever restored in Wyoming, many tribal members will have to reacquaint themselves with their original homelands in Wyoming by exercising their off-reservation treaty hunting rights. Although the Shoshone-Bannock Tribes have continued to exercise their treaty hunting in Idaho since the signing of the 1868 Fort Bridger Treaty, it is almost certain that the state of Wyoming, like Idaho, will continue to challenge the Treaty in every conceivable way. The fight to defend treaty promises is far from over—and the responsibility to protect them now lies with us.

Chapter 11 - Bibliography

House Bill No. 377, 66th Idaho Legislature, 1st Regular Session (2021). "Education—Dignity and Nondiscrimination in Public Education." Accessed May 18, 2025.
https://legislature.idaho.gov/sessioninfo/2021/legislation/H0377/.

Senate File No. SF0103, 66th Wyoming Legislature, 2022 Budget Session (introduced Feb. 15, 2022). "Education–Limitations on Teaching Critical Race History–2." Accessed May 18, 2025.
https://wyoleg.gov/Legislation/2022/SF0103.

The *Wihinakwate* Way

In the Fort Hall area, our people once called themselves *Wihinakwate* in Bannock or *Wihinai* in Shoshone—"From Iron", "On the Iron Side", or "From the Knife." Historically, this symbolized possessing iron tools—knives, guns, and implements gained through trade or taken from adversaries—representing strength, capability, and respect. Today, I give this word new meaning: minds and bodies forged like iron, sharpened like blades.

A person who embodies *Wihinakwate* is a protector, a provider, and a hard-working person driven by clear goals, integrity, and profound self-discipline. They continuously expand their knowledge, use their minds effectively, listen more than they speak, and avoid wasting energy on complaints or excuses. They stand prepared—physically, mentally, and spiritually—for whatever challenges may arise.

This message is for those getting crushed by life—sick of being soft, sick of being ignored, sick of living like they don't matter—and for those who feel lost or unable to find purpose. Life is a gift, and your family and community need you to rise and become more than you are now. You carry gifts, but many never sharpen them. You were made for more despite how you may think about yourself. The world isn't good or bad—and it isn't fair. It doesn't care, and no one is coming to save you. It just is. You either take control, or you get run over. Your story is yours—make it count.

The *Wihinakwate* way has always been about enduring, overcoming, and rising—no matter the odds. You will suffer. You will lose. You must take risks. But it's through that suffering, those losses, and the risks you take that you are forged. What matters is how you rise and push back. Walk the *Wihinakwate* path, and success will follow—not because you chased it, but because you earned it. You must grow your *Wihinakwate Puha* "From Iron Power".

A well-made blade that holds an edge, must go through the fire—again and again—before it's tempered. It takes heat, pressure, and pounding to make it hold an edge. The same goes for us. Pain, failure, and loss—they're not just suffering. They're the fire that hardens us. If you avoid the fire, you stay soft, weak, and brittle. If you go through it, and don't quit, you come out forged. Hardened. Ready. Durable.

I've lived the other side too—drunk, angry, blaming everyone but myself. I broke things. I destroyed relationships. I hurt people who didn't deserve it. I should be dead. But life doesn't care—and you should never expect it to. Your mind can be your strongest ally or your worst enemy. At some point you must recognize that change is necessary. Growth and change must happen together, and it takes time, pain, and sweat. No more excuses and no more complaining. It is now time to return to the *Wihinakwate* way. A human being of discipline, not chaos. Of clarity, not confusion. Of iron, not weakness. One who builds, not destroys. That's what it means to walk the path of the *Wihinakwate* way.

The path starts in the mind. Your thoughts create your world. Addiction, hate, self-pity, excuses—they all start in the mind too. Master your mind, or it will master you. It's your sharpest weapon—strong enough to crush your enemies or destroy your own life. If you don't sharpen it or use it right, it will dull or harm those you love and yourself. Drugs, alcohol, self-pity, bad people, lack of discipline will rot everything around you. Discard them. Focus on what you want to become and how to get there. Then act. Every day. Relentless focus and discipline—that is the *Wihinakwate* way.

Discipline is your backbone. Pain is your forge. Wake early. Train hard. Eat to fuel your body, not to please your tongue—keep it simple, clean, and disciplined. Learn martial arts and how to use weapons. That's how you armor your mind, body, and community. Embrace pain—pain is the hammer that shapes you. Every scar, every bruise, every hardship can make you stronger. And every moment of every day counts—it all counts.

As you grow older and wiser, leadership becomes more important—but it doesn't always mean taking control. Sometimes, true leadership is offering your insight, then stepping back. You can't—and shouldn't—try to control every outcome. Speak the truth, give guidance, and then let others make their own choices, even if it means they'll have to learn the hard way. That's how people grow. Pain teaches in ways words never can. A strong man knows when to act—and when to step aside so others can earn their own strength.

We are all called to lead, each with our own role and purpose. Men and women were not meant to trade places—each carries a distinct responsibility. When women or grandparents are left to raise children alone, that is not tradition—it is collapse. That is not the *Wihinakwate* way. Our ancestors didn't run from pain or hardship. They built a language and a culture to overcome it. They prepared for hard times and adapted. So must we.

Your possessions and the people you surround yourself with reflect who you are and the life you live. Keep your life in order and choose your circle wisely. Take care of what you have and be grateful for it—no matter how small or insignificant it may seem. If you can help the weak, the young, and the vulnerable do it—but take care of yourself first. If you don't care for yourself, you won't be able to care for anyone else—and someone else will have to take care of you!

Do not fear death, but do not chase it recklessly. Make peace with it, and live each day as if it could be your last. And when death does come, meet the Creator standing tall.

Show kindness and respect to others and yourself, and set a good example for all to follow, especially children. We should all reflect on the example we are setting for our children.

When a disciplined man stands beside a woman he honors, their mutual respect becomes the bedrock of a strong family—visible to all. The combined strength of man and woman far exceeds what either can achieve alone. When the family breaks down or is dysfunctional, our society will collapse. To forge a powerful tribe, it first begins with the individual and then the family.

We've lost sight of who is an outsider and who is kin. We no longer function as a warrior society tribe—and we've begun to forget what it means to live as a people bound by tradition, kinship, and purpose. It's time to remember. It's time to act like a tribe again—before what's left of us is lost forever.

A true tribe is forged when people stand together in purpose and weather adversity as one. Today, our greatest adversity isn't just outside us—it's within. We face addiction, poverty, distraction, hopelessness, laziness, the loss of purpose, and a flood of negative attitudes. We are being tested by entitlement, excuses, complaining, unchecked anger, and the absence of duty. If we don't face these head-on, we won't endure.

A tribe does not rise by blaming others or begging. It rises through strength, honor, innovation, focus, and responsibility—and by building real wealth through work, unity, and vision. We must become vigilant—guarding not only our land but also our minds, our families, and our sacred traditions. Outsiders—whether people, ideologies, or systems—can erode our culture, divide our unity, and dilute our language. We must uphold our *Tenichui* or *Deniwape*—the traditional teachings of behavior or philosophy.

Strong tribes uphold an unbreakable code of honor. They prize loyalty, courage, and unity. They value endurance over comfort and revere their elders and the *Damme Ape* "God", drawing wisdom from those who walked before. A real tribe holds its ground, outlasting any threat until the enemy tires and retreats. It draws power from the land and waters, defending them with unmatched ferocity. Yet it remains adaptable—shifting form and strategy to survive.

Unlike gangs or criminal organizations driven by greed and vice, warrior society tribes exist for their people alone—bound by shared blood, language, culture, memory, honor, pride, responsibility, and the sacred promise of mutual protection.

I'm not perfect. I'm not some ideal example. I still fall short and stray from the path of *Wihinakwate*—but I always return to it. It's time to let go of entitlement, complaining, laziness, and addiction. It's time to rebuild our homes and our community through hard work that comes from within. We must become independent, draw wealth from our own lands and waters, strengthen our family ties, treat one another with respect, and grow strong in both body and mind. We carry the weight of generational trauma—but we don't have to stay broken beneath it. It's time to rise.

If this message helps even one person stand up, reclaim their strength, and walk a straighter path—then it was worth writing. I don't care who mocks it or misunderstands it. I'm not here for their approval. I wrote it for the men and women who are ready to make it happen. This is *Wihinakwate*. This is "From Iron".

Appendix

Simplified *Panakwate* (Bannock) and *Newe Da̲igwape* (Shoshone) Pronunciation Guide and Orthography

The orthographic system employed for *Panakwate* (Bannock) derives from my own orthography, formulated during my master's thesis[1]. This system aligns closely with the one utilized in the Northern Paiute-Bannock Dictionary[2], but introduces an innovation by substituting the [e] symbol for the International Phonetic Alphabet's (IPA) [ɨ] phoneme, thereby facilitating ease of use and typing. Conversely, the orthography for *Newe Da̲igwape* (Shoshone) adheres to the standards set forth in Gould and Loether's "An Introduction to the Shoshoni Language"[3], which is been based in a Fort Hall dialect of Shoshone. Therefore, it was selected for its applicability and authenticity.

Throughout this work, meticulous attention has been paid to the identification of languages, with *Panawkate* and *Newe Da̲igwape* terms consistently italicized to aid in their recognition. To simplify the writing of these languages but to aid in differentiating the two languages without explicitly identifying which languages the term is derived from, a set of initial consonants were used to serve as a distinct marker of each language. For example, all *Panakwate* words invariably begin with the consonants [t], [tz], [k], [kw],[p], whereas all *Newe Da̲igwape* terms commence with [d], [dz], [g], [gw], and [b].

Although not always true, in general initial consonant use in *Panakwate* takes on a hard pronunciation, while in *Newe Da̲igwape* consonant typically takes on a soft pronunciation. The first consonant to discuss is the glottal stop, which is symbolized as ['], as in *da'oo'* the Shoshone term to describe "dried powdered meat". The glottal stop is ubiquitous in both languages and

---

[1] Cleve Davis, "*A Comparative and Historical Linguistic Analysis of the Bannock Dialect of the Northern Paiute Language*" (master's thesis, Idaho State University, 2010).
[2] Sven Liljeblad, Catherine S. Fowler, and Glenda Powell, compilers, *Northern Paiute-Bannock Dictionary* (Salt Lake City: University of Utah Press, 2012), 5-7.
[3] Drusilla Gould and Christopher Loether, *An Introduction to the Shoshoni Language* (Salt Lake City: University of Utah Press, 2002), 9-17.

pronounced by cutting off the flow of air in the throat as in "uh oh". Except for how initial consonants are used in the book, the following consonants can be used interchangeably in both languages — for the most part.

 b as the "p" in "spy"

 ch as in "church"

 d as the "t" in "stay"

 g as the "k" in "sky"

 k as in "cat"

 h as in "hat"

 m as in "mom"

 n as in "now"

 ng as in "finger" and not as in "singer"

 s as in "soon"

 sh as in "ship"

 t as in "tap"

 ts as in "cats"

 w as in "wind"

 y as in "yes"

 z as in "zoo"

The consonant [j] is used in *Newe Daigwape* and takes on the sound "j" as in "jam", but it does not exist in the *Panakwate* language. Similarly, the consonant [f] which produces a sound similar to that in "fight," is not found in *Panakwate*. Various combinations of consonants can also be used, especially in *Newe Daigwape*. But as a general rule, the combinations can be pronounced by simply merging the previously mentioned sounds.

 If one trains their ears and listens to these genetically related but mutually unintelligible languages, a significant distinction can be observed in the emphasis placed on vowels. Typically, in *Panakwate* the stress falls on the second vowel, whereas in *Newe Daigwape*, it is the first vowel that is emphasized. Both languages comprise the vowels: *a, e, i, o,* and *u.* These vowels can occur short and long, and when they written doubled the pronunciation is held twice as long. The vowels are pronounced in a manner similar to certain English vowels, as illustrated in the following examples:

a as in "hot"

e as in "put"

i as in "beet"

o as in "coat"

u as in "who"

Additionally, both languages feature instances where multiple vowel sounds merge into a single, fluid sound, technically known as diphthongs. Their pronunciation can be approximated as follows:

<u>*ai*</u> as in "hay".

ai as "igh" in English "high"

ea as "u" in "put" followed by "a" in "about"

ia as "ia" in "Maria"

oi as "oy" in "boy"

ua as "oo" in "too" followed by "a" in "father"

ui as "ewy" in "chewy"

Variations in diphthongs, particularly within *Newe Daigwape*, can be more extensive. However, a fundamental principle is that these diphthongs consist of blends of the individual vowels previously mentioned.

Appendix - Bibliography

Davis, Cleve. "A Comparative and Historical Linguistic Analysis of the Bannock Dialect of the Northern Paiute Language." Master's thesis, Idaho State University, 2010.

Gould, Drusilla, and Christopher Loether. An Introduction to the Shoshoni Language. Salt Lake City: University of Utah Press, 2002.

Liljeblad, Sven, Catherine S. Fowler, and Glenda Powell, compilers. Northern Paiute-Bannock Dictionary. Salt Lake City: University of Utah Press, 2012.

Glossary

Bannock Words

Aa: Horn.

Duupatehe'ya: Moose or "black water deer".

Hahveedziah: "Laying Girl", Bannock name of John Race Horse Sr's wife.

Iwau: Many.

Kuchu: Buffalo or in modern times, the domesticated cow.

Kusi-tzo: "Gray grandfather" or great-great-grandfather.

Manipenni: Do well; get along; status of things.

Nana'atakussu: Produces, grows, provides.

Neme: Indian people or more specifically Bannock and Shoshone speaking people.

Newe: Indian people or more specifically Bannock and Shoshone speaking people.

Newekuchu: Buffalo or "Indian cow".

O: Used to describe something or similar to the English "is".

Oteu: Because.

Panakwate: The name the Bannock people use for themselves, can be translated as "from the water".

Pateheya: Elk or "water deer".

Paaguchuha: The "Warm Water". Place name for Lava Hot Springs in southeastern Idaho.

Patotonoi Wakwami: "Water Comes out of Ground and Stands". The Bannock place name for the Yellowstone Caldera.

Pemma: With which (to accomplish something).

Pihaguyudeka': The "Sweet Root Eaters", lived along the Portneuf River, near its headwaters.

Pihaguye Nahukwa: The "Sweet Root River". The Bannock name of the Portneuf River in southeastern Idaho.

Pohave: "One Who Has Power" or "One Who Possesses Power." Bannock name of John Race Horse Sr.

Pozena: "Buffalo".

Puha: Supernatural power.

Sewoki'i: "Willows Standing in a Row". The name used to refer to the Shoshone and Bannock who lived along the Weiser and Payette Rivers in southwestern Idaho. The term is also the place name for this region.

Sehewoki'i: Variant of *Sewoki'i*.

Taggi: Bannock name of Chief Taghee. The Bannock Chief who signed the 1868 Fort Bridger Treaty.

Tebiwa: "Indian land" or "one's own country".

Tedebiwa'a: The "Poor People".

Tekkapema: "Food".

Tekkapekayu: Possess food.

Tuku: "Meat".

Tukudeka: "Meat eater" Shoshone and Bannock who hunted bighorn sheep, also known as the "Sheepeaters" in popular literature.

Tenichui: Traditional teachings of behavior or philosophy. It can also be a warning.

Wihi: "Knife" or "metal".

Wihinakwate: "On the Knife Side", "On the Iron Side", or "Possesses Iron". Historically this word referred to the technologically superior and mounted buffalo hunter Bannock and Shoshone Indians from the Fort Hall area.

Yakwi: To come with, to bring, or to hold.

Shoshone Words

Agaibaa: The Lemhi or Salmon Rivers.

Agaideka: The "Salmon Eaters". The Shoshone and Bannock people who lived along the Salmon and Lemhi Rivers in central Idaho.

Agaide'ka'a: Variant of *Agaideka*.

Appe: Father or father's brothers.

Badeheyadeka: "Water Deer Eaters" or elk eaters. The group of Shoshone and Bannock who hunted in Jackson Hole and Yellowstone regions.

Baingwideka: The "Fish Eaters". A name used to describe the Shoshone who lived or often visited the Bear River, Big and Little Lost Rivers.

Baki'ehe: The Blackfeet people or the "Raw Hide People".

Bannaite: "Bannock".

Bannaite' Doya': Yellowstone area or "Bannock Mountains".

Bia'agaideka': "Big Salmon Eaters". The Shoshone and Bannock who hunted salmon in southern Idaho, especially near the Shoshone Falls.

Boha Baa: "Power Water". A Shoshone place name for Lava Hot Springs in southeastern Idaho.

Bohogoi: The "Sagebrush Butte People", also the place name for Ferry Butte on the Fort Hall Indian Reservation. Literally means "Sagebrush Butte".

Bozheena: "Buffalo".

Debadeka: The "Pine Nut Eaters".

Daguwenede: The "Standing Thirst" dance, also known as the Sun Dance.

Daigwa: "Talk".

Dai'gwahni: "Talker".

Daibo'o: A white person or person of the Caucasian race.

Dedebiwa'ne'e: The "Poor People".

Deheyadekane'e: The "Deer Eater People". The mixed bands of Shoshone and Bannock who lived in the mountainous regions of western Idaho.

Deniwape: Traditional teachings of behavior or philosophy.

Dosawihi: The "White Knife" Shoshone. The term was used to describe the Western Shoshone communities from northeastern Nevada.

Doyanee: The "Mountain People". Another term to describe the people from the Yellowstone or other mountainous areas within the homeland of the Shoshone.

Dukudeka: "Meat eater". Shoshone and Bannock who hunted bighorn sheep, also known as the "Sheepeaters" in popular literature.

Duuwihi: The "Black Knife" Shoshone. Shoshone people who lived in the Yellowstone region.

Ga'mmudeka': "Rabbit eaters".

Gaihitsi: "No longer related" or great-great-great grandparent.

Gai Miawaite: No walk.

Gogohi': The Wind River Shoshone people named after the preference for eating or making use of the "guts" or "intestines" of buffalo.

Guhaape'e: Husband or husband's brother(s).

Gutsundeka: The "Buffalo Eaters". The horse-owning groups of Shoshone and Bannock that pursued buffalo into the northern plains.

Hekandeka: The "Wheat Grass Seed Eaters".

Hukandeka: The "Dust Eaters".

Isha: Wolf.

Izahpe'a: "Coyote". Term can also be used to describe a person who is a liar or trickster.

Nabidenge dai'gwahni: "War Talker" or war leader.

Nemi: To travel, wander, roam, and live. Singular form.

Newe: Indian people or more specifically Bannock and Shoshone speaking people.

Newe da'mmu: "Indian sinew" or "Indian thread".

Newe Daigwape: Shoshone (Peoples) language.

Seheewooki'nee': The "Willows Standing in a Row People". The name used to refer to the Shoshone and Bannock who lived along the Weiser and Payette Rivers in southwestern Idaho.

Soho'agaideka: "Cottonwood Salmon Eaters". A name for the Boise Valley Indians.

Sonigahni: "Grass lodge".

Sonipe: "Grass"

Sosoni: The word for "Shoshone".

Duku: "Meat".

Wihi: "Knife" or "Metal".

Wihinai: "On the Knife Side", "On the Iron Side", or "Possesses Iron". History technologically superior and mounted buffalo hunter Shoshone and Bannock Indians from the Fort Hall area.

Yahandeka: The "Rock Chuck Eaters" or yellow-bellied marmot eaters who lived in the lava fields of southern Idaho.

Yemega: To travel, wander, roam, and live. Plural form.

Index

Agaideka, 13, 195
alcohol, 29, 52, 53, 184
Andrew Johnson, 28
animals, ix, xi, 13, 22, 25, 26, 27, 29, 31, 32, 34, 36, 37, 41, 42, 44, 73, 100
appe, 29
armed, 2, 3
assimilation, 74, 91, 113, 178
Augur, 58, 60, 81, 152, 153, 157, 172
Bad Men, 59, 104
Badeheyadeka, 13, 195
Baingwideka, 15, 195
Bannaite, 52, 96, 195
Bannock, i, vi, vii, viii, ix, x, 2, 4, 5, 6, 9, 10, 11, 12, 13, 14, 15, 16, 17, 18, 19, 20, 21, 22, 23, 24, 28, 31, 32, 33, 34, 35, 36, 37, 38, 39, 40, 42, 43, 44, 46, 50, 51, 52, 57, 58, 59, 61, 63, 64, 65, 66, 67, 68, 69, 70, 71, 72, 74, 77, 78, 80, 82, 86, 88, 89, 90, 92, 93, 96, 97, 98, 99, 100, 102, 103, 104, 105, 107, 109, 110, 111, 112, 113, 115, 117, 122, 123, 124, 127, 128, 130, 131, 159, 160, 163, 164, 165, 166, 167, 168, 169, 170, 171, 172, 173, 174, 175, 177, 179, 180, 181, 183, 189, 192, 193, 194, 195, 196, 197
Bannock Trail, 36, 37, 38, 180

Barrett, 115, 119, 120, 122, 128
Bear Hunter, 55, 163
Bear River, 6, 15, 53, 54, 55, 56, 69, 72, 79, 82, 160, 162, 163, 174, 175, 195
Bear River Massacre, 6, 53, 54, 55, 56, 69, 72, 79, 82, 160, 162, 163, 174, 175
Bear River Mountains, 162
Ben Sinowan, 107
bighorn, 2, 16, 31, 53, 73, 156, 194, 196
Bighorn National Forest, 123, 124, 125, 128, 141
bighorn sheep, 2, 16, 31, 53, 73, 156
biologist, 2, 44, 139
bison, 31, 39, 40, 41, 42, 43, 45, 85
Black Hills, 33
Blackfeet, 9, 10, 48, 195
Boha Baa, 14, 195
Bohogoi, 14, 195
Boise, viii, 14, 15, 16, 19, 23, 51, 61, 66, 68, 81, 171, 197
Boise Valley, viii, 15, 197
Boldt, 136, 137
Boone and Crockett, 93
bounty hunters, 39
bozheena, 34
Brucellosis, 42, 43, 45, 46
Bruneau, 61, 171
Bu'ngu, 32, 33
buffalo, ix, 5, 9, 13, 26, 31, 33, 34, 35, 36, 37, 38, 39, 40, 41, 43, 44, 49, 63, 64,

73, 95, 139, 156, 163, 180, 194, 196, 197
Buffalo, ix, 13, 18, 31, 34, 39, 40, 41, 45, 46, 64, 65, 66, 67, 69, 70, 193, 194, 195, 196
Buffalo Bill, 40, 65
buffalo heart, 37
Buffalo Horn, 64, 65, 66, 67, 69, 70
Bureau of Land Management, 154
Cache Valley, 162
Camas Prairie, 37, 38, 59, 60, 61, 62, 64, 69
Ca-me-ah-wait, 48, 49, 50
Canada, 9, 10, 24, 33, 43, 46, 71, 79, 82, 114
Caroline Teton-Racehorse, 5
Ceded, 173
Celilo Falls, 10
ceremonies, v, ix, 28, 36, 77, 181
ceremony, ix, 13, 34, 36
Chad Colter, 43
Challis National Forest, 143
chief, viii, 52, 55, 66, 67, 162
Chief Moose Dung, 121
Christianity, vii
City of Rocks, 14
Clark, 47, 48, 49, 50, 70, 81, 82
Claudio Broncho, 43
Clayvin Herrera, 124, 141
Cleveland Brooks Racehorse, 5
colonialism, 79, 178
colonization, 6, 14, 21, 34, 48, 54, 72, 73, 179
Columbia, 51, 62, 135
Columbus, 48
Comanche, 31, 33, 45

commercial hunters, 39, 41
Commissioner of Indian Affairs, 53, 59, 64, 81, 87, 88, 89, 90, 94, 95, 96, 97, 98, 104, 105, 106, 109, 111, 115, 116, 127
Connor, 54, 55, 56, 57
conservation, 18, 28, 93, 129, 130, 133, 134, 135, 136, 137, 138, 139, 141, 145, 146, 154, 155, 180
conservation laws, 129, 130, 133, 134, 137, 180
Constitution, v, 139, 140, 166
contagious disease, 42
Corp of Discovery, 48, 50, 51
Corps of Discovery, 47, 48, 51
Court of Appeals for the Ninth Circuit, 159
Courts of the Conquer, 140
Coyote, 25, 27, 34, 196
Creator, ix, xi
critical race theory, 179
Crow, 4, 20, 58, 64, 65, 68, 70, 71, 82, 93, 94, 95, 117, 118, 119, 120, 121, 124, 125, 127, 128, 130, 131, 132, 133, 170, 177, 179
Crow Tribe, 4, 117, 118, 119, 120, 124, 125, 127, 128, 130, 131, 132, 133, 153, 157
cultural sensitivity, 161
cultural values, 161
culture, xi, 1, 22, 27, 28, 29, 33, 49, 74, 77, 78, 174, 177
Custer County, 2, 123

Cutler, 141, 142, 143, 144, 145, 147, 152, 153, 154, 155
da'mmu, 35, 197
Daguwenede, viii, ix, 36, 195
Daibo'o, 47, 195
Damme Ape, ix
Darren Parry, 54, 174
David Thompson, 9, 10
Debadeka, 14, 195
Dedebiwa'ne'e, 14, 196
deer, vii, 13, 25, 26, 27, 31, 43, 85, 90, 101, 138, 139, 143, 156, 193
Deer Eater, 13, 196
deheya, 13
Deheyadekane'e, 13, 196
deka, 13
Deniwape, 28, 29, 139, 196
Devon Boyer, 167
diseases, 50, 52, 72, 73, 138
District Court of Fremont County, 142
Donald McKenzie, 52
Doty, 57
Dukudeka, 6, 15, 16, 17, 85, 196
Dust Eaters, 14
Eagle Eye, 6
Eagle Protection Act, 126
East Fork of the Salmon, 1
Eastern Shoshone, 4, 38, 124, 128, 164, 167, 170
Eaters, 13, 14, 15, 16, 21, 193, 195, 196, 197
ecological, 40, 90, 91, 146, 148, 155, 156
education, 78, 82, 179, 181
Edward McGarry, 54
elk, 13, 26, 27, 31, 32, 42, 43, 44, 85, 90, 95, 100, 101, 108, 110, 111, 118, 120, 123, 124, 125, 129, 138, 141, 142, 143, 145, 148, 156, 195
Elk, 13, 42, 43, 46, 138, 139, 140, 193
Elk Eaters, 13
emigrants, 14, 52
Endangered Species Act, 126, 132, 155
European, 12, 14, 15, 31, 39, 48, 50, 72, 74, 78, 82
federal, v, xi, 4, 5, 43, 57, 59, 61, 79, 80, 87, 91, 95, 105, 112, 117, 122, 123, 126, 127, 133, 135, 137, 159, 164, 165, 166, 168, 170, 173, 174, 177, 178, 180, 181
Federal Land Policy and Management Act, 154
Ferry Butte, 14, 195
fish, 1, 14, 21, 22, 31, 85, 96, 118, 119, 126, 134, 135, 136, 138, 139, 161
Fish and Game Code, 180
Fish and Game Commission, 180
Fish and Wildlife Coordination Act, 147
Fish and Wildlife Department, 180
fishermen, 1, 2
fishing, vii, viii, 1, 2, 4, 5, 20, 89, 117, 122, 123, 124, 125, 134, 135, 136, 137, 139, 163, 164, 167, 168, 173, 177, 180
flora, 156
food, ix, xi, 18, 21, 25, 26, 27, 28, 31, 33, 34, 35, 44, 48, 55, 62, 63, 64, 68, 71, 72, 78, 92, 100, 111, 122,

124, 152, 156, 163, 172, 177, 178, 194
Fort Bridger Treaty, xi, 4, 5, 19, 38, 45, 57, 58, 59, 60, 61, 62, 68, 81, 89, 93, 96, 104, 110, 111, 117, 123, 124, 142, 143, 144, 145, 146, 147, 148, 149, 151, 152, 153, 154, 155, 157, 159, 160, 164, 165, 166, 167, 168, 170, 171, 172, 173, 181, 194
Fort Custer, 68
Fort Hall, i, v, vi, vii, viii, ix, 2, 5, 11, 12, 14, 17, 18, 20, 21, 22, 27, 29, 31, 36, 37, 38, 40, 44, 50, 57, 61, 62, 63, 64, 69, 74, 78, 80, 81, 85, 87, 89, 90, 92, 93, 94, 95, 96, 97, 98, 102, 105, 106, 109, 111, 112, 113, 115, 117, 123, 159, 163, 164, 165, 167, 168, 170, 173, 183, 189, 194, 195, 197
Fort Hall Business Council, 167, 173
Fort Hall Indian Reservation, v, vi, vii, 5, 22, 87, 195
France, 47
Ga'mmudeka', 14, 196
Gai Miawaite, 48, 196
game, vii, viii, 1, 7, 21, 26, 31, 38, 53, 56, 57, 58, 63, 69, 85, 87, 89, 90, 92, 93, 94, 95, 96, 97, 98, 99, 101, 111, 112, 117, 118, 119, 120, 121, 122, 123, 127, 138, 141, 142, 145, 146, 147, 152, 153, 154, 156, 159, 161, 163, 165, 170, 171, 172, 177, 178,180

game warden, 118
Gens du Serpent, 9
Gerald Cleo Tinno, 123
Gogohi', 13, 196
gold, viii, 16
gonorrhea, 50
Great Plains, 9, 33, 39, 163
Green River, 52, 98, 101
Greg Wooten, 159
Grover Cleveland, 128
guhaape'e, 29
gun, 9, 39, 40, 67, 70, 103
guns, vii, 39, 40, 46, 49, 52, 69, 101, 127
Gutsunambihi, 37
Gutsundeka, 13, 18, 196
habeas corpus, 105, 107, 108, 109, 110, 112
Hahveedziah, 5, 193
Harris, 42, 46, 86, 87, 88, 89, 92, 95, 115, 116
Herd Creek, 1
Herrera, 4, 7, 105, 115, 125, 127, 128, 129, 130, 131, 132, 133, 134, 137, 138, 140, 141, 168, 175
Herrera v. Wyoming, 4, 128, 129, 130
Hoback, 110
homeland, 36, 147, 162, 169, 171, 196
homelands, 11, 15, 21, 22, 31, 45, 56, 57, 60, 61, 149, 153, 162, 169, 170, 181
horse, 6, 13, 18, 31, 32, 33, 34, 44, 48, 67, 102, 163, 196
horses, viii, xi, 5, 9, 33, 44, 48, 49, 50, 62, 69, 102, 103, 127
Howard, 66, 81
Hukandeka, 14, 196

hunt, vii, xi, 2, 25, 26, 27, 29, 36, 38, 39, 43, 44, 45, 57, 58, 68, 78, 85, 92, 93, 95, 96, 102, 105, 112, 117, 118, 119, 120, 124, 125, 126, 127, 129, 138, 159, 161, 165, 168, 169, 170, 171, 172, 173, 177

hunting, v, vii, xi, 1, 2, 4, 5, 9, 17, 18, 20, 25, 27, 28, 29, 32, 33, 36, 38, 40, 41, 43, 44, 45, 49, 52, 58, 62, 64, 85, 87, 88, 89, 90, 92, 93, 94, 95, 96, 97, 98, 100, 105, 107, 110, 111, 113, 117, 118, 119, 120, 122, 123, 124, 125, 126, 128, 129, 133, 134, 137, 138, 139, 159, 160, 161, 163, 164, 165, 166, 167, 168, 170, 171, 172, 173, 174, 177, 180, 181

Hunting, i, viii, xi, 25, 178

hunting rights, v, xi, 2, 4, 5, 40, 44, 87, 93, 94, 98, 105, 107, 111, 117, 118, 123, 124, 128, 133, 139, 159, 160, 165, 166, 167, 168, 170, 171, 172, 173, 174, 177, 178, 180, 181

Idaho, i, vii, 1, 2, 5, 6, 7, 10, 11, 12, 13, 14, 16, 17, 18, 20, 21, 22, 23, 24, 31, 33, 35, 36, 37, 38, 41, 46, 48, 51, 52, 54, 57, 62, 63, 64, 66, 68, 69, 70, 71, 81, 82, 83, 88, 89, 90, 95, 96, 98, 99, 103, 109, 111, 115, 119, 123, 124, 132, 143, 145, 159, 160, 161, 162, 164, 165, 166, 167, 168, 171, 172, 173, 174, 175, 179, 180, 181, 182, 189, 192, 193, 194, 195, 196, 197

Idaho Fish and Game, 1, 145, 146, 159

Idaho National Laboratory, 38

Idaho Supreme Court, 142, 143, 144, 145, 146, 147, 148, 152, 155

Idaho v. Arthur, 154, 157

Idaho v. Coffee, 143, 157

Idaho v. Cutler, 157

Idaho v. Tinno, 143, 145, 152, 154, 157

independence, 41, 177, 178

Indian, i, v, vi, vii, viii, ix, x, xi, 1, 2, 4, 5, 6, 9, 10, 11, 12, 13, 16, 17, 18, 19, 20, 21, 22, 23, 24, 34, 36, 37, 39, 40, 41, 45, 46, 47, 48, 51, 52, 53, 55, 58, 59, 63, 64, 65, 66, 67, 68, 71, 72, 73, 74, 75, 76, 77, 78, 79, 80, 81, 82, 83, 85, 86, 87, 88, 89, 90, 91, 92, 93, 94, 95, 96, 97, 98, 100, 102, 103, 104, 105, 106, 109, 111, 112, 113, 114, 115, 116, 117, 118, 120, 121, 122, 123, 124, 125, 126, 127, 128, 131, 132, 134, 136, 137, 138, 139, 159, 160, 161, 162, 163, 164, 166, 168, 169, 171, 175, 177, 178, 179, 180, 181, 193, 194, 195, 197

Indian Nations, 48, 151, 156

Indian Peace Commission, 152

Indian rights, 111, 114, 123, 126, 156

Indians, vii, viii, ix, 2, 3, 4, 5, 7, 9, 10, 11, 12, 14, 15, 16, 17, 18, 21, 22, 23, 31, 33, 38, 39, 40, 46, 48, 50, 52, 53, 54, 55, 56, 57, 59, 61, 62, 63, 66, 68, 71, 72, 73, 75, 76, 77, 82, 83, 86, 87, 88, 89, 90, 92, 93, 94, 95, 96, 97, 98, 99, 100, 101, 102, 103, 104, 105, 106, 109, 110, 111, 112, 113, 114, 115, 117, 118, 119, 121, 122, 123, 124, 125, 127, 128, 130, 132, 133, 135, 137, 138, 140, 160, 163, 165, 169, 170, 172, 175, 177, 194, 197

indicia of occupancy, 155

injustice, 4, 113, 114, 178, 180

Isha, 25, 196

Izahpe'a, 25, 26, 27, 196

Jackson Hole, 13, 43, 85, 95, 97, 99, 100, 112, 195

James Duane Doty, 56

James Harlan, 153

John Race Horse Sr, 4, 5, 6, 107, 108, 109, 118, 193, 194

Jones v. Meehan, 121, 122, 132

Joseph Davis Jr., vii

Josephine Thorpe, 6

Kamas plains, 58, 60

Kamas Prairie, 169

Kiowa, 33

Klamath Tribes, 137

Knickerbocker Club, 93

Kootenai, 9

kuchu, 34

land, ix, xi, 17, 19, 21, 22, 32, 47, 50, 61, 67, 73, 74, 85, 91, 97, 110, 118, 119, 121, 122, 127, 128, 130, 137, 138, 139, 142, 143, 145, 146, 147, 148, 150, 151, 152, 154, 155, 156, 160, 161, 163, 164, 169, 170, 171, 174, 177, 178, 181, 194

landscape, 21, 85, 117, 141, 154, 155, 156, 163

language, v, viii, x, 1, 4, 11, 12, 18, 19, 20, 21, 22, 25, 29, 33, 44, 58, 61, 74, 78, 90, 117, 118, 119, 121, 122, 123, 126, 137, 138, 159, 168, 170, 171, 174, 189, 190, 197

languages, vi, viii, ix, x, 11, 12, 16, 19, 20, 21, 78, 113, 124, 189, 190, 191

Laramie Republican, 112, 113

Lemhi, 13, 33, 46, 47, 48, 50, 85, 87, 89, 90, 93, 94, 95, 195

Lemhi Reserve, 50

Lemhi River, 13, 47

Lewis, 47, 48, 49, 50, 74, 82

Liljeblad, 12, 13, 16, 17, 18, 20, 21, 23, 24, 31, 36, 41, 46, 124, 150, 157, 161, 175, 189, 192

livestock, 14, 43, 53, 95

Lost River, 88

Louisiana Purchase, 47, 51, 81

Mae Timbimboo Parry, 55, 174

Mammoth Hot Springs, 85

Manning, 96, 98, 99, 101, 102, 103, 104, 107, 113, 114

Marcia Racehorse-Robles, vii
Marysvale, 96, 101
Maude Pocatello-Racehorse, 5
McCormick, 106
Meehan, 121, 125
Mexico, 20, 33, 39, 47
Mike Davis, 1
military, vii, viii, 41, 54, 55, 56, 65, 66, 67, 68, 69, 75, 86, 162
Minnesota v. Mille Lacs Band of Chippewa, 4, 7, 125, 132, 138, 140, 169, 175
Missing and Murdered Indigenous Women, 114
MMIW, 114
Montana, 5, 9, 16, 17, 18, 20, 36, 37, 38, 40, 47, 64, 71, 87
Mormon, 57, 104
Moses Harris, 86
Nabidenge da̲i'gwahni, 57, 196
Napoleon Bonaparte, 47
Nathaniel P. Langford, 85
National Elk Wildlife Refuge, 43
native species, 156
Nazi, 48, 80, 82, 83
Nelson Racehorse, 5
Nevada, 14, 15, 18, 21, 33, 36, 162, 164, 174, 196
New York Zoological Park, 41
Newe, vi, 12, 13, 14, 15, 18, 20, 21, 25, 29, 31, 32, 33, 34, 35, 36, 38, 47, 49, 51, 52, 53, 54, 55, 56, 57, 85, 90, 91, 181, 189, 190, 191, 193, 197
Newe Da̲igwape, vi, 189, 190, 191, 197
Newekuchu, 34, 193

Nez Perce, 2, 10, 20, 22, 23, 66, 67, 69, 71, 72, 81
Ninth Circuit, 165, 168, 169, 170, 171, 172
Norris, 16, 17, 70, 82, 85, 86
Northwest Fur Company, 52
Northwestern Band, 54, 57, 82, 159, 162, 163, 164, 165, 166, 167, 168, 170, 171, 172, 173, 174, 175
Northwestern Band of the Shoshone, 54, 57, 164
Northwestern Band of the Shoshone Nation v. Wooten, 159, 163, 168, 175
O. O. Howard, 62, 66
Olympic National Park, 144
oral traditions, 6, 25, 35, 160
Oregon, 13, 21, 33, 51, 137, 140, 165, 175
Panakwate, vi, 12, 16, 189, 190, 193
Parry, 55, 82, 174
Patrick Edward Connor, 54
Payette, 14, 15, 194, 197
Peyote, ix
Philip Sheridan, 86
Pihaguyudeka', 14, 193
pinenuts, 156
plant, 20, 21, 28, 53, 62, 63, 74, 91, 154, 156
Pocatello, 6, 12, 15, 16, 18, 22, 23, 24, 31, 32, 36, 46, 56, 57, 76, 82, 160, 161, 162, 164, 165, 174, 175
Pohave, 4, 5, 107, 108, 194
Poor People, 14, 21, 194, 196
Portneuf, 14, 60, 61, 160, 162, 169, 193, 194
pozena, 34
prayers, ix, 29, 124

President, 47, 58, 61, 63, 93, 97, 98, 169
Province McCormick, 105
Puha, 183, 194
Puyallup, 133, 134, 135, 136, 137, 139, 140
Puyallup Tribe v. Department of Game of Washington, 133, 134, 139, 140
Puyallup Trilogy, 134, 136, 137
Race Horse, 4, 5, 6, 107, 108, 109, 110, 111, 112, 117, 118, 119, 121, 122, 123, 125, 126, 128, 129, 193, 194
Racehorse, viii, 5, 44, 45, 108
Raft River, 160, 162
railroad, 39, 40
Regulations, 43, 46, 139
Repsis, 118, 119, 120, 121, 122, 123, 124, 125, 126, 128, 129, 130, 131, 132
reservation, v, viii, x, xi, 1, 4, 6, 21, 22, 38, 40, 58, 59, 60, 61, 62, 63, 68, 76, 78, 87, 89, 90, 92, 93, 94, 96, 97, 98, 100, 109, 110, 111, 112, 117, 118, 120, 122, 124, 125, 126, 127, 128, 133, 137, 159, 164, 165, 168, 169, 170, 171, 172, 173, 174, 180, 181
resource, 123, 136, 137, 162, 180
Richards, 96, 105, 106, 110, 130
rock chucks, 14
Rock Creek, 98, 101
sacred, xi, 41, 161, 181
sacrifice, ix, 179
Sagebrush Butte, 14, 195

Sah-cah-gar-weah, 49
Salish, 9
salmon, vii, 1, 11, 14, 48, 73, 123, 135, 156, 173, 195
Salmon Eaters, 13, 15
Salmon River, 2, 15, 50, 123
Salt Lake, 16, 23, 31, 46, 53, 55, 56, 82, 87, 115, 162, 175, 189, 192
Salt Lake Road, 162
Sand Creek Ranch, 141, 142, 145, 146, 147, 148, 155
Sand Creek Wildlife Management Area, 142, 146, 147
Saskatchewan, 33
Secretary of Interior, 86, 89, 95
Seheewooki'nee', 14, 16, 197
Sehewoki'i, 14, 194
self-reliance, xi, 177
Sewoki'i, 14, 16, 194
Sharps .50 caliber rifle, 39
Sheridan, 129
Sherwin Racehorse, 44
Shoshone, i, vi, vii, viii, ix, x, 2, 4, 5, 6, 7, 9, 10, 11, 12, 13, 14, 15, 16, 17, 18, 19, 20, 21, 22, 23, 28, 29, 31, 32, 33, 34, 35, 36, 37, 38, 39, 40, 42, 43, 44, 47, 48, 49, 50, 51, 54, 55, 56, 57, 58, 61, 68, 69, 72, 74, 77, 78, 80, 82, 87, 89, 90, 93, 95, 96, 97, 98, 102, 105, 106, 110, 111, 115, 117, 123, 124, 127, 128, 131, 159, 160, 162, 163, 164, 165, 166, 167, 168, 169, 170, 171, 172, 173, 174, 175, 177, 179, 180, 181,

183, 189, 193, 194, 195, 196, 197
Shoshone-Bannock, 12, 13, 128, 141, 142, 147, 164, 167, 168, 173
Shoshone-Bannock Tribes, 5, 11, 12, 13, 15, 17, 42, 43, 57, 78, 80, 105, 115, 123, 127, 131, 164, 165, 166, 167, 168, 172, 173, 175, 180, 181
Sinowan, 109
smallpox, 9, 50, 72
Snake Indians, 9
Snake River, 11, 13, 14, 17, 51, 70, 87
Snakes, 9
sonigahni, 11
sosoni, 11
sovereignty, 5, 69, 117, 126, 130, 134, 141, 159, 161, 162, 180
Sovereignty, 178, 179
Spanish, 31
spear pole, 1
spearfishing, 1, 123
spiritual, viii, ix, 28, 85, 160
State of Idaho v. Warner, 165
steelhead, 1, 134, 135, 136
Stevens Treaties, 144
Stevens Treaty, 121
stockmen, 40
suffering, ix, 53, 72, 86, 87, 183
Sundance, ix, 77
Supreme Court, 4, 105, 110, 111, 115, 119, 121, 123, 124, 125, 126, 127, 128, 129, 130, 133, 134, 137, 138, 169, 177
Sven Liljeblad, 16, 23, 150, 160

Swim v. Bergland, 154, 157
syphilis, 51
Taggi, 19, 60, 194
Taggie, 58, 60, 64
Taghee, 19, 145, 150, 194
Tedebiwa'a, 14, 194
Ten Bears, 118, 123, 125
Tenichui, 28, 139, 194
Tenth Circuit Court of Appeals, 119, 130, 133
Teter, 96, 97, 98, 106, 109, 110, 112
Teton, viii, 18, 42, 43, 44, 87
Theodore Roosevelt, 93
Thomas B. Teter, 76
Thomas L. Ten Bears, 118
Tinno, 119, 123, 124, 132, 143, 145, 152
traditional, ix, xi, 9, 18, 21, 22, 28, 36, 61, 64, 77, 91, 95, 113, 123, 139, 161, 162, 163, 168, 169
trap, vii, 53
Treaty of Box Elder, 57, 59, 160, 164
Treaty of Hellgate, 143, 144, 157
Treaty of Olympia, 144, 157
treaty violations, 179
Treaty with the Eastern Band of Shoshoni and Bannock, 157
Treaty with the Nisqualli, Puyallup, and Other Tribes, 144, 157
Treaty with the Quinaielt, 144, 157
Tribal, i, ix, xi, 1, 2, 5, 6, 21, 22, 34, 38, 78, 79, 117, 120, 124, 135, 136, 159, 161, 167, 168, 173, 177, 181

trout, 85, 136, 156
Tuwahbahba, 28
U.S. v. Winans, 121, 122
Uinta, 109, 110, 112
United States v. Dion, 126, 132
United States v. Hicks, 144, 157
United States v. Shoshone Tribe of Indians, 144, 157
Utah, 16, 18, 21, 23, 31, 36, 46, 53, 54, 55, 56, 82, 87, 115, 160, 162, 164, 174, 175, 189, 192
venereal, 51
violence, 2, 4, 69, 72, 73, 138, 162, 163, 177
Virginia City, 58, 60
War, vii, 10, 29, 30, 48, 56, 62, 64, 65, 68, 69, 70, 83, 86, 96, 196
Ward v. Race Horse, 4, 7, 44, 110, 116, 117, 120, 123, 125, 132, 177, 180, 181
warfare, 54, 72, 74, 86, 178
Warner, 165, 175
warrior, xi, 10, 30, 55, 66
Wasatch, 162
Washakee, 56
Washakie, 56, 57, 58, 81, 145, 150, 160, 163, 164
Washington v. Washington State Commercial Passenger Fishing Vessel Association, 136, 140, 168, 175
Weiser, 14, 15, 194, 197
Western Shoshone, 15, 164, 196
Wheatland World, 112

wildlife, 2, 31, 42, 43, 44, 73, 85, 86, 118, 122, 133, 134, 138, 141, 143, 145, 146, 154, 155, 156, 161
Willows Standing in a Row, 14, 194, 197
Wind River, 13, 17, 21, 85, 87, 90, 93, 94, 95, 111, 160, 164, 165, 167, 168, 169, 175, 196
Wolf, 25, 27, 90, 116, 127, 196
women, x, 2, 29, 54, 55, 71, 76, 79, 99, 100, 104, 114, 162
Wooten, 159, 165, 166, 167, 170, 172, 173, 174, 175
Wyoming, i, 4, 5, 7, 15, 16, 17, 18, 20, 22, 23, 31, 36, 37, 38, 43, 44, 45, 52, 70, 71, 87, 89, 93, 94, 95, 96, 97, 99, 103, 105, 106, 107, 108, 109, 110, 111, 112, 114, 115, 117, 118, 119, 120, 122, 124, 125, 126, 127, 128, 129, 130, 131, 132, 133, 134, 137, 138, 140, 160, 164, 168, 175, 177, 178, 179, 180, 181, 182
Wyoming District Court, 118, 129, 130, 133
Yahandeka, 14, 197
Yankee Fork, 1, 123
Yellowstone, 11, 15, 16, 17, 18, 21, 22, 23, 32, 36, 37, 38, 41, 42, 43, 45, 46, 65, 70, 82, 85, 86, 87, 88, 90, 91, 92, 93, 94, 95, 96, 111, 115, 116, 130, 193, 195, 196

www.ingramcontent.com/pod-product-compliance
Lightning Source LLC
Chambersburg PA
CBHW071715160426
43195CB00012B/1686